The
DOCTRINE
— and —
COVENANTS

VOLUME 3

SECTIONS 77–107

SCRIPTURE CENTRAL  COMMENTARY ON

The
DOCTRINE
—and—
COVENANTS

VOLUME 3
SECTIONS 77–107

CASEY PAUL GRIFFITHS

CFI
An imprint of Cedar Fort, Inc.
Springville, Utah

Paperback ISBN 13: 978-1-4621-4682-6
eBook ISBN 13: 978-1-4621-4837-0

Published by CFI, an imprint of Cedar Fort, Inc.
2373 W. 700 S., Suite 100, Springville, UT 84663
Distributed by Cedar Fort, Inc., www.cedarfort.com

Library of Congress Cataloging Number: 2024936347

Cover design by Shawnda Craig
Cover design © 2024 Cedar Fort, Inc.
Edited and Typeset by Liz Kazandzhy

Printed in the United States of America

10 9 8 7 6 5 4 3 2 1

Printed on acid-free paper

For my students, who push me to be better.

CONTENTS

Introduction to Volume 3 1

Doctrine and Covenants 77 3

Doctrine and Covenants 78 17

Doctrine and Covenants 79 27

Doctrine and Covenants 80 31

Doctrine and Covenants 81 35

Doctrine and Covenants 82 41

Doctrine and Covenants 83 49

Doctrine and Covenants 84 55

Doctrine and Covenants 85 89

Doctrine and Covenants 86 97

Doctrine and Covenants 87 105

Doctrine and Covenants 88 113

Doctrine and Covenants 89 147

Doctrine and Covenants 90 159

Doctrine and Covenants 91 169

Doctrine and Covenants 92 175

Doctrine and Covenants 93 179

Doctrine and Covenants 94 195

Doctrine and Covenants 95 203

Doctrine and Covenants 96 211

Doctrine and Covenants 97 217

Doctrine and Covenants 98 227

Doctrine and Covenants 99 241

Doctrine and Covenants 100 247

Doctrine and Covenants 101............................... 255

Doctrine and Covenants 102 277

Doctrine and Covenants 103 289

Doctrine and Covenants 104 299

Doctrine and Covenants 105 315

Doctrine and Covenants 106 329

Doctrine and Covenants 107 333

About the Author 359

Introduction to Volume 3

THE THIRD VOLUME OF THIS COMMENTARY COVERS THE PERIOD FROM March 1832 to April 1835. This was only a small span in the early years of the Restoration, but it was filled with tremendous highs and lows for the early Saints. Only a few weeks after Joseph Smith and Sidney Rigdon saw a glimpse of the eternities in their vision of the three degrees of glory, their hopes came smashing back down to earth. On the night of March 24, 1832, a mob attacked the homes where Joseph and Sidney were staying, dragging them both out into the night. Joseph was beaten and then tarred and feathered by the mob, and Sidney was left half dead, his head covered with lacerations from being dragged across the frozen ground. The two men recuperated and were still able to fill an appointed mission to visit the Latter-day Saint colony in Missouri, but the mob attack was only a portent of more serious challenges threatening the Saints.

In the face of this opposition, Joseph continued his work on the translation of the Bible, and the Saints continued their quest to build the city of Zion. A revelation given in September 1832 commanded the Saints to build a temple at the heart of the city (see Doctrine and Covenants 84). Later revelations commanded them to build another "house of glory" in

1

the Church center in Kirtland, Ohio (Doctrine and Covenants 88:119). The Saints worked diligently to accomplish these commandments while the Lord continued to reveal profound truths through the revelations given to the Prophet.

In the summer of 1833 the Saints in Missouri were suddenly struck by a rash of mob violence that threatened to destroy their plans to build the city of Zion. The Lord told the Saints that Zion is the pure in heart (see Doctrine and Covenants 97:21) and hinted at even more severe trials to come. In the fall of 1833 the full fury of the mobs in Missouri came upon the Saints, and they were forced to leave their holy place as refugees. Joseph Smith, seeking to know the reason why this calamity came upon the Saints, again sought the Lord in revelation. The Lord answered, assuring the Saints that "Zion shall not be moved out of her place, notwithstanding her children are scattered" (Doctrine and Covenants 101:17). The Lord also commanded Joseph to organize a relief expedition to help the Saints, which was then called the camp of Israel and today commonly known as Zion's Camp (see Doctrine and Covenants 103).

Joseph Smith led a small but faithful band of men and women across a continent to help the distressed Saints in Missouri. The march of Zion's Camp failed to return the Saints to their homes in Zion, but it provided a critical opportunity for mentoring among the leaders who marched with the camp. Though they were unsuccessful in redeeming Zion, the Lord called many of the men of Zion's Camp to serve in the first Quorum of the Twelve and the Quorum of the Seventy in this dispensation (see Doctrine and Covenants 107). He also promised the Saints that Zion would eventually be redeemed, though how long and challenging that road might be was unknown.

During this crucial time, the Saints encountered serious opposition on the road to Zion, but with their gazed fixed upon the Celestial City, the Lord continued to bless them with light and truth. The quest for Zion would be more difficult than anyone could imagine, and even greater challenges lay ahead. But with a firm faith in Jesus Christ, and the hope of the gospel in their hearts and minds, the Saints pressed on.

*D*octrine and *C*ovenants
Section 77
The Seven Seals

*H*istorical *C*ontext

DURING THE WINTER OF 1832 JOSEPH SMITH CONTINUED TO WORK HIS way through the New Testament as part of his new translation of the Bible. Around this time, he likely reached the book of Revelation, one of the most challenging scriptural records to understand because of its rich symbolism. He turned to the Lord with his questions and received the revelation now found in Doctrine and Covenants 77. In a later history, the Prophet offered this simple introduction to the revelation, which was basically a question-and-answer session about the book: "About the first of march, in connection with the translation of the scriptures, I received the following explanation of the Revelations of Saint John."[1]

Joseph Smith does not provide an exact date for this revelation, but considering that he was in Kirtland, Ohio, between February 29 and March 4, this document was most likely written down between March 4 and March

20, when another revelation was given instructing Joseph and Sidney to "omit the translation for the present time" so that they could begin preparations to travel to Missouri.[2] If so, this is the last section of the Doctrine and Covenants given before Joseph and Sidney were attacked by a group of men in Hiram, Ohio, on the night of March 24, 1832. After the attack, Joseph Smith moved back to Kirtland and then traveled to Missouri to meet with Church leaders there.

When Joseph Smith returned from Missouri, he resumed his translation of the Bible, beginning with Revelation 12. This seems to explain why Doctrine and Covenants 77 answers questions concerning only the first eleven chapters of the book of Revelation. Unfortunately, there is no comparable revelation that serves as a guide to the remaining chapters.[3]

Doctrine and Covenants 77 was first published in the *Times and Seasons* on August 1, 1844. When Franklin D. Richards first put together the Pearl of Great Price in Great Britain in 1851, he included this section as one of the vital revelations he felt the British Saints should have on hand. It was added to the Doctrine and Covenants as section 77 in the 1876 edition of the book.[4]

*V*erse-by-*V*erse *C*ommentary

1 Q. What is the sea of glass spoken of by John, 4th chapter, and 6th verse of the Revelation? A. It is the earth, in its sanctified, immortal, and eternal state.

The revelations of Joseph Smith make it clear that the work of Jesus Christ saves and sanctifies not only men and women but also the entire ecosystem in which we live. A revelation given a few months after section 77 declares that "the earth abideth the law of a celestial kingdom, for it filleth the measure of its creation, and transgresseth not the law—Wherefore, it shall be sanctified; yea, notwithstanding it shall die, it shall be quickened again, and shall abide the power by which it is quickened, and the righteous shall inherit it" (Doctrine and Covenants 88:25–26).

In a later discourse, Joseph Smith also explained the existence of other sanctified worlds, teaching that "the angels do not reside on a planet like this earth; But they reside in the presence of God, on a globe like a sea of glass and fire, where all things for their glory are manifest, past, present, and future, and are continually before the Lord. The place where God resides is a great Urim and Thummim" (Doctrine and Covenants 130:6–8).

Because the earth fills the measure of its creation, it will eventually die and be resurrected as a glorified celestial world. Joseph Smith taught, "This earth, in its sanctified and immortal state, will be made like unto crystal and will be a Urim and Thummim to the inhabitants who dwell thereon, whereby all things pertaining to an inferior kingdom, or all kingdoms of a lower order, will be manifest to those who dwell on it; and this earth will be Christ's" (Doctrine and Covenants 130:9). This change will take place after the end of the Millennium. John saw this event in vision, writing, "And I saw a new heaven and a new earth: for the first heaven and the first earth were passed away; and there was no more sea" (Revelation 21:1).

> 2 Q. What are we to understand by the four beasts, spoken of in the same verse? A. They are figurative expressions, used by the Revelator, John, in describing heaven, the paradise of God, the happiness of man, and of beasts, and of creeping things, and of the fowls of the air; that which is spiritual being in the likeness of that which is temporal; and that which is temporal in the likeness of that which is spiritual; the spirit of man in the likeness of his person, as also the spirit of the beast, and every other creature which God has created.

John saw in vision four beasts surrounding the throne of God, and he described them as follows: "In the midst of the throne, and round about the throne, were four beasts full of eyes before and behind. And the first beast was like a lion, and the second beast like a calf, and the third beast had a face as a man, and the fourth beast was like a flying eagle. And the four beasts had each of them six wings about him; and they were full of eyes within: and they rest not day and night, saying, Holy, holy, holy, Lord God Almighty, which was, and is, and is to come" (Revelation 4:6–8).

The beasts are symbolic representations of the joy found in eternity. In mentioning the beasts, however, the Lord's explanation also teaches that the spirits of all living things appear in the likeness of their physical forms. The spirits of people are not ethereal and unrecognizable but exist in the same form as men and women do here on earth. This was illustrated when the premortal spirit of Jesus Christ appeared to the brother of Jared. On that occasion the Savior explained, "Behold, this body, which ye now behold, is the body of my spirit; and man have I created after the body of my spirit; and

5

even as I appear unto thee to be in the spirit will I appear unto my people in the flesh" (Ether 3:16).

The Savior gave this explanation to the brother of Jared partly to emphasize the connection between God and man. He taught, "Seest thou that ye are created after mine own image? Yea, even all men were created in the beginning after mine own image" (Ether 3:15). Speaking to Moses, the Lord declared that "I, the Lord God, created all things, of which I have spoken, spiritually, before they were naturally upon the face of the earth" (Moses 3:5). Our spirits, as well as our bodies, were created in the image of God and testify of our divine heritage as children of heavenly parents.

> 3 Q. Are the four beasts limited to individual beasts, or do they represent classes or orders? A. They are limited to four individual beasts, which were shown to John, to represent the glory of the classes of beings in their destined order or sphere of creation, in the enjoyment of their eternal felicity.

While section 77 notes that these beasts are figurative expressions, their presence in John's vision is meant to underline the broad nature of the atoning work of Jesus Christ, which saves not only mankind but all living things. Joseph Smith explained:

> John saw the actual beast in heaven, showing to John that beasts did actually exist there and not to represent figures of things on the earth. . . . I suppose John saw beings there of a thousand forms that had been saved from ten thousand times ten thousand earths like this;—strange beasts of which we have no conception—all might be seen in heaven. The grand secret was to show John what there was in heaven: John learned that God glorified himself by saving all that his hands had made, whether beasts, fowl, fishes, or men, and he will gratify himself with them.[5]

Joseph Smith decried those who would confine the saving work of Jesus Christ to only humanity. He taught:

> Says one, "I cannot believe in the salvation of beasts." Any man who would tell you that this could not be, would tell you that the revelations are not true. John heard the words of the beasts giving glory to God and understood them. God who made the beasts could understand every language spoken by them. The four beasts were four of the most noble animals that had filled the measure of their creation, and had been saved from other worlds, because they were perfect; they were like angels in their sphere; we

are not told where they came from, and I do not know; but they were seen and heard by John, praising and glorifying God.[6]

> 4 Q. What are we to understand by the eyes and wings, which the beasts had? A. Their eyes are a representation of light and knowledge, that is, they are full of knowledge; and their wings are a representation of power, to move, to act, etc.

While the book of Revelation and the Prophet Joseph Smith taught of animals enjoying eternal glory alongside men and women, the four beasts are only symbols of this principle. John's description that the beasts were "full of eyes before and behind" (Revelation 4:6) would have presented a horrifying sight to an uninitiated observer! The eyes are not literal, however; they are a symbol of the knowledge given to exalted beings.

In a similar fashion, wings are symbolic of the greater ability that exalted beings possess to travel and move throughout the universe. The prophet Isaiah saw similar symbolism when he saw seraphim (angels) in the temple in Jerusalem. Isaiah described one as having "six wings; with twain he covered his face, and with twain he covered his feet, and with twain he did fly" (Isaiah 6:2). It is likely that in both of these visions, the wings shown were meant to demonstrate the greater power of movement given to exalted beings. After His Resurrection, the Savior, now an exalted being, moved easily between different continents on earth. He ministered to His disciples in Palestine and to the Nephites in the Western Hemisphere; He also spoke of ministering to "other sheep, which are not of this land [where the Nephites lived], neither of the land of Jerusalem, neither in any parts of that land round about whither I have been to minister" (3 Nephi 16:1).

> 5 Q. What are we to understand by the four and twenty elders, spoken of by John? A. We are to understand that these elders whom John saw, were elders who had been faithful in the work of the ministry and were dead; who belonged to the seven churches, and were then in the paradise of God.

Along with the fantastic visions of the throne of God, the exalted earth, and the symbolic beasts, John saw the familiar faces of his fellow servants in the work. Seated around the throne were twenty-four elders from the churches John worked with who had passed beyond this life and gained an eternal reward. The poignance of seeing these elders perhaps needs to be emphasized. At this point, John was alone and exiled to the island of Patmos, while nearly all of the other leaders of the Church had died. Many of them had died violently, martyred at the hands of their persecutors.

The long night of apostasy was beginning in the world that John lived in. Within a few more centuries, the light of the gospel on the other side of the world, among the children of Lehi, would be extinguished as well. Yet in these dark moments, the Lord offered John and his fellow servants a glimpse of the dawn of eternity and of the reward waiting for their sacrifices made on earth.

> 6 Q. What are we to understand by the book which John saw, which was sealed on the back with seven seals? A. We are to understand that it contains the revealed will, mysteries, and the works of God; the hidden things of his economy concerning this earth during the seven thousand years of its continuance, or its temporal existence.
>
> 7 Q. What are we to understand by the seven seals with which it was sealed? A. We are to understand that the first seal contains the things of the first thousand years, and the second also of the second thousand years, and so on until the seventh.

The book seen by John represents the temporal existence of the earth— that is, the time from the Fall of Adam and Eve to the end of the Millennium. We do not know how old the earth is in total, but these seven thousand years contain the saga of the sons and daughters of God, their dealings with Him, and the covenants and blessings He has given to humankind stretching back to our first parents. The Prophet Joseph Smith explained, "John had the curtains of heaven withdrawn, and by vision looked through the dark vista of future ages, and contemplated events that should transpire throughout every subsequent period of time until the final winding up scene."[7]

Section 77 does not explain the symbols John saw with each of the seven seals, and John's revelation does not spend equal time on the history of each of the thousand years seen in vision. In fact, the first through fifth seals are covered in only eleven verses (see Revelation 6:1–11), and the events of the sixth seal are covered in fourteen verses (see Revelation 6:12–7:8). However, the events that take place after the opening of the seventh seal until the Second Coming of Jesus Christ are covered in 211 verses, or the totality of Revelation 8–19. Six verses then describe the Millennium (see Revelation 20:1–6). Nine verses cover the final scenes, including the last rebellion of the wicked and their ultimate destruction in the final great conflict (see Revelation 20:7–15). Finally, John's vision concludes with thirty-three verses containing his description of the earth in its celestial glory (see Revelation 21:1–22:6).

One of the most valuable contributions that Doctrine and Covenants 77 makes to our understanding of the book of Revelation is to show that the clear focus of the book is on the latter days. Therefore, we must view the symbols of the book through that lens. The timetable revealed in section 77 shows that most of the tribulations that John saw will take place after the opening of the seventh seal, or during the seventh thousand years (see Doctrine and Covenants 77:13).[8]

> 8 Q. What are we to understand by the four angels, spoken of in the 7th chapter and 1st verse of Revelation? A. We are to understand that they are four angels sent forth from God, to whom is given power over the four parts of the earth, to save life and to destroy; these are they who have the everlasting gospel to commit to every nation, kindred, tongue, and people; having power to shut up the heavens, to seal up unto life, or to cast down to the regions of darkness.

Angels played a key role in the Restoration of the gospel of Jesus Christ. This work of restoration took place during the sixth seal, through the work of these angels along with Joseph Smith and other men and women called to assist in the work. An angel holding a trumpet has become one of the most well-known symbols of the Restoration and adorns many of the Church's temples. While the angel on our temples is affectionately referred to as Moroni, the angel itself is a symbol of all of the angels involved in the work of the Restoration.

Moroni is identified in the Doctrine and Covenants as being given the specific commission to reveal the Book of Mormon, which contains "the fulness of my everlasting gospel" (Doctrine and Covenants 27:5). But Moroni was only the first of many angels who took part in the Restoration. Not all the angels who participated in the Restoration were named, but at least the following were involved: Moroni, John the Baptist, Peter, James, John, Moses, Elijah, Elias, Gabriel, Raphael, and Michael (see Doctrine and Covenants 13; 110; 128:19–21).

The four angels referred to in Doctrine and Covenants 77:8 are involved in the sealing of the servants of God. Joseph Smith taught that "four destroying angels [hold] power over the four quarters of the earth, until the servants of God are sealed in their foreheads which signifies sealing the blessing upon their heads meaning the everlasting covenant, thereby making their calling and election sure. When a seal is put upon the father and mother it secures their posterity so that they cannot be lost but will be saved by virtue of the covenant of their father and mother."[9]

> 9 Q. What are we to understand by the angel ascending from the east, Revelation 7th chapter and 2nd verse? A. We are to understand that the angel ascending from the east is he to whom is given the seal of the living God over the twelve tribes of Israel; wherefore, he crieth unto the four angels having the everlasting gospel, saying: Hurt not the earth, neither the sea, nor the trees, till we have sealed the servants of our God in their foreheads. And, if you will receive it, this is Elias which was to come to gather together the tribes of Israel and restore all things.

We do not know the precise identity of the Elias mentioned in this passage. According to the scriptures, several people have been identified as Elias. The Doctrine and Covenants identifies the ancient prophet Noah as an Elias and as the person to whom the Lord has "committed the keys of bringing to pass the restoration of all things" (Doctrine and Covenants 27:6). The prophet Elijah acts as an Elias preparing the way (see Malachi 4:5; Doctrine and Covenants 110:13–14). John the Baptist was identified as an Elias (see Matthew 17:10–13). John the Revelator is also identified as an Elias, based on how this revelation is interpreted (see Doctrine and Covenants 77:14).

Given that Elias can function as a calling and a title in addition to being a personal name, it is possible that the Elias referred to in this verse is a composite figure. This Elias may represent all the angels involved in the work of the Restoration of the latter days.[10] In the 1835 account of the First Vision, Joseph Smith mentioned that he saw not only the Father and the Son but also "many angels in this vision."[11] The Elias referred to in this passage may represent the many named and unnamed angels who participated and who still assist in the work of the Restoration, from the First Vision down to the present day.

One last possibility is that this Elias is not John the Baptist, John the Revelator, or any other prophet but Jesus Christ Himself. The Joseph Smith Translation of John 1:20–28 identifies another Elias who "was to restore all things" (Joseph Smith Translation, John 1:22 [in the Bible appendix]). In this passage, John the Baptist identifies Christ as this Elias, saying, "He it is of whom I bear record. He is that prophet, even Elias, who, coming after me, is preferred before me, whose shoe's latchet I am not worthy to unloose, or whose place I am not able to fill; for he shall baptize, not only with water, but with fire, and with the Holy Ghost" (Joseph Smith Translation, John 1:28 [in the Bible appendix]). If we are speaking of the restoration of "all things" (Doctrine and Covenants 77:9), then the person who serves as Elias in this instance is the Savior. He is the person who began the greatest of all restorations by reversing the work of death itself and redeeming humankind (see 1 Corinthians 15:22). He is the one who will carry out the "restitution of all things, which God hath spoken by the mouth of all his holy prophets since the world began" (Acts 3:21).

> 10 Q. What time are the things spoken of in this chapter to be accomplished? A. They are to be accomplished in the sixth thousand years, or the opening of the sixth seal.

We do not know the precise correlation between our time and God's time, and so it is difficult to know precisely when the sixth seal ends and the seventh seal begins. We should not assume, for instance, that the year AD 2000 corresponds with the opening of the seventh seal, and so forth. The Lord's answer to the question in verse 10 makes it clear that the initial work of the Restoration of the gospel took place in the sixth thousand years, but we do not know precisely when those thousand years end and the seventh thousand years, which are prophesied to be the Millennium of peace, begins.

> 11 Q. What are we to understand by sealing the one hundred and forty-four thousand, out of all the tribes of Israel—twelve thousand out of every tribe? A. We are to understand that those who are sealed are high priests, ordained unto the holy order of God, to administer the everlasting gospel; for they are they who are ordained out of every nation, kindred, tongue, and people, by the angels to whom is given power over the nations of the earth, to bring as many as will come to the church of the First-born.

The book of Revelation mentions that 144,000, or 12,000 from each of the tribes of Israel, will be sealed. The number twelve is associated symbolically with Israel. For instance, there are twelve tribes and twelve apostles called to minister to and judge those tribes (see 1 Nephi 12:9). Twelve multiplied by twelve, or twelve squared, represents the idea of Israel raised to a new order of magnitude, or the millennial Israel.[12] These high priests will be drawn from "every nation, kindred, tongue, and people" (verse 11), demonstrating the global reach of the Church in the latter days. As the gospel rolls forth throughout the world, it is encouraging to think of the formation of this select group of high priests. According to this passage, represented among the 144,000 will be members from Brazil, Russia, Malaysia, Italy, Ghana, and every other nation.

We should not make the assumption that the 144,000 will be the only ones who will receive blessings on that day. John also spoke of a "great multitude, which no man could number, of all nations, and kindreds, and people, and tongues" (Revelation 7:9) that stood before the throne of God. The Prophet Joseph tied the identity of the 144,000 and the great multitude to those who participate in temple ordinances for the dead. He taught:

> It is not only necessary that you should be baptized for your dead, but you will have to go through all the ordinances for them, same as you have gone through to save yourselves; there will be 144,000 Saviors on Mount Zion, and with them an innumerable host, that no man can number. Oh! I beseech you to go forward, and make your calling and your election sure; and if any man preach any other gospel than that which I have preached, he shall be cursed, and some of you who now hear me shall see it, and know that I testify the truth concerning them.[13]

12 Q. What are we to understand by the sounding of the trumpets, mentioned in the 8th chapter of Revelation? A. We are to understand that as God made the world in six days, and on the seventh day he finished his work, and sanctified it, and also formed man out of the dust of the earth, even so, in the beginning of the seventh thousand years will the Lord God sanctify the earth, and complete the salvation of man, and judge all things, and shall redeem all things, except that which he hath not put into his power, when he shall have sealed all things, unto the end of all things; and the sounding of the trumpets of the seven angels are the preparing and finishing of his work, in the beginning of the seventh thousand years—the preparing of the way before the time of his coming.

The seventh thousand years act effectively as the Sabbath of the earth's temporal existence. John wrote, "And when he had opened the seventh seal, there was silence in heaven about the space of half an hour. And I saw the seven angels which stood before God; and to them were given seven trumpets" (Revelation 8:1–2). This series of trumps sounding, and the events associated with them, are detailed in Doctrine and Covenants 88:95–107, which describes the Resurrection of all of God's children who came to earth. This Resurrection will culminate with the final trump, when "the angels be crowned with the glory of his might, and the saints shall be filled with his glory, and receive their inheritance and be made equal with him" (Doctrine and Covenants 88:107).

During this thousand-year-long Sabbath day, the Savior will carry out and complete His work of "the salvation of man," which is defined here as judging and redeeming all things. These blessings come to all those "which he hath not put into his power," meaning that the people in the telestial kingdom and the sons of perdition will not be able to partake of the blessings of the Millennium until near its end.

> 13 Q. When are the things to be accomplished, which are written in the 9th chapter of Revelation? A. They are to be accomplished after the opening of the seventh seal, before the coming of Christ.

The ninth chapter of Revelation contains some of the most terrifying imagery found in the book and speaks of wars and plagues poured out upon the earth in the latter days. Doctrine and Covenants 77:13 indicates that these events will take place *after* the opening of the seventh seal but *before* the coming of Christ. This seems to indicate not that the seventh thousand years will commence immediately with the coming of Christ but that His coming will be preceded by some of the most terrible of the events foreseen by John. Again, we do not know the precise time of the opening of the seventh seal or even whether we are currently living in the sixth or the seventh seal.

In this case, using the metaphor that each of the thousand years is like a day, and the seventh thousand years is the Sabbath of the earth's temporal existence, is instructive. A day does not begin when the sun emerges over the mountain; rather, it begins in the middle of the night, when the darkness is at its height. Likewise, the seventh thousand years begins in a dark place but eventually gives way to the gradual coming of the light. The coming of

Christ may be likened to the moment when the sun finally bursts over the horizon and bathes the earth in light.

> 14 Q. What are we to understand by the little book which was eaten by John, as mentioned in the 10th chapter of Revelation? A. We are to understand that it was a mission, and an ordinance, for him to gather the tribes of Israel; behold, this is Elias, who, as it is written, must come and restore all things.

John describes the book spoken of here using these words: "And I took the little book out of the angel's hand, and ate it up; and it was in my mouth sweet as honey: and as soon as I had eaten it, my belly was bitter" (Revelation 10:10). The sweetness and bitterness of the book speak to the bittersweet nature of John's mission. The Savior said of John, "He has undertaken a greater work; therefore I will make him as flaming fire and a ministering angel; he shall minister for those who shall be heirs of salvation who dwell on the earth" (Doctrine and Covenants 7:6). John was told he would "never taste of death" (3 Nephi 28:7), a sweet thing for sure. He was told that he would never have pain while in the flesh, the same blessing given to the three Nephite disciples.

But John and the three Nephite disciples were not made completely impervious to pain. The bitterness of their mission came in the Savior's promise that they would not know sorrow "save it be for the sins of the world" (3 Nephi 28:9). John watched as the early Christian Church fell into apostasy and disarray. He witnessed the depraved use of the name of Christ to carry out horrific acts of violence and prejudice over the centuries. But he also continued to labor to fulfill the mission the Lord had given to him. Only a year prior to this revelation, Joseph Smith was caught up by the Spirit and prophesied "that John the Revelator was then among the ten tribes of Israel who had been lead away by Salmanaser King of Israel, to prepare them for their return, from their Long dispersion, to again possess the land of their father's."[14]

John lived to see some of the worst and greatest events in the history of mankind, a bitter and sweet mission indeed.

> 15 Q. What is to be understood by the two witnesses, in the eleventh chapter of Revelation? A. They are two prophets that are to be raised up to the Jewish nation in the last days, at the time of the restoration, and to prophesy to the Jews after they

are gathered and have built the city of Jerusalem in the land of their fathers.

The two witnesses spoken of here are described by John as ministering to the people of Jerusalem for "a thousand two hundred and threescore days" (Revelation 11:3). They will have power to shut the heavens and smite the earth with plagues. When they have finished their testimony, they will be overcome by their enemies and killed. However, after three and a half days they will be resurrected and ascend into heaven (see Revelation 11:7–12). Doctrine and Covenants 77 identifies them as "two prophets that are to be raised up to the Jewish nation in the last days" (verse 15).

The title of "prophet" given to these two witnesses indicates that they will likely be leaders from The Church of Jesus Christ of Latter-day Saints, ordained and set apart by the heads of the Church. An earlier revelation to Joseph Smith declares that "it shall not be given to any one to go forth to preach my gospel, or to build up my church, except he be ordained by some one who has authority, and it is known to the church that he has authority and has been regularly ordained by the heads of the church" (Doctrine and Covenants 41:11). The designation of "prophets" raised up to the Jewish nation means that these witnesses will likely be called from among the General Authorities of the Church.

Another significant addition that this passage makes to the book of Revelation is that these prophets are to be called *after* the Jewish people have gathered and rebuilt the city of Jerusalem. This is a prophecy of Joseph Smith's that foresaw the modern establishment of the state of Israel in the wake of the Second World War. As Nephi prophesied, the Gentile nations will act as nursing fathers and mothers as the Jewish people return to Palestine (see 1 Nephi 21:7). The establishment of the state of Israel in 1948 constitutes another prophecy of Joseph Smith that has been fulfilled.

End Notes

1. Joseph Smith, in History, 1838–1856, volume A-1 [23 December 1805–30 August 1834], 192, josephsmithpapers.org.
2. Revelation, 20 March 1832, 1, josephsmithpapers.org.
3. See Richard D. Draper, "Historical Context and Overview of Doctrine and Covenants 77," in *Doctrine and Covenants Reference Companion* (Salt Lake City, UT: Deseret Book, 2015), 783.
4. See Kenneth W. Baldridge, "Pearl of Great Price," *Encyclopedia of Mormonism* (New York: Macmillan Publishing Company, 1992), 679–680. See also "Historical Introduction," Answers to Questions, between circa 4 and circa 20 March 1832 [D&C 77], josephsmithpapers.org.
5. Joseph Smith, in History, 1838–1856, volume D-1 [1 August 1842–1 July 1843], 1523, josephsmithpapers.org.
6. Joseph Smith, in History, 1838–1856, volume D-1 [1 August 1842–1 July 1843], 1523, josephsmithpapers.org.
7. Joseph Smith, in History, 1838–1856, volume C-1 [2 November 1838–31 July 1842], 69, josephsmithpapers.org.
8. See Joseph Fielding McConkie and Craig J. Ostler, *Revelations of the Restoration* (Salt Lake City, UT: Deseret Book, 2000), 555.
9. Joseph Smith, in History, 1838–1856, volume E-1 [1 July 1843–30 April 1844], 1690, josephsmithpapers.org.
10. See Joseph Fielding Smith, *Doctrines of Salvation*, comp. Bruce R. McConkie (1955), 1:170–174.
11. Journal, 1835–1836, 24, josephsmithpapers.org.
12. See Stephen E. Robinson and H. Dean Garrett, *A Commentary on the Doctrine and Covenants* (Salt Lake City, UT: Deseret Book, 2000), 2:344.
13. Joseph Smith, in History, 1838–1856, volume F-1 [1 May 1844–8 August 1844], 19, josephsmithpapers.org.
14. John Whitmer, History, 1831–circa 1847, 27, josephsmithpapers.org.

Doctrine and Covenants Section 78

That You May Be Equal in the Bonds of Heavenly Things

Historical Context

DURING THIS EARLY PERIOD OF CHURCH HISTORY, LEADERS CONSTANTLY worked to balance the needs of the Church in Ohio and Missouri. This revelation directed Joseph Smith, Sidney Rigdon, and Newel K. Whitney to travel to Missouri to organize several business ventures of the Church. In July 1831 a revelation commanded Sidney Gilbert, the business partner of Newel K. Whitney, to establish a store in Independence, Missouri, to raise funds "to buy lands for the good of the Saints" and to "plant them in their inheritance" (Doctrine and Covenants 57:8).

Another pressing concern was the need to raise funds for the publication of Joseph Smith's revelations. At a conference held in November 1831, several Church leaders were charged with the "sacred writings which they have entrusted to them to carry to Zion."[1] A revelation given at the conference created the Literary Firm, a consecrated effort by several Church leaders—including Joseph Smith, Oliver Cowdery, Sidney Rigdon, Martin Harris, and W. W. Phelps—to oversee the publication of the revelations. Funds raised from this venture were to be placed into a storehouse, and the leaders were instructed that "the benefits shall be consecrated unto the inhabitants of Zion, and unto their generations" (Doctrine and Covenants 70:8).

The revelation in Doctrine and Covenants 78 directed Church leaders to organize these ventures into one firm. It was originally called the United Firm, but the name was later edited in the revelations to be called the "order" or the "united order" (see Doctrine and Covenants 78:8; 82:20; 92:1; 104:1, 5, 10, 48).[2] Joseph Smith, Sidney Rigdon, and Newel K. Whitney were then asked to travel to Missouri to "sit in council with the saints which are in Zion" and organize the members of the Church in accordance with the revelations (Doctrine and Covenants 78:9).

Doctrine and Covenants 78 was the first of several revelations given to Joseph Smith that were published with code names throughout the text. For instance, when section 78 was first published in the 1835 Doctrine and Covenants, the code name *Enoch* was used for Joseph Smith, *Pelogoram* was used for Sidney Ridgon, and *Ahashdah* was used for Newel K. Whitney.[3] These code names did not appear in the original revelation. Elder Orson Pratt explained why the code names were used in the publication of these revelations: "It was thought wisdom, in consequence of the persecutions of our enemies in Kirtland and some of the regions around, that some of the names should be changed, and Joseph was called Baurak Ale, which was a Hebrew word, meaning God bless you. He was also called Gazelem, being a person to whom the Lord had given the Urim and Thummim. Sidney Rigdon was given the name Beneemy. And the revelation where it read so many dollars into the treasure was changed to talents. And the city of New York was changed to Cainhannoch."[4] Once the need to conceal identities had passed, the code names were removed from the Doctrine and Covenants and replaced with the original names.[5]

Verse-by-Verse Commentary

1 The Lord spake unto Joseph Smith, Jun., saying: Hearken unto me, saith the Lord your God, who are ordained unto the

high priesthood of my church, who have assembled yourselves together;

2 And listen to the counsel of him who has ordained you from on high, who shall speak in your ears the words of wisdom, that salvation may be unto you in that thing which you have presented before me, saith the Lord God.

3 For verily I say unto you, the time has come, and is now at hand; and behold, and lo, it must needs be that there be an organization of my people, in regulating and establishing the affairs of the storehouse for the poor of my people, both in this place and in the land of Zion—

4 For a permanent and everlasting establishment and order unto my church, to advance the cause, which ye have espoused, to the salvation of man, and to the glory of your Father who is in heaven;

The immediate context of this revelation is important in understanding how the revelation has developed. In the earliest version, the phrase "in regulating and establishing the affairs of the storehouse for the poor of my people" (verse 3) was not present. Instead, the revelation read that "it must needs be that there be an organization of the Literary and Mercantile establishments of my church."[6] The revelation referred to a group of Church leaders, known as the United Firm, who had consecrated their property to ensure the printing of the scriptures and other Church publications (see Doctrine and Covenants 70:1–5). The firm was also known as the United Order and the Order of Enoch.[7] This group covenanted to live an iteration of the law of consecration in which they gave of their resources to help ensure the printing of the scriptures. In exchange, their families were provided for from funds raised from the sale of the scriptures, and the surplus funds were used to operate the Church and to purchase land for the Saints in Ohio and Missouri.

By the time the Doctrine and Covenants was published in 1835, the United Firm had been reorganized as instructed in another revelation that provided individual members with specific stewardships (see Doctrine and Covenants 104). However, the principles found in the revelation were still valuable to guide the Church in its attempts to live the law of consecration, so the revelation was revised with new phrasing that better fit the general needs of the Church. The word *firm*, which appeared in the revelation, was also replaced with *order* (see Doctrine and Covenants 78:8). The united order referred only to this group, but in the late nineteenth and early twentieth centuries, it became common for Church leaders to refer to the united order and the law of consecration as the same thing.

> 5 That you may be equal in the bonds of heavenly things, yea, and earthly things also, for the obtaining of heavenly things.

> 6 For if ye are not equal in earthly things ye cannot be equal in obtaining heavenly things;

> 7 For if you will that I give unto you a place in the celestial world, you must prepare yourselves by doing the things which I have commanded you and required of you.

> 8 And now, verily thus saith the Lord, it is expedient that all things be done unto my glory, by you who are joined together in this order;

> 9 Or, in other words, let my servant Newel K. Whitney and my servant Joseph Smith, Jun., and my servant Sidney Rigdon sit in council with the saints which are in Zion;

> 10 Otherwise Satan seeketh to turn their hearts away from the truth, that they become blinded and understand not the things which are prepared for them.

> 11 Wherefore, a commandment I give unto you, to prepare and organize yourselves by a bond or everlasting covenant that cannot be broken.

> 12 And he who breaketh it shall lose his office and standing in the church, and shall be delivered over to the buffetings of Satan until the day of redemption.

In this revelation, the Lord says that the establishment of the law of consecration is necessary "for the salvation of man" (verse 4). That may seem like an overly dramatic statement, but these verses explain why consecration was and remains such an important law for the members of the Church. President Dieter F. Uchtdorf has taught that "like two sides of a coin, the temporal and spiritual are inseparable. . . . Unfortunately, there are those who overlook the temporal because they consider it less important. They treasure the spiritual while minimizing the temporal. While it is important to have our thoughts inclined toward heaven, we miss the essence of our religion if our hands are not also inclined toward our fellowman."[8]

The Lord teaches a similar principle in these verses. To be equal in heavenly things, we must strive to be united in earthly things. Those who cling too tightly to their temporal goods will have difficulty in living the laws of the gospel and gaining exaltation. Consecration was and is a sacred covenant for Church members, especially for those who have made temple covenants. The Lord warns that those who abuse or violate the law of consecration will lose their office and standing and be turned over to the buffetings of Satan. In particular, those who misuse the sacred funds of the Church or take advantage of the trust of Church members for financial gain are subject to severe penalties.

> 13 Behold, this is the preparation wherewith I prepare you, and the foundation, and the ensample which I give unto you, whereby you may accomplish the commandments which are given you;
>
> 14 That through my providence, notwithstanding the tribulation which shall descend upon you, that the church may stand independent above all other creatures beneath the celestial world;

Though the law of consecration asks members of the Church to depend on and trust each other and their leaders, the Lord instructs the Church to remain independent. Self-reliance is a term used in concert with consecration. Brigham Young counseled Church members, "Ye Latter-day Saints, learn to sustain yourselves. If you cannot obtain all you wish for today, learn to do without that which you cannot purchase and pay for; and bring your minds into subjection that you must and will live within your means."[9]

What the Church asks of its members, it also asks of itself. President Gordon B. Hinckley taught:

> In the financial operations of the Church, we have observed two basic and fixed principles: One, the Church will live within its means. It will not spend more than it receives. Two, a fixed percentage of the income will be set aside to build reserves against what might be called a possible "rainy day." For years, the Church has taught its membership the principle of setting aside a reserve of food, as well as money, to take care of emergency needs that might arise. We are only trying to follow the same principle for the Church as a whole.[10]

15 That you may come up unto the crown prepared for you, and be made rulers over many kingdoms, saith the Lord God, the Holy One of Zion, who hath established the foundations of Adam-ondi-Ahman;

16 Who hath appointed Michael your prince, and established his feet, and set him upon high, and given unto him the keys of salvation under the counsel and direction of the Holy One, who is without beginning of days or end of life.

The last clause of verse 15 and all of verse 16 were added in by Joseph Smith during the publication of the 1835 Doctrine and Covenants. By that time, Joseph Smith had received a revelation about Adam-ondi-Ahman being the place where Adam gathered his posterity to give them a final blessing before his death (see Doctrine and Covenants 107:53–57). Later, Spring Hill in Missouri was identified as the location of Adam-ondi-Ahman (see Doctrine and Covenants 116).

The Lord also identifies the authority of Michael as second to that of Jesus Christ Himself, or the Holy One. While many faiths disparage Adam for his role in the Fall, the revelations of the Doctrine and Covenants uphold him as Michael, the angel who fought against Satan and his minions in premortality (see Revelation 12:7–9). Joseph Smith taught:

The priesthood was first given to Adam, he obtained the first presidency and held the keys of it from generation to generation; he obtained it in the creation before the world was formed as in Gen. 1:26, 28 [and] he had dominion given him over every living creature. He is Michael the Archangel spoken of in the scriptures. Then to Noah who is Gabriel, he stands next in authority to Adam in the priesthood. He was called of God to this office and was the father of all living in his day and to him was given the dominion. These men held keys first on earth and then in heaven. The priesthood is an everlasting principle and existed with God from eternity, and will to eternity, without beginning of days or end of years.[11]

17 Verily, verily, I say unto you, ye are little children, and ye have not as yet understood how great blessings the Father hath in his own hands and prepared for you;

18 And ye cannot bear all things now; nevertheless, be of good cheer, for I will lead you along. The kingdom is yours and the blessings thereof are yours, and the riches of eternity are yours.

19 And he who receiveth all things with thankfulness shall be made glorious; and the things of this earth shall be added unto him, even an hundred fold, yea, more.

20 Wherefore, do the things which I have commanded you, saith your Redeemer, even the Son Ahman, who prepareth all things before he taketh you;

21 For ye are the church of the Firstborn, and he will take you up in a cloud, and appoint every man his portion.

22 And he that is a faithful and wise steward shall inherit all things. Amen.

Doctrine and Covenants 78:20 uses a term, "Son Ahman," that makes reference to a document, "Answers to Questions," that became Doctrine and Covenants 77. The document is inscribed in the handwriting of Church Historian John Whitmer and is labeled "A Sample of pure Language given by Joseph the Seer." The document reads as follows:

Question: What is the name of God in pure Language
Answer: Awmen.

Q: The meaning of the pure word A[w]men
A: It is the being which made all things in all its parts.

Q: What is the name of the Son of God.
A: The Son Awmen.

Q: What is the Son Awmen.
A: It is the greatest of all the parts of Awmen which is the Godhead the first born.

Q: What is man.
A: This signifies Sons Awmen. the human family the children of men the greatest parts of Awmen Sons the Son Awmen

Q: What are Angels called in pure language.
A: Awmen Angls-men

Q: What are the meaning of these words.
A: Awmen's Ministering servants Sanctified who are sent forth from heaven to minister for or to Sons Awmen the greatest part of Awmen Son. Sons Awmen Son Awmen Awmen.

Apparently, John Whitmer's spelling of the name was phonetic because in this and other revelations, the name is spelled as "Son Ahman" (Doctrine and Covenants 95:17). In Joseph Smith's translation of the book of Genesis, it is taught that "in the language of Adam, Man of Holiness is his name, and the name of his Only Begotten is the Son of Man, even Jesus Christ" (Moses 6:57). If the pure language referred to in this document is the same as the language of Adam, then God's name is Ahman, or Man of Holiness.

End Notes

1. Minutes, 12 November 1831, 18, josephsmithpapers.org.
2. See Craig J. Ostler, "Consecration," in *Doctrine and Covenants Reference Companion* (Salt Lake City, UT: Deseret Book, 2015), 107.
3. See Doctrine and Covenants, 1835, 204–205, josephsmithpapers.org.
4. Robert J. Woodford, "The Historical Development of the Doctrine and Covenants" (Provo, UT: Brigham Young University dissertation, 1974), 2:994.
5. See "Historical Introduction," Revelation, 1 March 1832 [D&C 78], josephsmithpapers.org.
6. Revelation, 1 March 1832 [D&C 78], 1, josephsmithpapers.org.
7. See Lyndon W. Cook, *The Revelations of the Prophet Joseph Smith: A Historical and Biographical Commentary of the Doctrine and Covenants* (Salt Lake City, UT: Deseret Book, 1985), 167.
8. Dieter F. Uchtdorf, "Providing in the Lord's Way," *Ensign* or *Liahona*, Nov. 2011, 53.
9. *Teachings of Presidents of the Church: Brigham Young* (1997), 231.
10. Gordon B. Hinckley, "The State of the Church," *Ensign*, May 1991, 53–54.
11. Discourse, between circa 26 June and circa 4 August 1839–A, as Reported by William Clayton, 11–12, josephsmithpapers.org.

Doctrine and Covenants Section 79

Proclaim Glad Tidings of Great Joy

Historical Context

JARED CARTER WAS A CONVERT TO THE CHURCH FROM CHENANGO, NEW York. He received the gospel and was baptized by Hyrum Smith on February 20, 1831. When the call came to gather to Ohio, Jared traveled along with members of the Colesville Branch, giving up his life and home in New York.[1] He spent much of the later part of 1831 and early 1832 preaching the gospel in Ohio, Pennsylvania, New York, and Vermont. A few weeks after he arrived home from his mission, he traveled to Hiram, Ohio, to meet with Joseph Smith, who was staying at the home of John and Elsa Johnson.

Jared wrote in his journal about the experience of being present when this revelation was given. "I at length went to Hiram to the Seer to inquire the will of the Lord concerning my ministry," he recorded. "The ensuing season and the word of the Lord came forth that showed that it was his will that I should go forth to the Eastern countries in the power of the ordinance wherewith I had been ordained which was to the high privilege of administering in the name of Jesus Christ even to seal on earth and to build up the Church of Christ and to work miracles in the name of Christ." He added, "Now I have received a revelation of the will of the Lord to me by the mouth of Joseph the Seer, that I should not only preach the gospel from place to place, but from city to city."[2]

Verse-by-Verse Commentary

1 Verily I say unto you, that it is my will that my servant Jared Carter should go again into the eastern countries, from place to place, and from city to city, in the power of the ordination wherewith he has been ordained, proclaiming glad tidings of great joy, even the everlasting gospel.

2 And I will send upon him the Comforter, which shall teach him the truth and the way whither he shall go;

3 And inasmuch as he is faithful, I will crown him again with sheaves.

4 Wherefore, let your heart be glad, my servant Jared Carter, and fear not, saith your Lord, even Jesus Christ. Amen.

Jared Carter had already made considerable sacrifices by serving a mission, but he was called once again to return to the mission field with the promise that the Lord "will crown him again with sheaves" (verse 3). After this mission was ended, he wrote in his journal:

Now while I make this record, I remember the goodness of the Lord to me in the mission that I have lately been to in the East. I have enjoyed health continually and the Lord, not withstanding the great opposition to the glorious work, has blessed me . . . in this mission which I have been gone six months and two days. The Lord has permitted me to administer the gospel to 79 souls and many others by my instrumentality have been convinced of this most glorious work, where I have been in this mission. All that have been baptized while I have been in the regions where I have been in this mission is 98, and many others have been convinced of the work that sooner or later I think will obey the work.[3]

End Notes

1. See "Biography: Carter, Jared," Joseph Smith Papers, accessed Feb. 19, 2023, https://www.josephsmithpapers.org/person/jared-carter.
2. Quoted in Lyndon W. Cook, *The Revelations of the Prophet Joseph Smith: A Historical and Biographical Commentary of the Doctrine and Covenants* (Salt Lake City, UT: Deseret Book, 1985), 169. See also "Historical Introduction," Revelation, 12 March 1832 [D&C 79], josephsmithpapers.org.
3. *Journal of Jared Carter,* spelling standardized, quoted in Cook, *The Revelations of the Prophet Joseph Smith*, 571. See also "Historical Introduction," Revelation, 7 March 1832 [D&C 80], josephsmithpapers.org.

$\mathcal{D}$octrine and $\mathcal{C}$ovenants
Section 80
Preach the Gospel to Every Creature

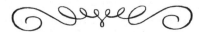

$\mathcal{H}$istorical $\mathcal{C}$ontext

STEPHEN BURNETT WAS JUST SEVENTEEN YEARS OLD WHEN HE WAS OR-dained to the high priesthood at a conference held in Kirtland, Ohio, in October 1831. A few months later, in January 1831, a revelation given at a conference in Amherst, Ohio, directed Stephen to preach the gospel with Ruggles Eames (see Doctrine and Covenants 75:35). It doesn't appear that Ruggles Eames or Stephen Burnett ever served the mission to which they were called in that revelation. A few weeks later, Stephen visited Joseph Smith, who received this revelation. The revelation instructed Stephen to begin a new mission with Eden Smith, a twenty-seven-year-old convert from Indiana.[1]

*V*erse-by-*V*erse *C*ommentary

1 Verily, thus saith the Lord unto you my servant Stephen Burnett: Go ye, go ye into the world and preach the gospel to every creature that cometh under the sound of your voice.

2 And inasmuch as you desire a companion, I will give unto you my servant Eden Smith.

3 Wherefore, go ye and preach my gospel, whether to the north or to the south, to the east or to the west, it mattereth not, for ye cannot go amiss.

4 Therefore, declare the things which ye have heard, and verily believe, and know to be true.

5 Behold, this is the will of him who hath called you, your Redeemer, even Jesus Christ. Amen.

Eden Smith and Stephen Burnett did not get the immediate chance to preach together. Instead, two weeks after this revelation was given, Stephen departed on a mission in the company of John Smith, Eden's father. The two traveled to southern Ohio to preach to John Smith's relatives. Stephen and Eden Smith were able to preach together in August 1832, after Eden's health had recovered.[2]

At this point in time, the Lord entrusted Stephen Burnett with the power to choose where he served, stating that it didn't matter where he went, "for ye cannot go amiss" (verse 3). This statement is another illustration of the Lord's admonition that "it is not meet that I should command in all things" (Doctrine and Covenants 58:26). Even something as significant as the place where a missionary labors can be left up to the wisdom and good judgment of the receiver in special cases. On other occasions, the Lord involves Himself deeply in the call of missionaries. Elder Ronald A. Rasband shared the experience of assigning mission calls in company with President Henry B. Eyring:

First, we knelt together in prayer. I remember Elder Eyring using very sincere words, asking the Lord to bless him to know "perfectly" where the missionaries should be assigned. The word "perfectly" said much about the faith that Elder Eyring exhibited that day.

As we were nearing the completion of that assignment meeting, a picture of a certain missionary appeared on the screen. I had the strongest prompting, the strongest of the morning, that the missionary we had before us was to be assigned to Japan. I did not know that Elder Eyring was going to ask me on this one, but amazingly he did. I rather tentatively and humbly said to him, "Japan?" Elder Eyring responded immediately, "Yes, let's go there." And up on the computer screen the missions of Japan appeared. I instantly knew that the missionary was to go to the Japan Sapporo Mission. Elder Eyring did not ask me the exact name of the mission, but he did assign that missionary to the Japan Sapporo Mission.

Privately in my heart I was deeply touched and sincerely grateful to the Lord for allowing me to experience the prompting to know where that missionary should go. At the end of the meeting Elder Eyring bore his witness to me of the love of the Savior, which He has for each missionary assigned to go out into the world and preach the restored gospel. He said that it is by the great love of the Savior that His servants know where these wonderful young men and women, senior missionaries, and senior couple missionaries are to serve. I had a further witness that morning that every missionary called in this Church, and assigned or reassigned to a particular mission, is called by revelation from the Lord God Almighty through one of these, His servants.[3]

End Notes

1. See "Biography: Smith, Eden," Joseph Smith Papers, accessed Feb. 19, 2023, https://www.josephsmithpapers.org/person/eden-smith.
2. See "Historical Introduction," Revelation, 7 March 1832 [D&C 80], josephsmithpapers.org. See also Lyndon W. Cook, *The Revelations of the Prophet Joseph Smith: A Historical and Biographical Commentary of the Doctrine and Covenants* (Salt Lake City, UT: Deseret Book, 1985), 170.
3. Ronald A. Rasband, "The Divine Call of a Missionary," *Ensign* or *Liahona*, May 2010, 52.

$\mathcal{D}$octrine and $\mathcal{C}$ovenants Section 81

The Keys of the Kingdom

$\mathcal{H}$istorical $\mathcal{C}$ontext

DOCTRINE AND COVENANTS 81 IS A BRIEF REVELATION THAT MARKS AN important step in the creation of the quorum of the First Presidency. At a conference held on January 25, 1832, in Amherst, Ohio, Joseph Smith was ordained as president of the high priesthood.[1] A few weeks later, on March 8, 1832, Joseph Smith chose and ordained Sidney Rigdon and Jesse Gause as his counselors in the First Presidency.[2] This revelation, received on March 15, declared that the keys of the kingdom rested with the presidency of the high priesthood and outlined some of the duties of a counselor in the First Presidency.

The revelation was originally received on behalf of Jesse Gause, but in the earliest copies of the revelation, Gause's name is crossed out and replaced with the name of Frederick G. Williams. Jesse Gause was a relatively new convert, baptized in late 1831 or early 1832, when he was called as a counselor in the First Presidency. Before joining the Church, Gause was a former member of the United Society of Believers in Christ's Second Appearing (Shakers). After joining the Church, he acted as Joseph Smith's scribe and accompanied Joseph and Sidney Rigdon on a trip to Missouri in the spring of 1832. Gause only served in his calling as a member of the First Presidency during the spring and summer of 1832 before he ran into difficulties.

On a mission to the Shaker community at North Union, Ohio, Gause apparently attempted to convince his wife, Minerva, to reunite with him and join the Church. She refused his offer. After Minerva's refusal to join him, Gause began to struggle on his mission. He became ill and parted company with his missionary companion. Gause continued to travel to the East, but he all but disappears from the records of the Church after separating from his companion.[3] A notation in Joseph Smith's journal written on December 3, 1832, seems to indicate that Gause was excommunicated.[4] In his place, Frederick G. Williams was appointed as a counselor in the First Presidency.

When this revelation was first published in the 1835 edition of the Doctrine and Covenants, the name of Frederick G. Williams was included instead of Jesse Gause's name. This modification has appeared in every edition of the Doctrine and Covenants produced since that time. This action seems to indicate that Joseph Smith and other Church leaders considered this revelation to be direction for whomever held the position of a counselor in the First Presidency generally, not for a specific person.[5]

Verse-by-Verse Commentary

1 Verily, verily, I say unto you my servant Frederick G. Williams: Listen to the voice of him who speaketh, to the word of the Lord your God, and hearken to the calling wherewith you are called, even to be a high priest in my church, and a counselor unto my servant Joseph Smith, Jun.;

2 Unto whom I have given the keys of the kingdom, which belong always unto the Presidency of the High Priesthood:

While this revelation represents an important step toward creating the highest quorum of the Church, the First Presidency as we know it did not come into being for another year. On March 18, 1833, Sidney Rigdon and Frederick G. Williams were given priesthood keys and sustained as members of the First Presidency (see Doctrine and Covenants 90:8).[6] Section 81 recognizes the creation of the presidency of the high priesthood. Today the First Presidency, consisting of the President of the Church and his counselors, serves as both the presidency of the Church (including all of its organizations) and the presidency of the high priesthood. The First Presidency as it now functions in the Church was organized later, on March 18, 1833.[7]

The Lord declares that Joseph Smith holds the "keys of the kingdom" and that these keys belong to the presidency of the high priesthood (verse 2). A year later, in Doctrine and Covenants 90, this matter of the keys belonging to the presidency of the high priesthood was further clarified when the Lord told Joseph that his counselors "are accounted as equal with thee in holding the keys of this last kingdom" (Doctrine and Covenants 90:6). These kingdom keys are those keys that were originally given to Joseph Smith and Oliver Cowdery by Peter, James, and John who appeared to them near the Susquehanna river "declaring themselves as possessing the keys of the kingdom and the dispensation of the fulness of times" (Doctrine and Covenants 128:20; see also Doctrine and Covenants 27:13–14). In their essence, these keys give those who hold them the authority to direct how the gospel will "roll forth unto the ends of the earth" to build up the kingdom of God on earth in preparation for Christ's return, at which time He will bring with Him the "kingdom of heaven" (Doctrine and Covenants 65:2–6).

While Joseph Smith possessed the keys of the kingdom conferred upon him by Peter, James, and John when this revelation was given in 1832, the restoration of keys pertaining to God's kingdom was not yet complete, and further keys were needed. When the Kirtland Temple was dedicated in 1836, Moses, Elias, and Elijah all appeared to Joseph Smith and Oliver Cowdery and provided further priesthood keys (see Doctrine and Covenants 110). Joseph Smith also began to pass the keys on to other leaders as the Church grew and became more complex. Joseph first passed the keys on to the other members of the First Presidency and later gave them to the Quorum of the Twelve so that they could lead the Church.[8]

> 3 Therefore, verily I acknowledge him and will bless him, and also thee, inasmuch as thou art faithful in counsel, in the office which I have appointed unto you, in prayer always, vocally and in thy heart, in public and in private, also in thy ministry in

proclaiming the gospel in the land of the living, and among thy brethren.

4 And in doing these things thou wilt do the greatest good unto thy fellow beings, and wilt promote the glory of him who is your Lord.

5 Wherefore, be faithful; stand in the office which I have appointed unto you; succor the weak, lift up the hands which hang down, and strengthen the feeble knees.

6 And if thou art faithful unto the end thou shalt have a crown of immortality, and eternal life in the mansions which I have prepared in the house of my Father.

7 Behold, and lo, these are the words of Alpha and Omega, even Jesus Christ. Amen.

When Jesse Gause left his calling, the blessings that God mentions in this revelation were given to Frederick G. Williams, though they remained conditional, based on his faithfulness (see verse 3). Though the apostasy of Jesse Gause must have been distressing at the time, the elevation of Frederick G. Williams into the Presidency became a great blessing for the Church.

Williams became a stalwart supporter of the Church and a key figure in many of its most important events. In an earlier revelation, he was counseled to not sell his farm (see Doctrine and Covenants 64:21). In the years that followed, the land from Williams's farm was generously deeded to the Church. The Church used this land to build a printing house for the scriptures and provide a place for many Church leaders to build homes. Eventually, the land became the spot where the Kirtland Temple itself was built. Williams was the scribe for many important documents, including architectural drawings for the city of Zion, several revelations, and the first written account of the First Vision. For a time, Joseph Smith's family boarded with Williams's family, and Williams was a frequent missionary companion of the Prophet. Joseph even named his second-born son Frederick Granger Williams Smith.[9]

In his journal, Joseph Smith wrote a personal tribute to Williams:

Brother Frederick [G. Williams] is one of those men in whom I place the greatest confidence and trust[;] for I have found him ever full of love and Brotherly kindness[;] he is not a man of many words but is ever wining [sic] because of his constant mind[;] he shall ever have place in my heart and is ever entitled to my confidence. He is perfectly honest and upright, and seeks with all his heart to magnify his presidency in the Church of Christ, but fails in many instances, in consequence of a want of confidence in himself: God grant that he may overcome all evil.[10]

Joseph and Frederick did eventually conflict over the difficulties surrounding the Kirtland Safety Society. These difficulties in Kirtland took a heavy toll on Church leadership. In May 1837 the Kirtland stake high council leveled charges of misconduct against Williams. At a conference of the Church held in Missouri in November 1837, Williams was released as a member of the First Presidency, and Hyrum Smith was chosen to take his place.[11] But although Williams was removed from the First Presidency, he remained a member in good standing. He followed the Church during its exodus from Missouri and settled in Quincy, just downriver from Nauvoo. He passed away on October 10, 1842, of a lung hemorrhage, though his son, Ezra, later said it was more of a broken heart. Williams's family was the only one from the original First Presidency to travel to Utah and stay active in the Church.[12]

End Notes

1. See Minutes, 26–27 April 1832, 24, josephsmithpapers.org.
2. See Note, 8 March 1832, 10–11, josephsmithpapers.org.
3. See D. Michael Quinn, "Jesse Gause: Joseph Smith's Little-Known Counselor," *BYU Studies* 23 (Fall 1993): 487–93.
4. See Journal, 1832–1834, 3, josephsmithpapers.org.
5. See "Historical Introduction," Revelation, 15 March 1832 [D&C 81], josephsmithpapers.org.
6. See Minutes, 18 March 1833, 17, josephsmithpapers.org.
7. See Minutes, 18 March 1833, josephsmithpapers.org.
8. See Appendix 3: Orson Hyde, Statement about Quorum of the Twelve, circa Late March 1845, 1, josephsmithpapers.org.
9. See Frederick G. Williams, "Frederick Granger Williams of the First Presidency of the Church," *BYU Studies* 12, no. 3 (1972): 3–5.
10. Journal, 1832–1834, 23–24, josephsmithpapers.org.
11. See Minutes, 7 November 1837, 83, josephsmithpapers.org.
12. See Williams, "Frederick Granger Williams of the First Presidency of the Church," 11.

$\mathcal{D}$octrine and $\mathcal{C}$ovenants
Section 82
Unto Whom Much Is Given Much Is Required

$\mathcal{H}$istorical $\mathcal{C}$ontext

IN THE SPRING OF 1832 JOSEPH SMITH TRAVELED IN THE COMPANY OF SEV-
eral Church leaders to Independence, Missouri. While he was there, he met
with Church leaders from the area to discuss the growing Church settlement
in Missouri and its business affairs. One of the major concerns of the conference was regarding some hard feelings created the summer before when
Bishop Edward Partridge, Sidney Rigdon, and Joseph Smith had a disagree-
ment over where the temple should be built. Another question of concern
was how the two Church centers in Ohio and Missouri stood in relation to
one another.

Joseph Smith placed section 82 into a later history with the following
introduction:

> On the 26th. of April I called a general council of the church, and was
> acknowledged as the President, of the High priesthood, according to a

previous ordination at a Conference of High-priests, elders, and members, held at Amherst, Ohio, on the 25th of January 1832. The right hand of fellowship was given to me by the Bishop Edward Partridge, in behalf of the Church. The scene was solemn, impressive, And delightful. During the intermission, a difficulty or hardness which had existed between Bishop Partridge and Elder Rigdon was amicably settled, and when we came together in the afternoon all hearts seemed to rejoice, and I received the following.[1]

*V*erse-by-*V*erse *C*ommentary

1 Verily, verily, I say unto you, my servants, that inasmuch as you have forgiven one another your trespasses, even so I, the Lord, forgive you.

2 Nevertheless, there are those among you who have sinned exceedingly; yea, even all of you have sinned; but verily I say unto you, beware from henceforth, and refrain from sin, lest sore judgments fall upon your heads.

3 For of him unto whom much is given much is required; and he who sins against the greater light shall receive the greater condemnation.

4 Ye call upon my name for revelations, and I give them unto you; and inasmuch as ye keep not my sayings, which I give unto you, ye become transgressors; and justice and judgment are the penalty which is affixed unto my law.

The Lord's admonition for His servants to forgive refers to the reconciliation of Sidney Rigdon and Edward Partridge, who in the months leading up to this revelation had been embroiled in conflict with each other. A few months before, in November 1831, Sidney wrote a letter to the Saints in Missouri in which he charged Partridge with defrauding funds, insulted Joseph Smith, and presumed to take authority over the Prophet. At a conference of the Church held in Missouri on March 10, 1832, Bishop Partridge asked a council of high priests to write a letter to Sidney in which Bishop Partridge answered the charges leveled against him and asked for forgiveness from those he had wronged. A month later, during the conference that

Joseph Smith called on April 26, Sidney and Bishop Partridge reconciled and ended the bad feelings between them that had persisted for several months.[2]

The dispute between Sidney Rigdon and Edward Partridge was just one of the problems the leaders of the Church worked through at the April 26 conference. The Lord uses the revelation in section 82 to teach His leaders that if they do not keep their covenants, they will be under great condemnation. As the Book of Mormon illustrates, some people fall away into sin and transgression after they have been enlightened by the Spirit of God and have had a great knowledge of things pertaining to righteousness. If they fall away, these people become more hardened and worse off than those who have never received the gospel (see Alma 24:30).

> 5 Therefore, what I say unto one I say unto all: Watch, for the adversary spreadeth his dominions, and darkness reigneth;
>
> 6 And the anger of God kindleth against the inhabitants of the earth; and none doeth good, for all have gone out of the way.
>
> 7 And now, verily I say unto you, I, the Lord, will not lay any sin to your charge; go your ways and sin no more; but unto that soul who sinneth shall the former sins return, saith the Lord your God.

After declaring to the elders present that "all of you have sinned" (Doctrine and Covenants 82:2), the Lord warns against the influence of the adversary (see verse 5). He points out the simple truth that "none doeth good" (verse 6), or as the Book of Mormon states it, all men and women are "unprofitable servants" (Mosiah 2:21). But while the Lord recognizes the faults and sins of the leaders and members of His Church, He still sees their potential for immense good. It is important for members of the Church to recognize the same potential in their leaders and themselves.

Elder Dale G. Renlund once quoted Nelson Mandela, who said, "I'm no saint—that is, unless you think a saint is a sinner who keeps on trying." Elder Renlund added:

> This statement—"a saint is a sinner who keeps on trying"—should reassure and encourage members of the Church. Although we are referred to as "Latter-day Saints," we sometimes flinch at this reference. The term *Saints* is commonly used to designate those who have achieved an elevated state of holiness or even perfection. And we know perfectly well that we are not perfect. . . .

God cares a lot more about who we are and who we are becoming than about who we once were. He cares that we keep on trying.[3]

> 8 And again, I say unto you, I give unto you a new commandment, that you may understand my will concerning you;
>
> 9 Or, in other words, I give unto you directions how you may act before me, that it may turn to you for your salvation.
>
> 10 I, the Lord, am bound when ye do what I say; but when ye do not what I say, ye have no promise.
>
> 11 Therefore, verily I say unto you, that it is expedient for my servants Edward Partridge and Newel K. Whitney, A. Sidney Gilbert and Sidney Rigdon, and my servant Joseph Smith, and John Whitmer and Oliver Cowdery, and W. W. Phelps and Martin Harris to be bound together by a bond and covenant that cannot be broken by transgression, except judgment shall immediately follow, in your several stewardships—
>
> 12 To manage the affairs of the poor, and all things pertaining to the bishopric both in the land of Zion and in the land of Kirtland;

The new commandment that the Lord mentions in verse 8 was to organize the United Firm (or united order), a consecrated effort to provide for the Saints in Missouri and Kirtland, especially the poor. One of the things that separates the law of consecration from the regular charitable acts that are expected of the Lord's disciples is the law's associated covenant. The Lord introduced consecration early in the Restoration, and it has remained as one of the vital covenants that Church members enter into as part of their discipleship.

The United Firm was an iteration of the law of consecration that was expressed through a business partnership between the leaders named in this section. In verse 11 the Lord counsels the members of the United Firm to be bound "by a bond and covenant that cannot be broken by transgression, except judgment shall immediately follow."

In verse 10 the Lord exhorts the members of the United Firm to keep their covenants by promising that He is bound when they keep their covenants. How can an omnipotent and infinite being be bound by anything? James E. Talmage explains:

[My religion] has taught me that God holds Himself accountable to law even as He expects us to do. He has set us the example in obedience to law. I know that to say this would have been heresy a few decades ago. But we have his divine word for it: [Doctrine and Covenants 82:10]. He operates by law and not by arbitrariness or caprice. He is no tyrant to be propitiated and placated by honeyed words. He cannot be moved by wordy oratory. He is not a judge sitting to be influenced by the specious pleas of crafty advocates; and yet there is an eloquence that moves Him; there is a plea that influences Him. The eloquence of prayer from a broken heart and contrite spirit prevails with him.[4]

> 13 For I have consecrated the land of Kirtland in mine own due time for the benefit of the saints of the Most High, and for a stake to Zion.
>
> 14 For Zion must increase in beauty, and in holiness; her borders must be enlarged; her stakes must be strengthened; yea, verily I say unto you, Zion must arise and put on her beautiful garments.
>
> 15 Therefore, I give unto you this commandment, that ye bind yourselves by this covenant, and it shall be done according to the laws of the Lord.
>
> 16 Behold, here is wisdom also in me for your good.

Verses 13 and 14 contain the first mention in the Doctrine and Covenants of a stake of Zion. The concept is taken from Isaiah, who likened Zion and the latter-day house of Israel to a great tent held securely by cords fastened to firm stakes. Isaiah admonished Israel to "enlarge the place of thy tent, and let them stretch forth the curtains of thine habitations: spare not, lengthen thy cords, and strengthen thy stakes" (Isaiah 54:2). In verse 13 the Lord refers to Kirtland as a stake, meaning it is to become a stronghold of Zion.

In Joseph Smith's time, some assumed that every member of the Church would eventually relocate to Zion in Missouri. Today some members still make the same assumption. But while the building of the New Jerusalem remains a central goal of the Restoration (see Doctrine and Covenants 101:17–19), the physical city has yet to be established. According to Isaiah's vision, the borders of Zion, like an expanding tent, are meant to be enlarged in an ever-expanding way until Zion covers the earth. Such a massive tent must be stabilized by many strong stakes. The Lord is here designating Kirtland as the first such stake of what would become a vast network of thousands of strong Church communities throughout the world.

> 17 And you are to be equal, or in other words, you are to have equal claims on the properties, for the benefit of managing the concerns of your stewardships, every man according to his wants and his needs, inasmuch as his wants are just—

> 18 And all this for the benefit of the church of the living God, that every man may improve upon his talent, that every man may gain other talents, yea, even an hundred fold, to be cast into the Lord's storehouse, to become the common property of the whole church—

> 19 Every man seeking the interest of his neighbor, and doing all things with an eye single to the glory of God.

> 20 This order I have appointed to be an everlasting order unto you, and unto your successors, inasmuch as you sin not.

In verse 17 the Lord admonishes the members of the United Firm to be equal. This counsel echoes the direction the Lord gave the members of the other consecrated effort operated by the Church, the Literary Firm (see Doctrine and Covenants 70:14). Members of both groups were admonished to place any profits beyond "their necessities and their wants" into the Lord's storehouse so that "the benefits thereof shall be consecrated unto the inhabitants of Zion and unto their generations" (Doctrine and Covenants 70:7–8). Both the United Firm and the Literary Firm were iterations of the law of consecration that served their purpose and then came to an end (see Doctrine and Covenants 104).

The "everlasting order" referred to in verse 20 is a reference to the United Firm but also the law of consecration generally. The United Firm, inspired by and governed by the principles of consecration, did eventually come to an end (see Doctrine and Covenants 104). But the principles of consecration that informed the governance of the firm are eternal. The fact that the law of consecration is everlasting does not mean that consecration will look exactly the same in every era of the Church. Even though consecration has been a part of the teachings and work of the Church from the time this law was first revealed, the consecrated effort by a Church of millions spread across the world will undoubtedly look different than the effort carried out by a small group of Saints in North America during the 1830s.

Some people incorrectly think that the law of consecration is solely a system of finance. The law of consecration is much more holistic: Saints contribute not only through material means but also through their time, talents, and any other way they can. A bishop who works long hours for the good of his ward is consecrating. A parent who acts as a chaperone at a youth activity is consecrating. Dedicated ministering brothers or sisters who drop off meals or assist with childcare are also consecrating. Material means are only part of the law; the Lord intends a person to consecrate their whole self.

> 21 And the soul that sins against this covenant, and hardeneth his heart against it, shall be dealt with according to the laws of my church, and shall be delivered over to the buffetings of Satan until the day of redemption.

> 22 And now, verily I say unto you, and this is wisdom, make unto yourselves friends with the mammon of unrighteousness, and they will not destroy you.

> 23 Leave judgment alone with me, for it is mine and I will repay. Peace be with you; my blessings continue with you.

> 24 For even yet the kingdom is yours, and shall be forever, if you fall not from your steadfastness. Even so. Amen.

The Lord's counsel to "make friends with the mammon of unrighteousness" (verse 22) may seem curious in light of His teachings on another occasion that "ye cannot serve God and mammon" (Matthew 6:24). President Joseph Fielding Smith explained:

> The commandment of the Lord that the Saints should make themselves "friends with the mammon of unrighteousness," seems to be a hard saying when not properly understood. It is not intended . . . that the brethren were to partake with them in their sins; to receive them into their bosoms, intermarry with them and otherwise come down to their level. [The brethren] were to so live that peace with their enemies might be assured. They were to treat them kindly, be friendly with them as far as correct and virtuous principles would permit, but never to swear with them or drink or carouse with them. If they could allay prejudice and show a willingness to trade with [them] and show a kindly spirit, it might help to turn them away from their bitterness. Judgement was to be left to the Lord.[5]

End Notes

1. Joseph Smith, in History, 1838–1856, volume A-1 [23 December 1805–30 August 1834], 210, josephsmithpapers.org.
2. See Minutes, 26–27 April 1832, josephsmithpapers.org.
3. Dale G. Renlund, "Latter-day Saints Keep on Trying," *Ensign* or *Liahona*, May 2015, 56.
4. James E. Talmage, in Conference Report, Apr. 1930, 96.
5. Joseph Fielding Smith, *Church History and Modern Revelation* (Salt Lake City, UT: Deseret Book, 1948), 2:89.

$\mathcal{D}$octrine and $\mathcal{C}$ovenants
Section 83

Concerning Women and Children

$\mathcal{H}$istorical $\mathcal{C}$ontext

DURING HIS TRIP TO MISSOURI IN THE SPRING OF 1832, JOSEPH SMITH RE-
ceived section 83 while in council with leaders of the Church in Missouri.
The revelation deals with the laws of the Church, specifically the law of
consecration and how it was administered to women and children who had
lost their husbands or fathers. The question of how to administer the law
of consecration may have been brought to the forefront of Joseph's mind
during a visit he made to a settlement consisting primarily of Saints from
Colesville, New York. These Saints had traveled to Missouri and settled at
Kaw Township, about twelve miles away from Independence, Missouri.
Some of these Saints were among Joseph's closest friends and the earliest
converts to the Church. Joseph later wrote that when he visited the Colesville
Saints, he "received a welcome only known by brethren and sisters united as
one in the same faith, and by the same baptism, and supported by the same

Lord." He also added, "The Colesville Branch, in particular, rejoiced as the Ancient Saints did with Paul. It is good to rejoice with the people of God."[1]

The Colesville Saints had been involved in some of the most dramatic and important events in the history of the young Church. They had heeded the call to gather to the Ohio, but the owner of the land that they were asked to settle on went back on his promise to live the law of consecration (see Doctrine and Covenants 54). They were commanded to relocate to Missouri and made the long journey there at great sacrifice, rejoicing with the Prophet when they arrived in the land of Zion (see Doctrine and Covenants 59). Among this dedicated company were at least two widows: Phebe Crosby Peck, who had four children, and Anna Slade Rogers, who had a daughter. Both women had lost their husbands in 1829 before the law of consecration was revealed. Joseph's friendship with them may have led to him asking the Lord how the law of consecration related to widows and the fatherless.[2]

Verse-by-Verse Commentary

1 Verily, thus saith the Lord, in addition to the laws of the church concerning women and children, those who belong to the church, who have lost their husbands or fathers:

2 Women have claim on their husbands for their maintenance, until their husbands are taken; and if they are not found transgressors they shall have fellowship in the church.

3 And if they are not faithful they shall not have fellowship in the church; yet they may remain upon their inheritances according to the laws of the land.

4 All children have claim upon their parents for their maintenance until they are of age.

In the family proclamation, the First Presidency and Quorum of the Twelve counsel that "by divine design, fathers are to preside over their families in love and righteousness and are responsible to provide the necessities of life and protection for their families." These three expectations for fathers—to preside, to provide, and to protect—remain in force today. At the same time, the proclamation explains that in fulfilling the responsibilities given to them, "fathers and mothers are obligated to help one another as equal partners."[3] Providing for families remains one of the Lord's important expectations for fathers. The Apostle Paul declares, "But if any provide not for his own, and specially for those of his own house, he hath denied the faith, and is worse than an infidel" (1 Timothy 5:8).

Commenting on Doctrine and Covenants 83:4, Elder D. Todd Christofferson teaches, "Breadwinning is a consecrated activity. Providing for one's family, although it generally requires time away from the family, is not inconsistent with fatherhood—it is the essence of being a good father. 'Work and family are overlapping domains.' This, of course, does not justify a man who neglects his family for his career or, at the other extreme, one who will not exert himself and is content to shift his responsibility to others."[4]

Even in situations in which divorce or other circumstances change typical family dynamics, fathers still have an obligation to do their best to see that their families are provided for. The *General Handbook* of the Church lists a person who "deliberately abandons family responsibilities, including nonpayment of child support and alimony" as one in danger of a membership council.[5]

In addition, providing for a family does not just mean providing financial support. Fathers have an obligation to provide love and emotional support. In an address to fathers, President Howard W. Hunter teaches, "You should express regularly to your wife and children your reverence and respect for her. Indeed, one of the greatest things a father can do for his children is to love their mother."[6]

> 5 And after that, they have claim upon the church, or in other words upon the Lord's storehouse, if their parents have not wherewith to give them inheritances.
>
> 6 And the storehouse shall be kept by the consecrations of the church; and widows and orphans shall be provided for, as also the poor. Amen.

Under the system of consecration that existed when section 83 was given, if parents did not have the resources to continue to support their children who came of age, these children could draw on the resources in the community storehouse to meet their needs until they could provide for themselves. Likewise, widows had the right to seek assistance from the Church. The number of references to widows and the fatherless in the scriptures demonstrates how seriously the Lord holds the Church responsible with regard to those who live in families with these kinds of challenges (see Exodus 22:22; Psalms 146:9; 1 Timothy 5:3; 2 Nephi 19:17).

A large part of the work of the Church is to provide a surrogate family to its members, particularly those who have lost family members. The family proclamation counsels that "disability, death, or other circumstances may necessitate individual adaptation" and that "extended families should lend support when needed."[7] Covenants of consecration allow the Church to form a large extended family that can offer support if a family has a parent missing or other challenging circumstances.

Elder Christofferson spoke to those who might face the challenge of living without a father: "To children whose family situation is troubled, we say, you yourself are no less for that. Challenges are at times an indication of the Lord's trust in you. He can help you, directly and through others, to deal with what you face. You can become the generation, perhaps the first in your family, where the divine patterns that God has ordained for families truly take shape and bless all the generations after you."[8] In our day, we deal not only with widowhood but also with divorced families, mixed-faith marriages, and a number of other circumstances. It is imperative for the Church to look after those who live in complex family situations.

End Notes

1. Joseph Smith, in History, 1838–1856, volume A-1 [23 December 1805–30 August 1834], 213, josephsmithpapers.org.
2. See William G. Hartley, *Stand by My Servant Joseph: Story of the Joseph Knight Family and the Restoration* (Salt Lake City, UT: Joseph Fielding Smith Institute, 2003), 112. See also "Historical Introduction," Revelation, 30 April 1832 [D&C 83], josephsmithpapers.org.
3. "The Family: A Proclamation to the World," Gospel Library.
4. D. Todd Christofferson, "Fathers," *Ensign* or *Liahona*, May 2016, 95.
5. *General Handbook: Serving in The Church of Jesus Christ of Latter-day Saints*, 32.6.2.5, Gospel Library.
6. *Teachings of Presidents of the Church: Howard W. Hunter* (2015), 224.
7. "The Family: A Proclamation to the World," Gospel Library.
8. D. Todd Christofferson, "Fathers," 96.

$\mathcal{D}$octrine and $\mathcal{C}$ovenants Section 84

The Oath and Covenant of the Priesthood

$\mathcal{H}$istorical $\mathcal{C}$ontext

WHILE WE KNOW THE EXACT DATE, RELATIVE LOCATION, AND CLOSE WORD-ing of the restoration of the Aaronic Priesthood, we have very little infor-mation about the restoration of the Melchizedek Priesthood. Doctrine and Covenants 84 is a landmark in our understanding of priesthood in general, but especially of the powers and promises associated with the Melchizedek Priesthood. This revelation came at the end of several months of great chal-lenges for Joseph Smith. A mob attacked Joseph and Sidney Rigdon at the John Johnson Farm on March 24, 1832. The beating was painful for both men, but it especially affected Sidney, whose head was badly lacerated as they dragged him across the frozen ground. Joseph seemed to recover more quickly, while Sidney was confined to bed for several days. Joseph visited Sidney a few days after the attack and later remembered, "I went to see Elder Rigdon, and found him crazy, and his head highly inflamed, for they had dragged him by his heels, and those, too, so high from the earth he could not raise his head from the rough frozen surface."[1]

Sidney recovered sufficiently to travel to Missouri in the spring of 1832 with Joseph Smith and other Church leaders. Their conversations with the Church leaders in Missouri were difficult, but Joseph managed to bring some harmony to the discussions before he left. On the way home, another hardship struck the travelers when the horses pulling their stagecoach had a runaway. Bishop Newel K. Whitney attempted to jump from the coach but caught his foot in the wheel and broke his leg in several places. Bishop Whitney was unable to travel, so Joseph elected to stay with him while the rest of the party journeyed home to Kirtland.[2]

Joseph spent a stressful four weeks at an inn in Greenville, Indiana, while Bishop Whitney recovered. He wrote in a letter to Emma Smith:

My Situation is a very unpleasant one although I will endeavor to be contented. The Lord assisting me I have visited a grove which is just back of the town almost every day where I can be secluded from the eyes of any mortal and there give vent to all the feelings of my heart. In meditation and prayer I have called to mind all the past moments of my life and am left to mourn and Shed tears of sorrow for my folly in suffering the adversary of my Soul to have so much power over me as he has had in times past.[3]

However, in the midst of his trials, Joseph also remembered the goodness of God in his life. "But God is merciful and has forgiven my sins," he wrote to Emma. "I rejoice that he sendeth forth the Comforter to as many as believe and humbleth themselves before him."[4]

On one occasion, Joseph believed he had been poisoned. "I rose from the dinner-table, I walked directly to the door and commenced vomiting most profusely," he later wrote. "I raised large quantities of blood and poisonous matter, and so great were the muscular contortions of my system that my jaw was dislocated in a few moments."[5] Joseph later recovered through a priesthood blessing, and he and Bishop Whitney left the inn the following day. By the time they returned to Kirtland, they had been gone nearly three months.

More trouble greeted Joseph when he arrived home. A letter from John Corrill, a counselor to Bishop Edward Partridge in Missouri, raised some points of conflict and animosity toward Joseph Smith and other Church leaders in Kirtland. Shortly after hearing these accusations, Sidney Rigdon suffered an episode where he became frantic and declared in public that "the keys are rent from this people."[6] Joseph was forced to travel to Kirtland from where he was staying in Hiram, Ohio, to remedy the situation. For a time, he was forced to remove Sidney from the First Presidency and revoke his priesthood.[7]

During these challenging months, Joseph Smith began to reflect on his experiences and record his history for the first time. He wrote an account of the First Vision and documented the appearance of angels who had given him his authority to minister. In this history, he suggested that he had received two different kinds of authority, noting that "the ministering of Angels" gave him an authority that allowed him "to administer the letter of the Gospel." He also wrote of receiving "the high Priesthood after the holy order of the son of the living God," giving him "power and ordinance from on high to preach the Gospel in the administration and demonstration of the spirit."[8]

Writing this history and enduring the tumultuous events surrounding the government of the Church were likely factors in the Prophet seeking further guidance on the nature of the priesthood. The revelation in section 84 traced the lineage of the two orders of the priesthood and explained the blessings associated with each. In a later history, Joseph Smith designated this revelation as simply "On Priesthood" and gave the following context for it: "The elders began to return from their Missions to the eastern states, and present the histories of their several stewardships in the Lord's vineyard; and while together in these seasons of joy, I inquired of the Lord and received the following: [Doctrine and Covenants 84]."[9]

The Prophet received the revelation over two days, September 22 and 23, 1832. Evidence from the earliest copies of the revelation suggests that it was received in two parts. We do not know exactly where the first part ends and the second part begins; however, several of the early scribes of the revelation, including Frederick G. Williams and John Whitmer, left a break after the phrase "for he is full of mercy, justice, grace and truth, and peace, forever and ever, Amen" (Doctrine and Covenants 84:102). This break suggests that Doctrine and Covenants 84:103–120 were received on September 23.[10]

*V*erse-by-*V*erse *C*ommentary

1 A revelation of Jesus Christ unto his servant Joseph Smith, Jun., and six elders, as they united their hearts and lifted their voices on high.

2 Yea, the word of the Lord concerning his church, established in the last days for the restoration of his people, as he has spoken by the mouth of his prophets, and for the gathering of his saints to stand upon Mount Zion, which shall be the city of New Jerusalem.

3 Which city shall be built, beginning at the temple lot, which is appointed by the finger of the Lord, in the western boundaries of the State of Missouri, and dedicated by the hand of Joseph Smith, Jun., and others with whom the Lord was well pleased.

No concept fired the imagination of the early Saints of this dispensation more than the construction of a holy city of God on the American continent. One survey found that in early Latter-day Saint literature, the most quoted passage from the Book of Mormon was Ether 13:4–8, in which the ancient prophet Moroni foretold "that a New Jerusalem should be built up upon this land, unto the remnant of the seed of Joseph" (Ether 13:6).[11] Interest in this New Jerusalem continued as Joseph Smith's translation of the Bible restored the knowledge of a city called Zion built by the prophet Enoch, where the people "were of one heart and one mind and dwelt in righteousness" (Moses 7:18).[12]

Early in the summer of 1833, a plat of the City of Zion was sent to Church leaders in Missouri. This plan illustrates not only the grand designs of the city but also the practical details of its creation. Created as a collaborative effort among the members of the First Presidency—Joseph Smith, Sidney Rigdon, and Frederick G. Williams—the plat is essentially the master plan for the city of God. Written around the edges of the plan are detailed notes about the nature of the city. The city was to be one square mile and have a grid system outlining rectangular blocks with lots laid out for homes and gardens. In many ways the plat resembled urban land division patterns utilized throughout the United States in the 1830s. In other ways the plat was highly unusual.[13]

Where the city's design diverged from that of other American communities was at the heart of the map, where two prominent rectangles sat with numbers from 1 to 24 inside of them. These rectangles designated a sacred place at the center of the city where a complex of twenty-four temples was to be built. According to the plans, these temples were intended for a different function than were later Latter-day Saint temples. Rather than being places where ordinances were performed for the living and the dead, these temples were intended to serve as administrative centers. In divisions of three, the temples were assigned to house various Church organizations. For example, temples 10, 11, and 12 were designated as "the house of the Lord for the presidency of the high and most holy priesthood." Other temple trios were identified by titles such as "the house of the Lord for the presidency of the high priesthood after the order of [Aaron]," "the house of the Lord for the teachers in Zion," "the house of the Lord for the Deacons in Zion," and so forth.[14] The offices of the priesthood had been revealed gradually, but the designations of the orders of the priesthood came from information provided in this revelation.

> 4 Verily this is the word of the Lord, that the city New Jerusalem shall be built by the gathering of the saints, beginning at this place, even the place of the temple, which temple shall be reared in this generation.
>
> 5 For verily this generation shall not all pass away until an house shall be built unto the Lord, and a cloud shall rest upon it, which cloud shall be even the glory of the Lord, which shall fill the house.

The city of Zion and its temples remain to be built. Some detractors have claimed that this passage proved to be false because the temple was not "reared in this generation" (verse 4). There are several reasons why this claim is not true.

First, it is possible that this commandment is not a *prophecy* but a *commandment*. When commandments are not kept, they are not invalidated. For example, the Lord commanded, "Thou shalt not bear false witness against thy neighbor" (Exodus 20:16). If a person does not keep that commandment, it is reflection of the weakness of the individual, not of the prophet who received the commandment or of the foreknowledge of God. In later revelations, the Lord provided two reasons why the temples were not built:

there were contentions, envyings, and strife among the Saints in Missouri (see Doctrine and Covenants 101:2, 6–8), and the enemies of the Saints were demonstrating intense opposition. In Doctrine and Covenants 124:49–50, the Lord refers to the charge to build the temples as a commandment that He rescinded because of persecution.[15]

Second, there is some uncertainty surrounding the use of the word *generation* in this passage. The Lord told Joseph Smith, "This generation shall have my word through you" (Doctrine and Covenants 5:10). It seems that in this case, the word *generation* is used as a synonym for *dispensation*. *Generation* as used here does not appear to refer to the time between parents' birth and the birth of their children but as an epoch of time in this history of the human race.[16]

Finally, the passage declares that "this generation shall not all pass away until *an* house shall be built unto the Lord" (verse 5; emphasis added). It is possible that this passage specifies only that *a* house will be built, not necessarily that the temples in Zion will be built. If this is the case, a house *was* built in Kirtland, Ohio (see Doctrine and Covenants 109–110). Another house was built by this generation in Nauvoo, Illinois. Many of those who lived in the days of Joseph Smith survived long enough to see temples rise in Utah at St. George, Logan, Manti, and Salt Lake City. A smaller number who lived into the 1920s even saw temples dedicated in Cardston, Canada, and Laie, Hawaii. In this sense, the word of the Lord was more than fulfilled.

> 6 And the sons of Moses, according to the Holy Priesthood which he received under the hand of his father-in-law, Jethro;
>
> 7 And Jethro received it under the hand of Caleb;
>
> 8 And Caleb received it under the hand of Elihu;
>
> 9 And Elihu under the hand of Jeremy;
>
> 10 And Jeremy under the hand of Gad;
>
> 11 And Gad under the hand of Esaias;
>
> 12 And Esaias received it under the hand of God.
>
> 13 Esaias also lived in the days of Abraham, and was blessed of him—

The priesthood of Moses is traced back to Adam, who received it from God Himself (see Abraham 1:2–4). One interesting addition to our understanding of the priesthood is the knowledge that Moses received his priesthood from his father-in-law, Jethro. Jethro was a descendant of Midian, one of the children Abraham fathered with his wife Keturah after the death of his first wife, Sarah (see Genesis 25:2). It is significant that Moses's priestly lineage comes through a route outside of Israel. This lineage seems to indicate a number of the servants of Jehovah who were not descendants of Jacob (Israel) but were nonetheless key figures in the scriptures. Just as the Book of Mormon indicates, there are stories of God's works that are yet to be told but that will someday be known.

Other illuminating names in Moses's priestly lineage include Esaias (see Doctrine and Covenants 84:13). Esaias is a name for Isaiah used in the King James Version of the New Testament. This Esaias lived long before Isaiah's time and appears to have been a contemporary of Melchizedek and Abraham. Other than what is written in these verses and a brief mention in Doctrine and Covenants 76:100, we have little information about Esaias. We know he was ordained under the hand of God, but the phrase "under the hand of God" likely means that he was ordained by someone who acted under God's direction. For instance, Joseph Smith taught that "all the Prophets had the Melchizedek Priesthood and was ordained by God himself."[17] In Joseph's teaching, as well as in this passage, it is likely that one of God's servants carried out the ordination. In this instance, it was probably Abraham who ordained Esaias, as indicated in verse 13 and given the fact that Melchizedek and his city were taken into heaven (see Joseph Smith Translation, Genesis 14:33–34 [in the Bible appendix]).

> 14 Which Abraham received the priesthood from Melchizedek, who received it through the lineage of his fathers, even till Noah;
>
> 15 And from Noah till Enoch, through the lineage of their fathers;
>
> 16 And from Enoch to Abel, who was slain by the conspiracy of his brother, who received the priesthood by the commandments of God, by the hand of his father Adam, who was the first man—
>
> 17 Which priesthood continueth in the church of God in all generations, and is without beginning of days or end of years.

Little is known about Melchizedek, except that Abraham, considered the father of the faithful, paid homage to him after the Battle of Kings (see Genesis 14:18–20). Scriptures restored in the latter days greatly assist in our understanding of Melchizedek. The book of Alma provides a larger part of

Melchizedek's backstory, including that "there were many before him, and also there were many afterwards, but none were greater" (Alma 13:19).[18]

Some Church members speculate that Melchizedek, the king of Salem, and Shem, the son of Noah, are the same person. Based on the information given in section 84, however, it seems unlikely that this is the case. Another passage, Doctrine and Covenants 138:41, calls Shem "the great high priest" and fails to list Melchizedek among the prophets Joseph F. Smith saw in vision. However, verse 15 of section 84 says that Melchizedek received the priesthood "through the lineage of his fathers, even till Noah." Although it does not definitively settle the controversy, this lineage seems to indicate that there is no father-son connection between Noah and Melchizedek. In addition, no writer in the Bible or the Book of Mormon explicitly made a connection between the two. Bible writers often paid attention to names and pointed out when a biblical figure went by two different names, such as Abram-Abraham, Sarai-Sarah, Jacob-Israel, Esau-Edom, and so on. That not one writer made this connection between Shem and Melchizedek is telling.

Another important figure illuminated in this lineage is Abel, who was identified as having received the priesthood from Adam. A similar priestly lineage given in Doctrine and Covenants 107:42–43 connects the priesthood from Adam to Seth, but this lineage recognizes the role of Abel as the first heir to Adam's priesthood. The Prophet Joseph Smith taught that Abel "magnified the Priesthood which was conferred upon him and died a righteous man, and therefore has become an Angel of God by receiving his body from the dead, [and is] therefore [still] holding the Keys of his dispensation."[19] Abel's office as a priesthood holder also elevates the seriousness of Cain's murder of Abel. In taking the life of his brother, Cain not only shed the blood of his own kin but also took the life of one of the Lord's anointed and the heir to the priesthood.

> 18 And the Lord confirmed a priesthood also upon Aaron and his seed, throughout all their generations, which priesthood also continueth and abideth forever with the priesthood which is after the holiest order of God.
>
> 19 And this greater priesthood administereth the gospel and holdeth the key of the mysteries of the kingdom, even the key of the knowledge of God.

20 Therefore, in the ordinances thereof, the power of godliness is manifest.

21 And without the ordinances thereof, and the authority of the priesthood, the power of godliness is not manifest unto men in the flesh;

22 For without this no man can see the face of God, even the Father, and live.

The greater priesthood referenced in these verses is the Melchizedek Priesthood, which administers the gospel and holds the keys and ordinances necessary to enter again into the presence of God. The purpose of the priesthood is to bring men and women back into the presence of God in this life and in the life to come. There are a number of ways in which this goal can be accomplished. Ordinances such as baby blessings, blessings of healing or comfort, or patriarchal blessings bring the power of God into the lives of their recipients by providing guidance, solace, and recovery. Ordinances required for salvation allow the receivers to enter into sacred covenants that open the door of salvation and unlock the powers of godliness. "Godliness" is the power to become like God and is made possible by the covenants and ordinances facilitated through the priesthood.

When this revelation declares that "without this no man can see the face of God, even the Father, and live" (verse 22), the *this* referred to is the power of godliness, not the priesthood. Many individuals, including Joseph Smith, have received the privilege of seeing the face of God without being ordained to the priesthood. Typically, the power of godliness necessary to see God is given to a person through the ordinances of the gospel, though there can be exceptions to this rule under unusual circumstances. One exception is transfiguration, in which an individual is temporarily changed by the power of the Spirit to be able to exist in the presence of God (see Doctrine and Covenants 67:11; Moses 1:9, 11, 15). Transfiguration is most likely the way that Joseph Smith was able to behold the presence of God during his First Vision despite not holding the priesthood or receiving the ordinances yet. Other individuals have been granted this privilege, but for most men and women, the way to enter the presence of God is to receive the power to do so through the ordinances of the gospel.

23 Now this Moses plainly taught to the children of Israel in the wilderness, and sought diligently to sanctify his people that they might behold the face of God;

24 But they hardened their hearts and could not endure his presence; therefore, the Lord in his wrath, for his anger was kindled against them, swore that they should not enter into his rest while in the wilderness, which rest is the fulness of his glory.

25 Therefore, he took Moses out of their midst, and the Holy Priesthood also;

This passage affirms that the laws Moses gave to Israel during their sojourn in the wilderness were not the fulness of the gospel but a temporary set of provisions to prepare them for the higher law. The prophet Abinadi taught that this lesser law of "performances and ordinances" was only a type of things to come. The true power of God to save was not solely bound in keeping the law but in accepting the atoning sacrifices of Jesus Christ. Abinadi taught "that salvation doth not come by the law alone; and were it not for the atonement, which God himself shall make for the sins and iniquities of his people, that they must unavoidably perish, notwithstanding the law of Moses" (Mosiah 13:28).

It was not Moses's original intent to give the children of Israel this lesser law, but because of the hardness of their hearts, a change was required. The Joseph Smith Translation of this episode explains:

And the Lord said unto Moses, Hew thee two other tables of stone, like unto the first, and I will write upon them also, the words of the law, according as they were written at the first on the tables which thou brakest; but it shall not be according to the first, for I will take away the priesthood out of their midst; therefore my holy order, and the ordinances thereof, shall not go before them; for my presence shall not go up in their midst, lest I destroy them.

But I will give unto them the law as at the first, but it shall be after the law of a carnal commandment; for I have sworn in my wrath, that they shall not enter into my presence, into my rest, in the days of their pilgrimage. Therefore do as I have commanded thee. (Joseph Smith Translation, Exodus 34:1–2 [in Exodus 34:1, footnote a])

26 And the lesser priesthood continued, which priesthood holdeth the key of the ministering of angels and the preparatory gospel;

27 Which gospel is the gospel of repentance and of baptism, and the remission of sins, and the law of carnal commandments, which the Lord in his wrath caused to continue with the house of Aaron among the children of Israel until John, whom God raised up, being filled with the Holy Ghost from his mother's womb.

28 For he was baptized while he was yet in his childhood, and was ordained by the angel of God at the time he was eight days old unto this power, to overthrow the kingdom of the Jews, and to make straight the way of the Lord before the face of his people, to prepare them for the coming of the Lord, in whose hand is given all power.

The "preparatory gospel," as it is referred to in verse 26, was present among the Israelites until the coming of John. The importance of John the Baptist is sometimes overshadowed by the nearness of his ministry to that of Jesus Christ. John was the proper heir to the office held anciently by Aaron and could trace his authority directly to him (see Doctrine and Covenants 68:15–18; 107:16, 70, 76). This passage explains that John was baptized while he was in his childhood and had been "ordained" by an angel when he was eight days old. The word *ordained* in this context does not mean that John was ordained to the Aaronic or Melchizedek Priesthood or any office of the priesthood. In the time of Joseph Smith, the term was used in the same way that *set apart* or *blessed* is used in the modern Church. For instance, Emma Smith was "ordained" to "expound scriptures, and to exhort the Church" but was not given the priesthood or a priesthood office (Doctrine and Covenants 25:7).

In a similar fashion, John was ordained "*unto this power*, to overthrow the kingdom of the Jews, and to make straight the way of the Lord before the face of his people, to prepare them for the second coming of the Lord" (verse 28; emphasis added). John was ordained by an angel because his father, Zacharias, held only the Aaronic Priesthood and lacked the authority to give such a blessing to an infant.

During his ministry, John preached the gospel of faith, repentance, and baptism by immersion for the remission of sins—the first three principles of the gospel. However, he lacked the authority to provide the fourth principle of the gospel, baptism by fire and the Holy Ghost. He also lacked the authority to administer the other ordinances of the Melchizedek Priesthood. Hence, when Jesus began His ministry, John directed his disciples toward Him, explaining that "He [Christ] must increase, but I must decrease" (John 3:30). Having fulfilled his mission as the most important of forerunners, John allowed the true Messiah to take the lead.[20]

The submission John showed to Jesus was another sign of his greatness. The Savior Himself taught that "among those born of women there is not a greater prophet than John the Baptist" (Luke 7:28). In an 1843 discourse, Joseph Smith provided three reasons why the Savior had given such high praise to John:

It could not have been on account of the miracles John performed, for he did no miracles; but it was, *first*, because he was trusted with a divine mission, of preparing the way before the face of the Lord. Who was trusted with such a mission, before or since? *No man.*

Second, He was trusted, and it was required at his hands, to baptise the son of man. Who ever did that? Who ever had so great a privilege or glory? Who ever led the Son of God into the waters of baptism, beholding the *Holy Ghost* descend upon him in the *sign* of the Dove? *No man.*

Third, John, at that time, was the only legal administrator, holding the keys of power, there was on earth: The keys, the kingdom, the power, the glory, had departed from the Jews; and John, the son of Zachariah, by the holy anointing, and decree of heaven, held the keys of power at the time.[21]

29 And again, the offices of elder and bishop are necessary appendages belonging unto the high priesthood.

30 And again, the offices of teacher and deacon are necessary appendages belonging to the lesser priesthood, which priesthood was confirmed upon Aaron and his sons.

31 Therefore, as I said concerning the sons of Moses—for the sons of Moses and also the sons of Aaron shall offer an acceptable offering and sacrifice in the house of the Lord, which house shall be built unto the Lord in this generation, upon the consecrated spot as I have appointed—

32 And the sons of Moses and of Aaron shall be filled with the glory of the Lord, upon Mount Zion in the Lord's house, whose sons are ye; and also many whom I have called and sent forth to build up my church.

In this passage, the offices of elder and bishop are established as "necessary appendages" of the Melchizedek Priesthood, and it is assumed that those holding the office of bishop, which is an office of the Aaronic Priesthood, will be high priests set apart as bishops. An earlier revelation explained that literal descendants of Aaron have a right to the office of bishop if they are found worthy and set apart by those holding the keys of the Melchizedek Priesthood (see Doctrine and Covenants 68:15–20). The offices of teacher and deacon are given as necessary appendages of the Aaronic Priesthood because those offices did not exist as part of the Aaronic or Levitical Priesthood in Old Testament times.

The concept of an acceptable offering from the sons of Moses and the sons of Aaron goes back to the initial appearance of John the Baptist to restore the Aaronic Priesthood (see Doctrine and Covenants 13). Joseph Smith commented on the Aaronic Priesthood in an 1840 discourse, explaining:

It is generally supposed that sacrifice was entirely done away when the great sacrifice was offered up, and that there will be no necessity for the ordinance of Sacrifice in future; but those who assert this, are certainly not acquainted with the duties, privileges, and authority of the priesthood, or with the prophets. The offering of sacrifice has ever been connected and forms a part of the duties of the priesthood. It began with the priesthood and will be continued until after the coming of Christ, from generation to generation. We frequently have mention made of the offering of Sacrifice by the Servants of the most High in Ancient days prior to the law of Moses.[22]

He continued, "These sacrifices as well as every ordinance belonging to the priesthood will, when the temple of the Lord shall be built and the sons of Levi be purified, be fully restored and attended to in all their powers, ramifications and blessings; this ever did and will exist when the powers of the Melchizedek Priesthood are sufficiently manifest. Else how can the restitution of all things spoken of by all the Holy Prophets be brought to pass?"[23]

33 For whoso is faithful unto the obtaining these two priesthoods of which I have spoken, and the magnifying their calling, are sanctified by the Spirit unto the renewing of their bodies.

34 They become the sons of Moses and of Aaron and the seed of Abraham, and the church and kingdom, and the elect of God.

The central part of this revelation is commonly known as the oath and covenant of the priesthood and constitutes verses 33–44. Every Church member should understand and become familiar with this passage. The oath makes the men who receive the priesthood and fully enter into it adopted sons of Aaron, Moses, and Abraham, heirs to the powers of God, and "heirs of God, and joint-heirs with Christ" (Romans 8:17). To "obtain" these two priesthoods is more than just to be ordained to an office within the priesthood. A later revelation to Joseph Smith explains that "many are called, but few are chosen," and only those who can wield the power of the priesthood "upon the principles of righteousness are fully chosen" (Doctrine and Covenants 121:36).

To obtain the priesthood is to magnify one's calling within the priesthood. President Thomas S. Monson provided a simple definition of what it means to magnify one's calling: "What does it mean to magnify a calling? It means to build it up in dignity and importance, to make it honorable and commendable in the eyes of all men, to enlarge and strengthen it, to let the light of heaven shine through it to the view of other men. And how does one magnify a calling? Simply by performing the service that pertains to it."[24]

In return for their faithful service, priesthood holders are "sanctified," or "made holy." The Lord also promises a renewal of their bodies. This blessing can happen in this life but comes to full fruition in the First Resurrection, when the priesthood holder is blessed to receive a celestial body and be truly renewed to become like God and Jesus Christ.

35 And also all they who receive this priesthood receive me, saith the Lord;

36 For he that receiveth my servants receiveth me;

37 And he that receiveth me receiveth my Father;

The phrase "receive the priesthood" most likely has a double meaning. It is true that men receive the priesthood when they are ordained to a priesthood office, but in a larger sense anyone, male or female, can receive the priesthood by accepting those who have been sent to minister of God. While this passage refers specifically to the oath and covenant pertaining to the priesthood, in a larger sense, when those who hold the keys give priesthood authority to worthy Church members, these members hold the priesthood—and this group encompasses both men and women. President Dallin H. Oaks taught:

> We are not accustomed to speaking of women having the authority of the priesthood in their Church callings, but what other authority can it be? When a woman—young or old—is set apart to preach the gospel as a full-time missionary, she is given priesthood authority to perform a priesthood function. The same is true when a woman is set apart to function as an officer or teacher in a Church organization under the direction of one who holds the keys of the priesthood. Whoever functions in an office or calling received from one who holds priesthood keys exercises priesthood authority in performing her or his assigned duties. Whoever exercises priesthood authority should forget about their rights and concentrate on their responsibilities.[25]

The oath and covenant of the priesthood can be understood in multiple contexts and applications. A person who participates in the ordinances of the temple enters into an oath and covenant with God that facilitates their entrance into the celestial kingdom. A couple sealed in the temple might understand the "oath and covenant" to be in part fulfilled by their entering into "this order of the priesthood," meaning the new and everlasting covenant of marriage (see Doctrine and Covenants 131:2). Those who enter into these promises receive the same blessing as Adam and Eve, Abraham and Sarah, Isaac and Rebekah, and so forth.

> 38 And he that receiveth my Father receiveth my Father's kingdom; therefore all that my Father hath shall be given unto him.
>
> 39 And this is according to the oath and covenant which belongeth to the priesthood.
>
> 40 Therefore, all those who receive the priesthood, receive this oath and covenant of my Father, which he cannot break, neither can it be moved.
>
> 41 But whoso breaketh this covenant after he hath received it, and altogether turneth therefrom, shall not have forgiveness of sins in this world nor in the world to come.

In a letter written to his uncle Silas Smith in September 1833, Joseph Smith commented on the blessings received in this promise and the potential the promise held for all men and women everywhere. He wrote:

> Abraham, Isaac, and Jacob, had the promise of eternal life confirmed to them by an oath of the Lord, but that promise or oath was no assurance to them of their salvation; but they could by walking in the footsteps and continuing in the faith of their fathers, obtain, for themselves an oath for confirmation that they were meet to be partakers of the inheritance, with the Saints in light. . . .
>
> Must I not rather obtain for myself by my own faith and diligence in keeping the commandments of the Lord, an assurance of salvation for myself? And have I not an equal privilege with the ancient Saints? And will not the Lord hear my prayers and listen to my cries as soon as he ever did to theirs, if I come to him in the manner they did? Or, is he a respecter of persons?[26]

This statement captures as much as anything the essence of the latter-day Restoration of the gospel. God made oaths and covenants with His sons and daughters anciently, but He offers the same blessings to His children in the latter days.

> 42 And wo unto all those who come not unto this priesthood which ye have received, which I now confirm upon you who are present this day, by mine own voice out of the heavens; and even I have given the heavenly hosts and mine angels charge concerning you.
>
> 43 And I now give unto you a commandment to beware concerning yourselves, to give diligent heed to the words of eternal life.
>
> 44 For you shall live by every word that proceedeth forth from the mouth of God.
>
> 45 For the word of the Lord is truth, and whatsoever is truth is light, and whatsoever is light is Spirit, even the Spirit of Jesus Christ.
>
> 46 And the Spirit giveth light to every man that cometh into the world; and the Spirit enlighteneth every man through the world, that hearkeneth to the voice of the Spirit.

47 And every one that hearkeneth to the voice of the Spirit cometh unto God, even the Father.

48 And the Father teacheth him of the covenant which he has renewed and confirmed upon you, which is confirmed upon you for your sakes, and not for your sakes only, but for the sake of the whole world.

49 And the whole world lieth in sin, and groaneth under darkness and under the bondage of sin.

50 And by this you may know they are under the bondage of sin, because they come not unto me.

51 For whoso cometh not unto me is under the bondage of sin.

52 And whoso receiveth not my voice is not acquainted with my voice, and is not of me.

53 And by this you may know the righteous from the wicked, and that the whole world groaneth under sin and darkness even now.

A marvelous contrast is made in these verses between the Light of Christ and the darkness of sin. A revelation received shortly after Doctrine and Covenants 84 was given revealed that the Light of Christ is "the light which is in all things, which giveth life to all things, which is the law by which all things are governed, even the power of God who sitteth upon his throne, who is in the bosom of eternity, who is in the midst of all things" (Doctrine and Covenants 88:13). This radiant light, energy, and intelligence was to be the focus of the next phase of teaching the early Saints about the nature and power of Jesus Christ. The Light of Christ is highlighted again in Doctrine and Covenants sections 88 and 93. As men and women accept and live the truths of the gospel, this light, and their capacity to bear it and use it, becomes greater and greater.

In contrast, if people move away from the commandments and truths of the gospel, they receive less light and are more susceptible to the bondage of sin. These truths apply broadly to humanity since this passage is discussing the Light of Christ and not the gift of the Holy Ghost. While the Holy Ghost can inspire people everywhere, only those who have entered into covenants through ordinances can gain the gift of the Holy Ghost, and then only those who keep their covenants have the constant companionship of the Spirit.

But all children of God, regardless of their religious background, are given the Spirit of Christ to enlighten them. As the revelation declares, "[The] Spirit [of Christ] giveth light to every man that cometh into the world" (verse 46). President Brigham Young taught:

> Honest hearts, the world over, desire to know the right way. They have sought for it, and still seek it. There have been people upon the earth all the time who sought diligently with all their hearts to know the ways of the Lord. These individuals have produced good, inasmuch as they had the ability. And to believe that there has been no virtue, no truth, no good upon the earth for centuries, until the Lord revealed the Priesthood through Joseph the Prophet, I should say is wrong. There has been more or less virtue and righteousness upon the earth at all times, from the days of Adam until now. That we all believe.[27]

54 And your minds in times past have been darkened because of unbelief, and because you have treated lightly the things you have received—

55 Which vanity and unbelief have brought the whole church under condemnation.

56 And this condemnation resteth upon the children of Zion, even all.

57 And they shall remain under this condemnation until they repent and remember the new covenant, even the Book of Mormon and the former commandments which I have given them, not only to say, but to do according to that which I have written—

58 That they may bring forth fruit meet for their Father's kingdom; otherwise there remaineth a scourge and judgment to be poured out upon the children of Zion.

59 For shall the children of the kingdom pollute my holy land? Verily, I say unto you, Nay.

60 Verily, verily, I say unto you who now hear my words, which are my voice, blessed are ye inasmuch as you receive these things;

61 For I will forgive you of your sins with this commandment—that you remain steadfast in your minds in solemnity and the spirit of prayer, in bearing testimony to all the world of those things which are communicated unto you.

One of the most powerful ways to increase the light and truth in our lives is through regular study of the scriptures. In these verses, the Lord declares condemnation on the Saints for their vanity, unbelief, and neglect of the new covenant—the Book of Mormon. They treated lightly this sacred book—the sign of a "new covenant" between God and His children in the latter days. In response to this warning, a few months after the revelation was received, William W. Phelps dedicated several pages of *The Evening and the Morning Star*, the Church newspaper in Missouri, to the Book of Mormon. He wrote, "The inhabitants of Zion are brought under condemnation for neglecting the book of Mormon, from which they not only received the new covenant, but the fulness of the gospel. Has this been done for the sake of hunting mysteries in the prophecies? or has it come to pass by carelessness?"[28]

The censure offered to the early Saints in this revelation has also been applied to the Saints in our day. President Ezra Taft Benson declared:

> Unless we read the Book of Mormon and give heed to its teachings, the Lord has stated in section 84 of the Doctrine and Covenants that the whole Church is under condemnation: "And this condemnation resteth upon the children of Zion, even all" (Doctrine and Covenants 84:56). The Lord continues: "And they shall remain under this condemnation until they repent and remember the new covenant, even the Book of Mormon and the former commandments which I have given them, not only to say, but to do according to that which I have written" (Doctrine and Covenants 84:57). . . .
>
> The Book of Mormon has not been, nor is it yet, the center of our personal study, family teaching, preaching, and missionary work. Of this we must repent.[29]

To date, no prophet of the Church has removed the condemnation found in these verses for the neglect of the Book of Mormon. More recently, President Monson has pleaded:

> If you are not reading the Book of Mormon each day, please do so. If you will read it prayerfully and with a sincere desire to know the truth, the

Holy Ghost will manifest its truth to you. If it is true—and I solemnly testify that it *is*—then Joseph Smith was a prophet who saw God the Father and His Son, Jesus Christ.

Because the Book of Mormon is true, The Church of Jesus Christ of Latter-day Saints is the Lord's Church on the earth, and the holy priesthood of God has been restored for the benefit and blessing of His children.

If you do not have a firm testimony of these things, do that which is necessary to obtain one. It is essential for you to have your own testimony in these difficult times, for the testimonies of others will carry you only so far.[30]

62 Therefore, go ye into all the world; and unto whatsoever place ye cannot go ye shall send, that the testimony may go from you into all the world unto every creature.

63 And as I said unto mine apostles, even so I say unto you, for you are mine apostles, even God's high priests; ye are they whom my Father hath given me; ye are my friends;

64 Therefore, as I said unto mine apostles I say unto you again, that every soul who believeth on your words, and is baptized by water for the remission of sins, shall receive the Holy Ghost.

65 And these signs shall follow them that believe—

66 In my name they shall do many wonderful works;

67 In my name they shall cast out devils;

68 In my name they shall heal the sick;

69 In my name they shall open the eyes of the blind, and unstop the ears of the deaf;

70 And the tongue of the dumb shall speak;

71 And if any man shall administer poison unto them it shall not hurt them;

72 And the poison of a serpent shall not have power to harm them.

73 But a commandment I give unto them, that they shall not boast themselves of these things, neither speak them before the world; for these things are given unto you for your profit and for salvation.

74 Verily, verily, I say unto you, they who believe not on your words, and are not baptized in water in my name, for the remission of their sins, that they may receive the Holy Ghost, shall be damned, and shall not come into my Father's kingdom where my Father and I am.

75 And this revelation unto you, and commandment, is in force from this very hour upon all the world, and the gospel is unto all who have not received it.

76 But, verily I say unto all those to whom the kingdom has been given—from you it must be preached unto them, that they shall repent of their former evil works; for they are to be upbraided for their evil hearts of unbelief, and your brethren in Zion for their rebellion against you at the time I sent you.

In 1832, the year this revelation was given, the Quorum of the Twelve was yet to be organized in this dispensation. When the Savior declares that "you are mine apostles" (verse 63), He is using the word *apostle* in its broadest sense as "one sent forth."[31] The list given here is very similar to the instructions Jesus gave to the Twelve in Jerusalem and the Americas (see Mark 16:15–18; Mormon 9:23–25). Everyone sent forth by Jesus Christ to minister to the children of men are, in a sense, apostles, and they carry with them the power to perform miracles in His name. The promise that they would be kept safe if poison was administered to them must have been extremely meaningful to Joseph Smith. Only a few months earlier, during his return journey from Missouri, he was poisoned while staying at a boarding house in Greenville, Indiana.[32]

Many of the Church's early missionaries experienced the blessings found in these verses to heal and bless those they served. A few months prior to this revelation, William McLellin recorded in his journal that "Sister Sarah St. John's child was scalded badly and Br. [Samuel] was there and laid his hands upon it and healed it in so much that it did not even so much as blister." A few days later, a woman who was ill approached McLellin. He wrote, "I prayed for her and laid my hands upon her and she was restored to health." Only a few days after this, McLellin himself fell ill and was healed by Joseph Smith.[33]

Healings like this were common in the early Church and continue to happen in the Church in our day. However, the Saints were commanded that "they shall not boast themselves of these things, neither speak them before the world; for these things are given unto you for your profit and for salvation" (verse 73). The Savior's instructions to avoid boasting or speaking of these miracles is echoed in the modern counsel of Boyd K. Packer, who said, "I have come to believe also that it is not wise to continually talk of unusual spiritual experiences. They are to be guarded with care and shared only when the Spirit itself prompts you to use them to the blessing of others."[34]

77 And again I say unto you, my friends, for from henceforth I shall call you friends, it is expedient that I give unto you this commandment, that ye become even as my friends in days when I was with them, traveling to preach the gospel in my power;

78 For I suffered them not to have purse or scrip, neither two coats.

79 Behold, I send you out to prove the world, and the laborer is worthy of his hire.

80 And any man that shall go and preach this gospel of the kingdom, and fail not to continue faithful in all things, shall not be weary in mind, neither darkened, neither in body, limb, nor joint; and a hair of his head shall not fall to the ground unnoticed. And they shall not go hungry, neither athirst.

81 Therefore, take ye no thought for the morrow, for what ye shall eat, or what ye shall drink, or wherewithal ye shall be clothed.

82 For, consider the lilies of the field, how they grow, they toil not, neither do they spin; and the kingdoms of the world, in all their glory, are not arrayed like one of these.

83 For your Father, who is in heaven, knoweth that you have need of all these things.

84 Therefore, let the morrow take thought for the things of itself.

85 Neither take ye thought beforehand what ye shall say; but treasure up in your minds continually the words of life, and it shall be given you in the very hour that portion that shall be meted unto every man.

86 Therefore, let no man among you, for this commandment is unto all the faithful who are called of God in the church unto

the ministry, from this hour take purse or scrip, that goeth forth to proclaim this gospel of the kingdom.

87 Behold, I send you out to reprove the world of all their unrighteous deeds, and to teach them of a judgment which is to come.

88 And whoso receiveth you, there I will be also, for I will go before your face. I will be on your right hand and on your left, and my Spirit shall be in your hearts, and mine angels round about you, to bear you up.

89 Whoso receiveth you receiveth me; and the same will feed you, and clothe you, and give you money.

90 And he who feeds you, or clothes you, or gives you money, shall in nowise lose his reward.

91 And he that doeth not these things is not my disciple; by this you may know my disciples.

The instructions given in this passage are directed primarily to missionaries, who are promised divine protection for their service. In the early Restoration, missionaries were sent forth without "purse or scrip," a phrase meaning roughly "without much money or belongings." Missionaries in this time were instructed to trust in the Lord for their food, housing, and other needs. As the conditions in which missionaries served changed, the policies changed as well, and now missionaries serve with support from their families and home wards. Missionaries are still instructed to see those funds as sacred and to seek to use them responsibly and honestly.[35]

The Lord also promises the missionaries sent forth that they will be accompanied by the angels of God and will act as the angels of God. Wilford Woodruff recorded an experience in which he and several other apostles were protected by angels during their 1840 mission to the British Isles:

Brother Kimball, Brother George A. Smith and myself had a similar experience in London, at a house where we were stopping. It seemed as if there were legions of spirits there. They sought our destruction; and on one occasion, after Brother Kimball had left, these powers of darkness fell upon us to destroy our lives, and both Brother Smith and myself would have been killed, apparently, had not three holy messengers come into the room and filled the room with light. They were dressed in temple clothing.

They laid their hands upon our heads and we were delivered, and that power was broken, so far as we were concerned.

Why did the Lord send these men to us? Because we could not have lived without it; and, as a general thing, angels do not administer to anybody on the earth unless it is to preserve the lives of good men, or to bring the Gospel, or perform a work that men cannot do for themselves. . . .

Lucifer may appear to man in the capacity of an angel of light; but there is no deception with the Holy Ghost. We do not particularly need the administration of angels unless we are in a condition similar to that in which Brother Kimball, Brother Smith and myself were placed, when we could not save our lives without them.[36]

> 92 He that receiveth you not, go away from him alone by yourselves, and cleanse your feet even with water, pure water, whether in heat or in cold, and bear testimony of it unto your Father which is in heaven, and return not again unto that man.
>
> 93 And in whatsoever village or city ye enter, do likewise.
>
> 94 Nevertheless, search diligently and spare not; and wo unto that house, or that village or city that rejecteth you, or your words, or your testimony concerning me.
>
> 95 Wo, I say again, unto that house, or that village or city that rejecteth you, or your words, or your testimony of me;
>
> 96 For I, the Almighty, have laid my hands upon the nations, to scourge them for their wickedness.
>
> 97 And plagues shall go forth, and they shall not be taken from the earth until I have completed my work, which shall be cut short in righteousness—

The cleansing of the feet mentioned here appears to be a variation of shaking the dust off the feet explained earlier in the Doctrine and Covenants (see commentary for Doctrine and Covenants 24:15–19). Earlier in the revelation, the Lord tells missionaries that they are being sent out to "reprove the world of all their unrighteous deeds, and to teach them of a judgment which is to come" (verse 87). The Lord's promise here that He will lay His hands upon the nations and "scourge them for their wickedness" shows that part of missionary work is simply warning people of the judgments coming upon humankind.

In another sense, this cleansing is symbolic of the act of Church members fulfilling their stewardship to preach the gospel to their fellow brothers and sisters. Elder Orson Pratt explained, "The Lord has commanded us to purify ourselves, to wash our hands and our feet, that he may testify to his Father and to our Father—to his God and our God, that we are clean from the blood of this generation."[37]

> 98 Until all shall know me, who remain, even from the least unto the greatest, and shall be filled with the knowledge of the Lord, and shall see eye to eye, and shall lift up their voice, and with the voice together sing this new song, saying:
>
> 99 The Lord hath brought again Zion;
> The Lord hath redeemed his people, Israel,
> According to the election of grace,
> Which was brought to pass by the faith
> And covenant of their fathers.
>
> 100 The Lord hath redeemed his people;
> And Satan is bound and time is no longer.
> The Lord hath gathered all things in one.
> The Lord hath brought down Zion from above.
> The Lord hath brought up Zion from beneath.
>
> 101 The earth hath travailed and brought forth her strength;
> And truth is established in her bowels;
> And the heavens have smiled upon her;
> And she is clothed with the glory of her God;
> For he stands in the midst of his people.
>
> 102 Glory, and honor, and power, and might,
> Be ascribed to our God; for he is full of mercy,
> Justice, grace and truth, and peace,
> Forever and ever, Amen.

This passage contains a song that will be sung after the Savior has accomplished all of His great works and has brought them to full fruition. The song speaks of "the election of grace," borrowing a phrase from Paul (Romans 11:5), and praises the glory, honor, mercy, grace, and truth of God. These verses emphasize that though men and women are called to assist in bringing about this great work, the power behind this transformation is found in Jesus Christ and the grace He extends to all humanity.

Several times in this revelation, the Lord has told the Saints that they have a responsibility to take the gospel to the world. The doctrine of the election of grace is crucial to understanding the gathering of Israel on both sides of the veil and preparing the world for the Second Coming of Christ. In the current Latter-day Saint Bible Dictionary, "election" is defined as follows:

> A theological term primarily denoting God's choice of the house of Israel to be the covenant people with privileges and responsibilities, that they might become a means of blessing to the whole world (Rom. 9:11; 11:5, 7, 28). Election is an opportunity for service and is both on a national and an individual basis. On a national basis the seed of Abraham carry the gospel to the world. But it is by individual faithfulness that it is done.
>
> The elect are chosen even "before the foundation of the world," yet no one is unconditionally elected to eternal life. Each must, for himself, hearken to the gospel and receive its ordinances and covenants from the hands of the servants of the Lord in order to obtain salvation. If one is elected but does not serve, his election could be said to have been in vain, as Paul expressed in 2 Cor. 6:1. . . .
>
> An "election of grace" spoken of in Doctrine and Covenants 84:98–102 and Rom. 11:1–5 has reference to one's situation in mortality; that is, being born at a time, at a place, and in circumstances where one will come in favorable contact with the gospel. This election took place in the premortal existence. Those who are faithful and diligent in the gospel in mortality receive an even more desirable election in this life and become the elect of God. These receive the promise of a fulness of God's glory in eternity (Doctrine and Covenants 84:33–41).

Another important phrase here is the recognition that after Satan is bound, "time is no longer" (verse 100). Latter-day Saints commonly use the phrase "time and eternity." *Time* commonly refers to linear time, the state of past, present, and future that we live in during mortality. *Eternity* is different than time. Church members often raise the question, "After millions of years in the celestial kingdom, will we grow tired of our existence?" This question assumes that time operates the same way in eternity as it does in mortality. However, the scriptures teach that "time only is measured unto men" (Alma 40:8) and that after the fulfillment of God's plan, "there should be time no longer" (Revelation 10:6). Trying to comprehend this concept in our mortal state is like trying to describe color to a person who was born blind, but it remains a valid teaching. There is no danger of boredom in heaven, because time is no more.

Latter-day Saints see the Restoration as only the beginning of the change that the Savior will carry out on the earth. In a letter written to the Queen of England, Parley P. Pratt declared:

Know assuredly that the world in which we live is on the eve of a revolution, more rapid in its progress—more powerful in its operations—more extensive in its effects—more lasting in its influence—and more important in its consequences, than any which man has yet witnessed upon the earth; a revolution in which all the inhabitants of the earth are vitally interested, both religiously and politically—temporally and spiritually; one on which the fate of nations is suspended, and upon which the future destiny of all the affairs of earth is made to depend. Nay, the angels have desired to look into it, and heaven itself has waited with longing expectation for its consummation.[38]

103 And again, verily, verily, I say unto you, it is expedient that every man who goes forth to proclaim mine everlasting gospel, that inasmuch as they have families, and receive money by gift, that they should send it unto them or make use of it for their benefit, as the Lord shall direct them, for thus it seemeth me good.

104 And let all those who have not families, who receive money, send it up unto the bishop in Zion, or unto the bishop in Ohio, that it may be consecrated for the bringing forth of the revelations and the printing thereof, and for establishing Zion.

105 And if any man shall give unto any of you a coat, or a suit, take the old and cast it unto the poor, and go on your way rejoicing.

106 And if any man among you be strong in the Spirit, let him take with him him that is weak, that he may be edified in all meekness, that he may become strong also.

107 Therefore, take with you those who are ordained unto the lesser priesthood, and send them before you to make appointments, and to prepare the way, and to fill appointments that you yourselves are not able to fill.

108 Behold, this is the way that mine apostles, in ancient days, built up my church unto me.

109 Therefore, let every man stand in his own office, and labor in his own calling; and let not the head say unto the feet it hath no need of the feet; for without the feet how shall the body be able to stand?

110 Also the body hath need of every member, that all may be edified together, that the system may be kept perfect.

In the midst of the soaring declarations about the power and promises of the ordinances and covenants of the gospel, there is a return to the practical work of the Church to improve the lives of the people it serves. After the lofty song of Zion, the revelation returns to more earthly concerns: addressing the bishop in Zion (Edward Partridge) and the bishop in Ohio (Newel K. Whitney). The bishops are instructed to continue to carefully use Church funds to look after the poor and to see to the needs of the Church, especially the printing of the revelations.

While the earlier passages in the revelation speak of a hierarchy of priesthood and the adoptive and literal children of Moses and Aaron who are carrying out the work, it is important to remember that the humblest callings in the kingdom are vital to its success. The Lord declares, "The body hath need of every member, that all may be edified together, that the system may be kept perfect" (verse 110).

President Oaks reminded us that though we speak in terms of organizational hierarchy within the Church, there is no hierarchy of righteousness. He taught:

> At this conference we have seen the release of some faithful brothers, and we have sustained the callings of others. In this rotation—so familiar in the Church—we do not "step down" when we are released, and we do not "step up" when we are called. There is no "up or down" in the service of the Lord. There is only "forward or backward," and that difference depends on how we accept and act upon our releases and our callings. I once presided at the release of a young stake president who had given fine service for nine years and was now rejoicing in his release and in the new calling he and his wife had just received. They were called to be the nursery leaders in their ward. Only in this Church would that be seen as equally honorable![39]

111 And behold, the high priests should travel, and also the elders, and also the lesser priests; but the deacons and teachers

should be appointed to watch over the church, to be standing ministers unto the church.

112 And the bishop, Newel K. Whitney, also should travel round about and among all the churches, searching after the poor to administer to their wants by humbling the rich and the proud.

113 He should also employ an agent to take charge and to do his secular business as he shall direct.

114 Nevertheless, let the bishop go unto the city of New York, also to the city of Albany, and also to the city of Boston, and warn the people of those cities with the sound of the gospel, with a loud voice, of the desolation and utter abolishment which await them if they do reject these things.

115 For if they do reject these things the hour of their judgment is nigh, and their house shall be left unto them desolate.

116 Let him trust in me and he shall not be confounded; and a hair of his head shall not fall to the ground unnoticed.

117 And verily I say unto you, the rest of my servants, go ye forth as your circumstances shall permit, in your several callings, unto the great and notable cities and villages, reproving the world in righteousness of all their unrighteous and ungodly deeds, setting forth clearly and understandingly the desolation of abomination in the last days.

118 For, with you saith the Lord Almighty, I will rend their kingdoms; I will not only shake the earth, but the starry heavens shall tremble.

119 For I, the Lord, have put forth my hand to exert the powers of heaven; ye cannot see it now, yet a little while and ye shall see it, and know that I am, and that I will come and reign with my people.

120 I am Alpha and Omega, the beginning and the end. Amen.

Following the commandment given in this revelation, Bishop Whitney traveled to New York City, with Joseph Smith accompanying him. During his stay, Joseph wrote a letter to Emma Smith that captured the conflicting feelings of compassion he felt toward the people in the city alongside his sorrow for their wickedness. Joseph wrote:

> This day I have been walking through the most splendid part of the city of New Y[ork]— the buildings are truly great and wonderful to the astonishing of every beholder, and the language of my heart is like this—can the great God of all the Earth maker of all things magnificent and splendid be displeased with man for all these great inventions sought out by them? My answer is no, it cannot be seeing these works are calculated to make men comfortable wise and happy.
>
> Therefore, not for the works can the Lord be displeased only against man is the anger of the Lord kindled because they give him not the glory. Therefore, their iniquities shall be visited upon their heads and their works shall be burned up with unquenchable fire. The iniquity of the people is printed in every countenance, and nothing but the dress of the people makes them look fair and beautiful. All is deformity, there is something in every countenance that is disagreeable with few exceptions. Oh, how long, oh Lord, shall this order of things exist and darkness cover the Earth and gross darkness cover the people? After beholding all that I had any desire to behold I returned to my room to meditate and calm my mind and behold the thoughts of home of Emma and Julia [M. Smith] rushes upon my mind like a flood and I could wish for a moment to be with them. My breast is filled with all the feelings and tenderness of a parent and a husband and could I be with you I would tell you many things yet when I reflect upon this great city like Ninevah not discerning their right hand from their left. Yea, more than two hundred thousand souls. My bowels [are] filled with compassion towards them, and I am determined to lift up my voice in this city and leave the event with God who holdeth all things in his hands and will not suffer an hair of our heads unnoticed to fall to the ground.
>
> I hope God will give you strength that you may not faint [Emma was expecting her fourth child]. I pray God to soften the hearts of those around you to be kind to you and take the burden off your shoulders as much as possible and not afflict you. I feel for you, for I know your state and that others do not, but you must comfort yourself knowing that God is your friend in heaven and that you have one true and living friend on Earth your Husband, Joseph Smith Jr.[40]

Also of note is the charge in these verses to warn the cities of New York, Albany, and Boston. Wilford Woodruff may have been referring to this passage of section 84 when he prophesied of the destruction of these three cities.

In 1863 he prophesied of a time when people in the Millennium would recall, "That was before New York was destroyed by an earthquake; it was before Boston was swept into the sea, by the sea heaving itself beyond its bounds; it was before Albany was destroyed by fire; yea, at that time you will remember the scenes of this day. Treasure them up and forget them not.'" President Brigham Young stood up afterward and declared, "What Brother Woodruff has said is revelation and will be fulfilled."[41]

End Notes

1. Joseph Smith, in History, 1838–1856, volume A-1 [23 December 1805–30 August 1834], 208, josephsmithpapers.org.
2. See History, 1838–1856, volume A-1 [23 December 1805–30 August 1834], 214, josephsmithpapers.org.
3. Letter to Emma Smith, 6 June 1832, 1, josephsmithpapers.org; spelling corrected and punctuation added.
4. Letter to Emma Smith, 6 June 1832, 1–2, josephsmithpapers.org; spelling corrected and punctuation added.
5. Joseph Smith, in History, 1838–1856, volume A-1 [23 December 1805–30 August 1834], 215, josephsmithpapers.org.
6. "Book 13," Lucy Mack Smith, History, 1844–1845, 5, josephsmithpapers.org.
7. See "Historical Introduction," Letter to William W. Phelps, 31 July 1832, josephsmithpapers.org.
8. History, circa Summer 1832, 1, josephsmithpapers.org.
9. Joseph Smith, in History, 1838–1856, volume A-1 [23 December 1805–30 August 1834], 229, josephsmithpapers.org.
10. See Revelation Book 1, 155, josephsmithpapers.org. In this copy of the revelation, John Whitmer actually wrote "Received on the 23 day of September 1832" before the rest of the revelation. See also "Historical Introduction," Revelation, 22–23 September 1832 [D&C 84], josephsmithpapers.org.
11. See Grant Underwood, "Book of Mormon Usage in Early LDS Theology," *Dialogue* 17, no. 3 (Autumn 1984): 39.
12. See Old Testament Revision 1, 16, josephsmithpapers.org.
13. See Richard Francaviglia, *The Mapmakers of New Zion: A Cartographic History of Mormonism* (Salt Lake City, UT: University of Utah Press, 2015), 31.
14. Plat of the City of Zion, circa Early June–25 June 1833, 2, josephsmithpapers.org.
15. See Stephen E. Robinson and H. Dean Garrett, *A Commentary on the Doctrine and Covenants* (Salt Lake City, UT: Deseret Book, 2000), 3:26.
16. See Joseph Fielding McConkie and Craig J. Ostler, *Revelations of the Restoration* (Salt Lake City, UT: Deseret Book, 2000), 588.
17. Discourse, 5 January 1841, as Reported by William Clayton, 5, josephsmithpapers.org.

18. Other illuminating passages about Melchizedek include Joseph Smith Translation, Genesis 14:17 (in Genesis 14:18, footnote *d*); Joseph Smith Translation, Genesis 14:25–40 (in the Bible appendix); Joseph Smith Translation, Hebrews 7:3 (in Hebrews 7:3, footnote *a*); and Doctrine and Covenants 107:1–4.
19. Joseph Smith, in History, 1838–1856, volume C-1 [2 November 1838–31 July 1842], 17 (addenda), josephsmithpapers.org.
20. See Robinson and Garrett, *A Commentary on the Doctrine and Covenants*, 3:38.
21. Discourse, 29 January 1843, as Reported by Willard Richards–B, 2, josephsmithpapers.org.
22. Joseph Smith, in History, 1838–1856, volume C-1 [2 November 1838–31 July 1842], 18 (addenda), josephsmithpapers.org.
23. Joseph Smith, in History, 1838–1856, volume C-1 [2 November 1838–31 July 1842], 18 (addenda), josephsmithpapers.org.
24. Thomas S. Monson, "The Sacred Call of Service," *Ensign* or *Liahona*, May 2005, 54.
25. Dallin H. Oaks, "The Keys and Authority of the Priesthood," *Ensign* or *Liahona*, May 2015, 51.
26. Letter to Silas Smith, 26 September 1833, 4–5, josephsmithpapers.org.
27. Brigham Young, in *Journal of Discourses*, 6:170.
28. William W. Phelps, "Some of Mormon's Teaching," *The Evening and the Morning Star*, Jan. 1833, 4, quoted in Revelation, 22–23 September 1832 [D&C 84], 3, footnote 28, josephsmithpapers.org.
29. Ezra Taft Benson, "Cleansing the Inner Vessel," *Ensign*, May 1986, 5.
30. Thomas S. Monson, "The Power of the Book of Mormon," *Ensign* or *Liahona*, May 2017, 86–87.
31. *Lexham Bible Dictionary* (Bellingham, WA: Lexham Press, 2016), s.v. "apostle."
32. See History, 1838–1856, volume A-1 [23 December 1805–30 August 1834], 215, josephsmithpapers.org.
33. See William McLellin, *The Journals of William E. McLellin, 1831-1836*, ed. Jan Shipps and John Welch (Provo, UT: Brigham Young University Studies, 1994), 66–67.
34. Boyd K. Packer, "The Candle of the Lord," *Ensign*, Jan. 1983, 53.
35. See *Missionary Standards for Disciples of Jesus Christ*, 4.8.4.
36. *Collected Discourses: Delivered by Wilford Woodruff, His Two Counselors, the Twelve Apostles and Others*, ed. Brian H. Stuy (Burbank, CA: B.H.S. Publishing, 1987–1992), 1:218.

37. David J. Whittaker, *The Essential Orson Pratt (Classics in Mormon Thought Series)* (Salt Lake City, UT: Signature Books, 1991), 127–128.

38. Parley P. Pratt, "A Letter to the Queen Touching the Signs of the Times and the Political Destiny of the World," *Writings of Parley Parker Pratt,* ed. Parker Pratt Robison (Salt Lake City, UT: Parker Pratt Robison, 1952), 97; emphasis in original.

39. Dallin H. Oaks, "The Keys and Authority of the Priesthood," 49.

40. Letter to Emma Smith, 13 October 1832, 1–2, josephsmithpapers.org.

41. N. B. Lundwall, *Temples of the Most High* (Salt Lake City, UT: by the author, 1941), 97–98.

Doctrine and Covenants Section 85

Set in Order the House of God

Historical Context

DOCTRINE AND COVENANTS 85 IS AN EXCERPT FROM A LETTER JOSEPH Smith wrote to William W. Phelps on November 27, 1832. The letter highlights the continuing difficulty between Church leaders in Kirtland, Ohio, and the Church leadership in Independence, Missouri. At the time, it was a requirement for all Church members who wished to emigrate to Missouri to commit to live the law of consecration (see Doctrine and Covenants 72:15, 24–26). However, during this time, some members of the Church were relocating to Missouri without entering into the law of consecration. William McLellin, for example, did not meet with Edward Partridge, the bishop in Zion, to consecrate his property to the Church. Instead, McLellin purchased two lots on Main Street in his own name.[1] Incidents such as this caused distress to the leaders of the Church in Missouri, who were earnestly striving to live the law of consecration.

Joseph anticipated these concerns over how the law would be administered among the Saints in Missouri. He wrote:

> I fancy to myself that you are saying or thinking something similar to these words: My God, great and mighty art thou, therefore shew unto thy servant what shall become of all these who are assaying to come up unto Zion in order to keep the commandments of God, and yet receive not their inheritance by consecration, by order or deed from the bishop, the man that God has appointed in a legal way agreeable to the law given to organize and regulate the church and all the affairs of the same.[2]

Despite some trouble the previous summer, during which Joseph had reprimanded Phelps for his "cold and indifferent manner,"[3] the Prophet offered warm words of encouragement and support in the following letter: "Brother William, in the love of God[,] having the most implicit confidence in you as a man of God[,] having obtained this confidence by a vision of heaven. Therefore I will proceed to unfold to you some of the feelings of my heart and proceed to answer the question." The letter contains instructions from Joseph and a revelation given by inspiration providing instruction to the Saints in Zion. After receiving this letter, Phelps promptly published portions of it in the January 1833 issue of *The Evening and the Morning Star*. The full letter, except a brief postscript, was published in Nauvoo in *Times and Seasons* on October 15, 1844. In 1876 Elder Orson Pratt, acting under the direction of President Brigham Young, placed portions of the 1833 letter into the Doctrine and Covenants as section 85.[4]

Verse-by-Verse Commentary

1 It is the duty of the Lord's clerk, whom he has appointed, to keep a history, and a general church record of all things that transpire in Zion, and of all those who consecrate properties, and receive inheritances legally from the bishop;

2 And also their manner of life, their faith, and works; and also of the apostates who apostatize after receiving their inheritances.

3 It is contrary to the will and commandment of God that those who receive not their inheritance by consecration, agreeable to his law, which he has given, that he may tithe his people, to

prepare them against the day of vengeance and burning, should have their names enrolled with the people of God.

4 Neither is their genealogy to be kept, or to be had where it may be found on any of the records or history of the church.

5 Their names shall not be found, neither the names of the fathers, nor the names of the children written in the book of the law of God, saith the Lord of Hosts.

The Lord's clerk referred to in this passage is John Whitmer, the Church Historian. He was directed to keep a history of the Saints in Zion, including those who consecrated and received inheritances from the bishop in Missouri, Edward Partridge. Whitmer was also directed to record those who left the Church after entering into consecration. The Lord had earlier given instructions about what was to happen if a person left the Church after entering into consecration. The individual was allowed to retain the stewardship that was given to them, but the portion of their means that had been consecrated to the Lord remained with the Church (see Doctrine and Covenants 51:4–6; 54:4–5). The reference to tithing made here (see verse 3) is not the same as the law of the tithe, which was later given in July 1838 (see Doctrine and Covenants 119), and appears to be a more general reference to the principle of tithing.

Unfortunately, it is a fact that people sometimes leave the Church. Not everyone who makes gospel covenants will keep them. At times the Church must also withdraw membership from individuals because of serious sins or transgressions.[5] As taught in this revelation, leaving the Church causes an individual to lose many of the blessings that come from being a member of the Church. Such actions should not be taken lightly. These actions can also cause heartache for the loved ones of the person who leaves.

Even though it can be difficult for us when people leave the Church, we should also remember to deal gently with those who have chosen a different path. President Uchtdorf counseled, "In this Church that honors personal agency so strongly, that was restored by a young man who asked questions and sought answers, we respect those who honestly search for truth. It may break our hearts when their journey takes them away from the Church we love and the truth we have found, but we honor their right to worship Almighty God according to the dictates of their own conscience, just as we claim that privilege for ourselves."[6]

If we continue to love and build our relationships with loved ones who leave the Church, we can be instruments in the Lord's hand in holding on to them. Elder Ulisses Soares taught:

> It is hard to understand all the reasons why some people take another path. The best we can do in these circumstances is just to love and embrace them, pray for their well-being, and seek for the Lord's help to know what to do and say. Sincerely rejoice with them in their successes; be their friends and look for the good in them. We should never give up on them but preserve our relationships. Never reject or misjudge them. Just love them! The parable of the prodigal son teaches us that when children come to themselves, they often desire to come home. If that happens with your dear ones, fill your hearts with compassion, run to them, fall on their neck, and kiss them, like the father of the prodigal son did.[7]

> 6 Yea, thus saith the still small voice, which whispereth through and pierceth all things, and often times it maketh my bones to quake while it maketh manifest, saying:

> 7 And it shall come to pass that I, the Lord God, will send one mighty and strong, holding the scepter of power in his hand, clothed with light for a covering, whose mouth shall utter words, eternal words; while his bowels shall be a fountain of truth, to set in order the house of God, and to arrange by lot the inheritances of the saints whose names are found, and the names of their fathers, and of their children, enrolled in the book of the law of God;

These verses and the reference to "one mighty and strong" who will set in order the house of God (verse 7) have been the source of frequent speculation. Some splinter groups from the Church have used this passage to justify their attempts to reform the Church or start their own Church. The most authoritative commentary on this passage comes from a statement issued in 1905 by the First Presidency, consisting of Joseph F. Smith, John R. Winder, and Anthon H. Lund. In an official statement, the First Presidency discussed the circumstances of this revelation and the identity of the "one mighty and strong":

> It is to be observed first of all that the subject of this whole letter, as also the part of it subsequently accepted as a revelation, relates to the affairs of the Church in Missouri, the gathering of the Saints to that land and

obtaining their inheritances under the law of consecration and steward-ship; and the Prophet deals especially with the matter of what is to become of those who fail to receive their inheritances by order or deed from the bishop. . . .

It was while these conditions of rebellion, jealousy, pride, unbelief and hardness of heart prevailed among the brethren in Zion—Jackson County, Missouri—in all of which Bishop Partridge participated, that the words of the revelation taken from the letter to William W. Phelps, of the 27th of November, 1832, were written. The "man who was called and appointed of God" to "divide unto the Saints their inheritance"—Edward Partridge—was at that time out of order, neglecting his own duty, and putting "forth his hand to steady the ark"; hence, he was warned of the judgment of God impending, and the prediction was made that another, "one mighty and strong," would be sent of God to take his place, to have his bishopric—one having the spirit and power of that high office resting upon him, by which he would have power to "set in order the house of God, and arrange by lot the inheritance of the Saints"; in other words, one who would do the work that Bishop Edward Partridge had been appointed to do, but had failed to accomplish. . . .

And inasmuch as through his repentance and sacrifices and suffer-ing, Bishop Edward Partridge undoubtedly obtained a mitigation of the threatened judgment against him of falling "by the shaft of death, like as a tree that is smitten by the vivid shaft of lightning," so the occasion for sending another to fill his station—"one mighty and strong to set in order the house of God, and to arrange by lot the inheritances of the Saints"—may also be considered as having passed away and the whole incident of the prophecy closed.[8]

> 8 While that man, who was called of God and appointed, that putteth forth his hand to steady the ark of God, shall fall by the shaft of death, like as a tree that is smitten by the vivid shaft of lightning.
>
> 9 And all they who are not found written in the book of remem-brance shall find none inheritance in that day, but they shall be cut asunder, and their portion shall be appointed them among unbelievers, where are wailing and gnashing of teeth.

The phrase "to steady the ark" makes reference to an episode in the Old Testament in which David was bringing the ark of the covenant back to Jerusalem after the Philistines returned it. During the journey, the ark was shaken by the oxen pulling it, and a man named Uzzah put forth his hand to steady the ark. The record reads, "Uzzah put forth his hand to the ark of God, and took hold of it; for the oxen shook it. And the anger of the Lord was kindled against Uzzah; and God smote him there for his error; and there he died by the ark of God" (2 Samuel 6:6–7).

The record gives us no insight into Uzzah's motives for reaching out to steady the ark. But the phrase "to steady the ark" has become shorthand for stepping outside of a person's given stewardship to interfere in a matter in which he or she has no authority. We may be sincere in our concern or our desire to help, but we must also show faith and trust in those the Lord has placed in positions of leadership. As explained in this and other revelations, concerns need to go through the proper channels of authority. In this case, God warns Edward Partridge, the bishop in Zion, to follow the counsel of Church leaders. Bishop Partridge repented and remained a faithful steward in the Church and a wise leader among the Saints in Missouri.

> 10 These things I say not of myself; therefore, as the Lord speaketh, he will also fulfil.
>
> 11 And they who are of the High Priesthood, whose names are not found written in the book of the law, or that are found to have apostatized, or to have been cut off from the church, as well as the lesser priesthood, or the members, in that day shall not find an inheritance among the saints of the Most High;
>
> 12 Therefore, it shall be done unto them as unto the children of the priest, as will be found recorded in the second chapter and sixty-first and second verses of Ezra.

Those who refuse to follow counsel given in revelation by the Lord's chosen leaders, however, lose the blessings promised to them. Verse 12 refers to Ezra 2:61–62, which reads, "And of the children of the priests: the children of Habaiah, the children of Koz, the children of Barzillai; which took a wife of the daughters of Barzillai the Gileadite, and was called after their name: These sought their register among those that were reckoned by genealogy, but they were not found: therefore were they, as polluted, put from the priesthood."

These verses refer to the time when the Jews returned from their Babylonian captivity around 539 BC. As the returning people worked to rebuild the temple, they also sought to reconstitute the priesthood of the temple. During this time, it became clear that many who claimed the priesthood through the lineage of Levi could not prove their claim through any kind of official records. Because of this, they were dismissed from priesthood service (see Ezra 2:62; Nehemiah 7:64). In a similar fashion, those who do not honor their covenants in our time will similarly not find their names in the sacred records kept both on earth and in heaven that documents the works of the faithful. The scriptures themselves frequently refer to records of those who fulfill their covenants (see Daniel 7:10; Revelation 20:12; 2 Nephi 29:11; 3 Nephi 27:25–26; Doctrine and Covenants 128:6–7).

End Notes

1. See Steven C. Harper, *Making Sense of the Doctrine & Covenants: A Guided Tour Through Modern Revelations* (Salt Lake City, UT: Deseret Book, 2008), 304.
2. Letter to William W. Phelps, 27 November 1832, 1, josephsmithpapers.org; spelling and punctuation modernized.
3. Letter to William W. Phelps, 31 July 1832, 1, josephsmithpapers.org; punctuation modernized.
4. See "Historical Introduction," Letter to William W. Phelps, 27 November 1832, josephsmithpapers.org.
5. See *General Handbook: Serving in The Church of Jesus Christ of Latter-day Saints*, 32.11.4, Gospel Library.
6. Dieter F. Uchtdorf, "Come, Join with Us," *Ensign* or *Liahona*, Nov. 2013, 22.
7. Ulisses Soares, "How Can I Understand?," *Ensign* or *Liahona*, May 2018, 8.
8. *Messages of the First Presidency of The Church of Jesus Christ of Latter-day Saints*, 1833-1964, ed. James R. Clark (Salt Lake City, UT: Bookcraft, 1965), 4:112, 115, 117.

Doctrine and Covenants Section 86

The Wheat and the Tares

Historical Context

IN THE WANING MONTHS OF 1832, JOSEPH SMITH AND SIDNEY RIGDON continued to work on the new translation of the Bible. In his journal on December 6, 1832, Joseph wrote that he was "translating and received a Revelation explaining the Parable [of] the wheat and the tears [tares] &c."[1] Joseph had already worked through this parable more than a year earlier, but he returned to it at this time. The parable of the wheat and the tares in the King James Bible reads as follows:

> The kingdom of heaven is likened unto a man which sowed good seed in his field:
>
> But while men slept, his enemy came and sowed tares among the wheat, and went his way.
>
> But when the blade was sprung up, and brought forth fruit, then appeared the tares also.

So the servants of the householder came and said unto him, Sir, didst not thou sow good seed in thy field? from whence then hath it tares?

He said unto them, An enemy hath done this. The servants said unto him, Wilt thou then that we go and gather them up?

But he said, Nay; lest while ye gather up the tares, ye root up also the wheat with them.

Let both grow together until the harvest: and in the time of harvest I will say to the reapers, Gather ye together first the tares, and bind them in bundles to burn them: but gather the wheat into my barn. (Matthew 13:24–30)

Somewhere in the translation process, Joseph and Sidney altered the order of the parable from "I will say to the reapers, gather ye together first the tares" to "gather ye together first the wheat into my barn, and the tares are bound in bundles to be burned" (Joseph Smith Translation, Matthew 13:29 [in Matthew 13:30, footnote *b*]).[2]

We do not know if this edit inspired section 86 or if it was the other way around. But this new order aligns more closely with earlier revelations given to Joseph Smith that revealed that the righteous would be gathered out from among the wicked before the destructions surrounding the Second Coming of Jesus Christ (see Doctrine and Covenants 133:12–14). This revelation recontextualizes the parable of the wheat and the tares as an explanation of the Great Apostasy and the Restoration of the gospel in the latter days. This passage, along with the First Vision and Doctrine and Covenants 1, provides explanations from the Savior Himself about how the Apostasy took place and why there was a need for the gospel to be restored to the earth again.[3]

*V*erse-by-*V*erse *C*ommentary

1 Verily, thus saith the Lord unto you my servants, concerning the parable of the wheat and of the tares:

2 Behold, verily I say, the field was the world, and the apostles were the sowers of the seed;

3 And after they have fallen asleep the great persecutor of the church, the apostate, the whore, even Babylon, that maketh all nations to drink of her cup, in whose hearts the enemy, even Sa-

tan, sitteth to reign—behold he soweth the tares; wherefore, the tares choke the wheat and drive the church into the wilderness.

When Jesus was asked why He spoke in parables, He told His Apostles, "Because it is given unto you to know the mysteries of the kingdom of heaven, but to them it is not given. For whosoever hath, to him shall be given, and he shall have more abundance: but whosoever hath not, from him shall be taken away even that he hath. Therefore speak I to them in parables: because they seeing see not; and hearing they hear not, neither do they understand" (Matthew 13:11–13). Parables are a way of opening gospel mysteries to those with the Spirit and keeping the mysteries of the kingdom of God closed to those who are not ready to receive them. In this revelation, the Savior interprets the parable of the wheat and the tares.

As the Lord explains, the field refers to the world, and the sowers represent the Apostles. In the original parable, the Savior identifies Himself as the sower. But by the end of His ministry, He gives the charge to His Apostles to "go ye therefore, and teach all nations" (Matthew 28:19), enlisting them to serve as sowers as well. However, after the Apostles had "fallen asleep," or died, "the apostate, the whore, even Babylon" sowed tares (verse 3). A tare is a kind of weed that looks like wheat in its early stages but ultimately chokes the wheat it grows around. In a revelation given just a few weeks later, Christ identifies the tares as "that great church, the mother of abominations, that made all nations drink of the wine of the wrath of her fornication, that persecuteth the saints of God, that shed their blood—she who sitteth upon many waters, and upon the isles of the sea" (Doctrine and Covenants 88:94).

Beyond interpreting the parable, the Savior, more importantly, witnesses that the early Christian Church apostatized. The true Church of Jesus Christ was driven into the wilderness, causing the need for the Restoration of the gospel through the work of Joseph Smith and others called in the latter days.

> 4 But behold, in the last days, even now while the Lord is beginning to bring forth the word, and the blade is springing up and is yet tender—
>
> 5 Behold, verily I say unto you, the angels are crying unto the Lord day and night, who are ready and waiting to be sent forth to reap down the fields;

6 But the Lord saith unto them, pluck not up the tares while the blade is yet tender (for verily your faith is weak), lest you destroy the wheat also.

7 Therefore, let the wheat and the tares grow together until the harvest is fully ripe; then ye shall first gather out the wheat from among the tares, and after the gathering of the wheat, behold and lo, the tares are bound in bundles, and the field remaineth to be burned.

With the Restoration of the true Church of Jesus Christ, there is new hope and a new harvest of wheat to be gathered. The "harvest" symbolizes the day of Christ's return in glory to the earth. Until that day, God allows the wheat and tares to grow alongside each other. The Lord even goes so far as to say that if the tares were plucked up too soon, the wheat might also be destroyed. Even the wicked (the tares) play a role in helping the righteous (the wheat) undergo the tests and trials they need to become purified and refined.

Given the foreknowledge of God, people sometimes ask why God allows wicked people to remain on the earth where they can harm or cause grief to the righteous. If God knows whom He will eventually exalt and whom He will not, why did He not just assign His children to their final places of glory without sending them to earth first? The answer is set forth in the explanation given of the parable. Tares must have the time to fully become tares, and wheat must to have the time to fully mature as wheat. The issue at hand is not God's omniscience but the agency and accountability of mankind. God might know all things, but we do not. He allows us a chance to use our agency to develop and become what we choose to be: a purified person who is worthy of God's kingdom, or a person who chooses a different path outside of the Lord's presence. The passage even suggests that the wheat need the tares to fully mature.

The time is drawing nearer when both the wheat and the tares must come to a full reckoning of what they really are. Speaking of the angels "crying . . . day and night" to be sent forth to reap, President Wilford Woodruff declared:

> God has held the angels of destruction for many years, lest they should reap down the wheat with the tares. But I want to tell you now, that those angels have left the portals of heaven, and they stand over this people and this nation now, and are hovering over the earth waiting to pour out the

judgments. And from this very day they shall be poured out. Calamities and troubles are increasing in the earth, and there is a meaning to these things. Remember this, and reflect upon these matters. If you do your duty, and I do my duty, we'll have protection, and shall pass through the afflictions in peace and safety.[4]

> 8 Therefore, thus saith the Lord unto you, with whom the priesthood hath continued through the lineage of your fathers—
>
> 9 For ye are lawful heirs, according to the flesh, and have been hid from the world with Christ in God—
>
> 10 Therefore your life and the priesthood have remained, and must needs remain through you and your lineage until the restoration of all things spoken by the mouths of all the holy prophets since the world began.
>
> 11 Therefore, blessed are ye if ye continue in my goodness, a light unto the Gentiles, and through this priesthood, a savior unto my people Israel. The Lord hath said it. Amen.

The final part of this revelation pivots from explaining the parable of the wheat and the tares to directly calling the descendants of the house of Israel to come forward and take part in the great and last Restoration. Shortly after he was ordained as the first patriarch of the Church, Joseph Smith Sr. pronounced the following blessings on his son Joseph: "I bless thee with the blessings of thy fathers Abraham, Isaac and Jacob; and even the blessings of thy father Joseph, the son of Jacob. Behold, he looked after his posterity in the last days, when they should be scattered and driven by the Gentiles, and wept before the Lord: he sought diligently to know from whence the son should come who should bring forth the word of the Lord, by which they might be enlightened, and brought back to the true fold."[5]

Joseph Smith was just one of a multitude of descendants of the house of Israel whose lineage was preserved and kept hidden from the world so that he and others could play their part in restoring the covenants given to Israel. The descendants of Israel who honor their heritage and those who join Israel's descendants by adoption will be the instruments God uses to set up His kingdom in the last days. There is no distinction in the blessings God gives to a person who is a literal descendant of Israel versus a person who is adopted into Israel's linage through the sacred covenants of the gospel. Later revelations given to Joseph Smith explain how members of the Church in the latter days mirror the work of the Savior of all mankind by becoming saviors of their ancestors as well.

End Notes

1. Journal, 1832–1834, 4, josephsmithpapers.org.
2. See Scott H. Faulring, Kent P. Jackson, and Robert J. Matthews, eds., *Joseph Smith's New Translation of the Bible: Original Manuscripts* (Salt Lake City, UT: Deseret Book, 2004), 153–228.
3. See "Historical Introduction," Revelation, 6 December 1832 [D&C 86], josephsmithpapers.org.
4. Wilford Woodruff, *The Discourses of Wilford Woodruff* (Salt Lake City, UT: Bookcraft, 1990), 229–30.
5. Blessing from Joseph Smith Sr., 9 December 1834, 3, josephsmithpapers.org.

$\mathcal{D}$octrine and $\mathcal{C}$ovenants Section 87

Stand Ye in Holy Places

$\mathcal{H}$istorical $\mathcal{C}$ontext

THIS SECTION, COMMONLY KNOWN AS "THE REVELATION ON WAR," WAS RE-ceived on Christmas Day, 1832. Joseph Smith later recorded that the reve-lation came during a time when he was deeply troubled over the state of the world. In his history he wrote the following: "Appearances of troubles among the nations, became more visible, this season, than they had previously done, since the church began her journey out of the wilderness. The ravages of the cholera were frightful, in almost all the large cities on the globe; and the plague broke out in India; while the United States, amid all her pomp and greatness, was threatened with immediate dissolution."[1] Many of these troubles had been highlighted a few days earlier in the *Painesville Telegraph*, a nearby newspaper. In some ways, God gave the revelation in Doctrine and Covenants 87 in response to Joseph Smith experiencing a feeling that is common to many of us—anxiety after reading the news.

Of particular concern to Joseph Smith was the nullification crisis involving South Carolina. Joseph Smith wrote that "the people of South Carolina, in convention assembled, passed ordinances, declaring their state, a free and Independent Nation; and appointed Thursday the 31st. day of January 1833, as a day of humiliation and prayer, to implore Almighty God to vouchsafe his blessings, and restore liberty and happiness within their borders. President [Andrew] Jackson issued his proclamation against this rebellion; called out a force sufficient to quell it and implored the blessings of God to assist the Nation to extricate itself from the horrors of the approaching and solemn Crisis."[2] The crisis Joseph Smith expressed concern over was resolved in March 1833 when a compromise tariff averted a potential civil war in the United States.

Though this revelation was received in 1832, Brigham Young noted that it was intentionally left out of the 1835 edition of the Doctrine and Covenants. In an 1860 discourse, Brigham declared: "That revelation was reserved at the time the compilation for that book was made by Oliver Cowdery and others, in Kirtland. It was not wisdom to publish it to the world, and it remained in the private *escritoire* [a small writing desk]. Brother Joseph had that revelation concerning this nation at a time when the brethren were reflecting and reasoning with regard to African slavery on this continent, and the slavery of the children of men throughout the world."[3] Section 87 was first published in the 1851 edition of the Pearl of Great Price and was included in the 1876 edition of the Doctrine and Covenants.[4]

$\mathcal{V}$erse-by-$\mathcal{V}$erse $\mathcal{C}$ommentary

> 1 Verily, thus saith the Lord concerning the wars that will shortly come to pass, beginning at the rebellion of South Carolina, which will eventually terminate in the death and misery of many souls;

Though the nullification crisis in 1832 ultimately did not lead to a civil war in the United States, Joseph Smith stood by the accuracy of this prophesy, even after the crisis had passed. In a discourse given on April 2, 1843, he declared, "I prophesy, in the name of the Lord God, that the commencement of the difficulties which will cause much bloodshed previous to the coming of the Son of Man will be in South Carolina. It may probably arise through the slave question. This a voice declared to me, while I was praying earnestly on the subject, December 25th, 1832" (Doctrine and Covenants 130:12–13). He was eventually proven correct. On April 12, 1861, the American Civil War began when Confederate forces fired on Fort Sumter, a sea fort near Charleston, South Carolina.

In many ways the American Civil War was the beginning of the wars leading up to the Second Coming of Jesus Christ. The war proved to be far more bloody and costly than anyone could have imagined. The prophecy given to Joseph Smith said the war would terminate in the "death and misery of many souls," and to this day, there is no war in the history of the United States that approaches the Civil War on the death scale. A conservative estimate puts the number of Civil War deaths at 618,000. By comparison, in other major wars fought by the United States, the number of estimated deaths range from 4,435 in the American Revolution; 2,260 in the War of 1812; 13,283 in the Mexican War; 2,446 in the Spanish-American War; 116,516 in World War I; 405,399 in World War II; 36,574 in the Korean War; 58,220 in the Vietnam War; 383 in the Gulf War; and 6,773+ in Iraq/Afghanistan. However, these estimates only take into account the soldiers killed in the war, not the massive civilian casualties and the destruction of property wrought in the conflicts.[5]

> 2 And the time will come that war will be poured out upon all nations, beginning at this place.
>
> 3 For behold, the Southern States shall be divided against the Northern States, and the Southern States will call on other nations, even the nation of Great Britain, as it is called, and they shall also call upon other nations, in order to defend themselves against other nations; and then war shall be poured out upon all nations.

If this revelation is read only as a prophecy of the Civil War, it would be remarkable on its own. Depending on how the prophecy is read, however, it may also be a prophecy of the world wars fought in the first half of the twentieth century. The prophecy declares that the Southern nations will call upon other nations, even Great Britain, for assistance in the war. During the Civil War, William L. Yancey led a group of commissioners from the Southern states that met with Lord John Russell, the British secretary of state for foreign affairs, and with Napoleon III of France. Other commissioners from the South approached Spain and Belgium for help in the war.[6]

The prophecy further states that "they," possibly meaning Great Britain and other European nations, would in turn call upon other nations for assistance. Parts of this prophecy came to fulfillment during the first and second world wars, during which Britain called upon the United States and other nations to come to their assistance. During WWI and WWII, war was poured out upon all nations. The toll of the death and misery experienced by both military members and civilians in these wars has yet to be exceeded. One historical group estimates that fifteen million soldiers and twenty-five million civilians were killed in WWII—but these are conservative numbers. Depending on how casualties are counted, there may have been more than fifty million civilian deaths just in the nation of China.[7] Taken as a prophecy of not just the American Civil War but also the world wars of the twentieth century, this revelation becomes even more remarkable.

> 4 And it shall come to pass, after many days, slaves shall rise up against their masters, who shall be marshaled and disciplined for war.

This prophecy was partially fulfilled during the American Civil War, during which around 180,000 Black men served in the Union army, which constituted about 10 percent of the total force. Most of these soldiers—by one estimate, about 90,000—were former slaves from the Confederate States who had fled and joined the Northern forces.[8] By the end of the war, the Southern states became so strained for resources that the Confederate Congress passed a bill allowing the armies of the South to draft enslaved workers as soldiers in the war. The war ended before these soldiers arrived in large numbers. But the act alone would have been unthinkable in 1832 when Joseph Smith received section 87.[9]

Taken as a prophecy larger than just regarding the American Civil War, this revelation may also speak of larger upheavals throughout the world. When the revelation was given to Joseph Smith, a small number of European nations ruled the majority of the people on the earth. The millennial wars of the twentieth century completely overthrew this system, creating hundreds of new nation states. Dozens of new nations came into being as a result of the world wars, and other nations went through dramatic changes. Even in our time, wars and rumors of war continue among the sons and daughters of God.

5 And it shall come to pass also that the remnants who are left of the land will marshal themselves, and shall become exceedingly angry, and shall vex the Gentiles with a sore vexation.

6 And thus, with the sword and by bloodshed the inhabitants of the earth shall mourn; and with famine, and plague, and earthquake, and the thunder of heaven, and the fierce and vivid lightning also, shall the inhabitants of the earth be made to feel the wrath, and indignation, and chastening hand of an Almighty God, until the consumption decreed hath made a full end of all nations;

We do not know the precise identity of the "remnants" described in this passage. This could refer to the remnants of the Book of Mormon peoples found in the Western Hemisphere. It may also be a reference to the remnants of the house of Israel. When Jesus Christ ministered among the people of the Americas, he uttered a prophecy that holds some parallels to the wording used here: "Then shall the remnants, which shall be scattered abroad upon the face of the earth, be gathered in from the east and from the west, and from the south and from the north; and they shall be brought to the knowledge of the Lord their God, who hath redeemed them" (3 Nephi 20:13). The Savior continued, "If the Gentiles do not repent after the blessing which they shall receive, after they have scattered my people—then shall ye, who are a remnant of the house of Jacob, go forth among them; and ye shall be in the midst of them who shall be many; and ye shall be among them as a lion among the beasts of the forest, and as a young lion among the flocks of sheep" (3 Nephi 20:15–16).

The Savior concludes the prophecy with the following: "And I will gather my people together as a man gathereth his sheaves into the floor. For I will make my people with whom the Father hath covenanted, yea, I will make thy horn iron, and I will make thy hoofs brass. And thou shalt beat in pieces many people; and I will consecrate their gain unto the Lord, and their substance unto the Lord of the whole earth. And behold, I am he who doeth it" (3 Nephi 20:19; see also Micah 5:8). These words indicate that the restored house of Israel will assist in bringing about "the end of nations." While this does not mean that the people of these nations will be destroyed, it does mean that their governments will be dissolved as the kingdom of God spreads throughout the earth (Articles of Faith 1:10).

7 That the cry of the saints, and of the blood of the saints, shall cease to come up into the ears of the Lord of Sabaoth, from the earth, to be avenged of their enemies.

8 Wherefore, stand ye in holy places, and be not moved, until the day of the Lord come; for behold, it cometh quickly, saith the Lord. Amen.

The words of this prophecy convey a world of chaos and calamity leading up to the Second Coming. As indicated here and in other places, the Saints will not entirely escape this destruction (see Revelation 16:6; 17:6; 18:24; 2 Nephi 28:10; Mormon 8:27, 41). However, this does not mean that the Lord is not in control or will not protect His disciples. He is reassuringly referred to here as "the Lord of Sabaoth" (*Sabaoth* is a Hebrew term referring to both human and angelic armies), which phrase is often translated as "the Lord of Hosts."[10] The Lord of Hosts will intervene in the conflicts leading up to the Second Coming, bear His power to end bloodshed on earth, and reign as the Prince of Peace.

Those who live in troubled times need not be troubled themselves. We can find peace by standing in holy places, as the Lord counsels in this revelation. The Lord is overseeing events, and we can take comfort in knowing that whatever happens on earth, there is joy waiting in the next life. In anticipating these blessings, the Saints should not give up on their efforts to build Zion and make the world a better place. Shortly after the terrorist attacks of September 11, 2001, President Hinckley addressed the Church in a general conference. Many in the audience, both in the United States and around the world, were still reeling from the horrific acts of violence that had been acted out in front of them. President Hinckley spoke to the Church, declaring with firm certainty, "Are these perilous times? They are. But there is no need to fear. We can have peace in our hearts and in our homes. We can be an influence for good in this world, every one of us."[11]

End Notes

1. Joseph Smith, in History, 1838–1856, volume A-1 [23 December 1805–30 August 1834], 244, josephsmithpapers.org.
2. Joseph Smith, in History, 1838–1856, volume A-1 [23 December 1805–30 August 1834], 244, josephsmithpapers.org.
3. Brigham Young, in *Journal of Discourses,* 8:68.
4. See Lyndon W. Cook, *The Revelations of the Prophet Joseph Smith: A Historical and Biographical Commentary of the Doctrine and Covenants* (Salt Lake City, UT: Deseret Book, 1985), 180. See also "Historical Introduction," Revelation, 25 December 1832 [D&C 87], josephsmithpapers.org.
5. See Matthew Green, "How Many Soldiers Died in Each U.S. War?," KQED, May 25, 2017, https://www.kqed.org/lowdown/22209/interactive-american-war-deaths-by-the-numbers.
6. See Shelby Foote, *The Civil War: A Narrative* (New York: Vintage, 1986), 1:134–37.
7. See "Research Starters: Worldwide Deaths in World War II," The National WWII Museum, accessed Mar. 25, 2021, https://www.nationalww2museum.org/students-teachers/student-resources/research-starters/research-starters-worldwide-deaths-world-war.
8. See "Black Civil War Soldiers," History.com, last modified Nov. 22, 2021, https://www.history.com/topics/american-civil-war/black-civil-war-soldiers.
9. See "Confederacy Approves Black Soldiers," History.com, last modified Mar. 10, 2021, https://www.history.com/this-day-in-history/confederacy-approves-black-soldiers.
10. *Lexham Bible Dictionary* (Bellingham, WA: Lexham Press, 2016), s.v. "hosts."
11. Gordon B. Hinckley, "The Times in Which We Live," *Ensign,* Nov. 2001, 74.

Doctrine and Covenants
Section 88
The Olive Leaf

Historical Context

THE REVELATION RECEIVED ON CHRISTMAS DAY, 1832 (DOCTRINE AND Covenants 87), must have been very disturbing for Joseph Smith and the Saints in Kirtland. The "prophecy on war," as it has come to be known, contained striking predictions of a world full of turmoil and wars that would cause death and misery among the children of men. Only two days later, Joseph Smith received this revelation, which he described as "the Olive leaf which we have plucked from the tree of paradise" and "the Lord's message of peace to us."[1] In contrast to the revelation on war, which is eight verses long in the current Doctrine and Covenants, the "message of peace" is 141 verses long—currently the lengthiest revelation in this book of scripture.

Joseph Smith received the revelation over three days in two parts that were combined and published together in the 1835 Doctrine and Covenants.[2] Verses 1–126 were received on December 27 and 28 in the translation room of the Whitney store in Kirtland, Ohio, during a conference of high priests held in Kirtland. The minutes of the conference note that "Bro Joseph arose and said, to receive revelation and the blessings of heaven it was necessary to have our minds on god and exercise faith and become of one heart and of one mind." Joseph asked each of the brethren present to pray separately "for the Lord to reveal his will unto us concerning the upbuilding of Zion." After this, each person in the room rose to share "his feelings, and determination to keep the commandments of God." Joseph then began to dictate the revelation and continued until nine o'clock at night. Starting at 9 a.m. the following morning, he finished the first part of the revelation (see Doctrine and Covenants 88:1–126).[3]

Verses 127–141 came on January 3, 1833, and were designated as "instructions [on] how to regulate the Elders school."[4] In the earlier part of the revelation, God instructed the Church to establish a school and also to build a "house of God" that would serve as a "house of learning" (Doctrine and Covenants 88:119). Later, in verses 117–141, God explains how to conduct the school in the house of the Lord. These instructions included the salutation that the elders gave when entering and the "ordinance of the washing of feet" (Doctrine and Covenants 88:139). This section provides vital information about the nature and power of Jesus Christ, the signs of the times, and the Resurrection of all people. It also contains the command to build the house of the Lord in Kirtland, a sacred structure where the truths and keys necessary to carry out temple work in the last days would be given, and a house where the Savior Himself would appear.[5]

$\mathcal{V}$erse-by-$\mathcal{V}$erse $\mathcal{C}$ommentary

1 Verily, thus saith the Lord unto you who have assembled yourselves together to receive his will concerning you:

2 Behold, this is pleasing unto your Lord, and the angels rejoice over you; the alms of your prayers have come up into the ears of the Lord of Sabaoth, and are recorded in the book of the names of the sanctified, even them of the celestial world.

3 Wherefore, I now send upon you another Comforter, even upon you my friends, that it may abide in your hearts, even the

Holy Spirit of promise; which other Comforter is the same that
I promised unto my disciples, as is recorded in the testimony of
John.

4 This Comforter is the promise which I give unto you of eternal
life, even the glory of the celestial kingdom;

5 Which glory is that of the church of the Firstborn, even of
God, the holiest of all, through Jesus Christ his Son—

After the frightening prophecies found in Doctrine and Covenants
87, the Lord begins this revelation by again referring to Himself as "the
Lord of Sabaoth," or the "Lord of Hosts" (see commentary for Doctrine
and Covenants 87:7). In section 87, the title "Lord of Hosts" appears in the
context of judgment coming down upon the heads of those who would persecute the Saints. Here the "Lord of Hosts" is used to describe Jesus Christ
as a being of infinite power, able to overthrow the forces of wickedness and
provide the righteous with their reward. While Doctrine and Covenants
87 discusses a world descending into chaos, the first part of Doctrine and
Covenants 88 (verses 1–118) explains the vast power and influence of the
Lord. In a world that seems to be spinning out of control, the Savior asserts
that He manages an entire universe through His power and that the struggles of our world are only a brief and temporary part of the Father's grand
plan. The righteous will eventually receive their reward and find their names
in the book of the sanctified.

In the midst of these challenges, the Savior promises His disciples the
peace of the Comforter, or the Holy Ghost. In the Gospel of John, the Holy
Ghost is the First Comforter. Here, as in John, the Savior tells of another
Comforter who brings with Him the promise of eternal life (see John 14:16).
In an 1839 discourse, Joseph Smith commented on the other Comforter spoken of here and in John 14. He said, "Now what is this other Comforter[?]
It is no more or less than the Lord Jesus Christ himself[,] and this is the
sum and substance of the whole matter, that when any man obtains this last
Comforter he will have the personage of Jesus Christ to attend him or appear unto him from time to time. Even he will manifest the Father unto him
and they will take up their abode with him, and the visions of the heavens
will be opened unto him and the Lord will teach him face to face."[6]

The Holy Ghost, or the First Comforter, brings peace as we endure the
trying conditions of our world. The Second Comforter, who is the resurrected Jesus Christ, brings an assurance of eternal life and exaltation in the

next life, provided that a person does not commit the unpardonable sin (see Doctrine and Covenants 76:34–35).

> 6 He that ascended up on high, as also he descended below all things, in that he comprehended all things, that he might be in all and through all things, the light of truth;
>
> 7 Which truth shineth. This is the light of Christ. As also he is in the sun, and the light of the sun, and the power thereof by which it was made.
>
> 8 As also he is in the moon, and is the light of the moon, and the power thereof by which it was made;
>
> 9 As also the light of the stars, and the power thereof by which they were made;
>
> 10 And the earth also, and the power thereof, even the earth upon which you stand.
>
> 11 And the light which shineth, which giveth you light, is through him who enlighteneth your eyes, which is the same light that quickeneth your understandings;
>
> 12 Which light proceedeth forth from the presence of God to fill the immensity of space—
>
> 13 The light which is in all things, which giveth life to all things, which is the law by which all things are governed, even the power of God who sitteth upon his throne, who is in the bosom of eternity, who is in the midst of all things.

Part of what makes this revelation "the Lord's message of peace" is the explanation of the vastness of His power. Jesus Christ is a resurrected, glorified being with a body of flesh and bone (see Doctrine and Covenants 130:22). Jesus ascended up on high by overcoming death and gaining exaltation. He also descended below all things, enduring infinite suffering to provide salvation for all men and women (see Alma 34:9–10). He is omniscient. He knows and comprehends all things. Paul and Alma both testified that through His experience and suffering, Jesus gained infinite compassion and understanding for the children of God.

Additionally, Jesus Christ is omnipresent. How can He have a physical body and yet be omnipresent? The answer is through the medium of the Light of Christ. The Light of Christ is different from the Holy Ghost. It is not a personage but a force, or a power. Elder James E. Talmage referred to it as the "'divine essence' by means of which the Godhead operates upon man and in nature."[7] President Joseph F. Smith explained:

> The question is often asked, Is there any difference between the Spirit of the Lord and the Holy Ghost? The terms are frequently used synonymously. We often say the Spirit of God when we mean the Holy Ghost; we likewise say the Holy Ghost when we mean the Spirit of God. The Holy Ghost is a personage in the Godhead, and is not that which lighteth every man that cometh into the world. It is the Spirit of God which proceeds through Christ to the world, that enlightens every man that comes into the world, and that strives with the children of men, and will continue to strive with them, until it brings them to a knowledge of the truth and the possession of the greater light and testimony of the Holy Ghost.[8]

Here the Light of Christ is not just referred to as the power "given to every man, that he may know good from evil," though that is one of its most important functions (Moroni 7:16). It is the essence of light, the power that makes the universe a livable place. This power "fill[s] the immensity of space" and is that "which is in all things, which giveth life to all things, which is the law by which all things are governed" (verses 12–13). There is no more direct and comprehensive statement about the power of Jesus Christ anywhere in scripture. The testimony given here assures us that whatever challenges we face, with Christ as our Advocate, we can overcome them. For a being whose stewardship and power bring life to the universe and fills all things, the challenges we face are small by comparison.

> 14 Now, verily I say unto you, that through the redemption which is made for you is brought to pass the resurrection from the dead.
>
> 15 And the spirit and the body are the soul of man.
>
> 16 And the resurrection from the dead is the redemption of the soul.

After explaining the infinite immensity of His power, the Savior pivots to explain the intimate miracles He provides for our redemption. The "soul of man" is described here as "the spirit and the body" that is redeemed with physical resurrection. Resurrection serves as a major theme of this revelation, with the Lord explaining in detail when this blessing comes to all people.

In most verses in scripture, *soul* is used as another word for *spirit*. For instance, Abraham referred to our spirits in the premortal realm as souls (see Abraham 3:23), and Alma referred to the deceased in the spirit world as souls awaiting resurrection (see Alma 40:11–14). In Doctrine and Covenants 88:16, "the redemption of the soul" is the reuniting of the spirit and the body, a gift given by Christ to all people. A unique trait of Latter-day Saint beliefs is the concept that the physical body functions not as a prison but as an essential component of an eternal being. Elder Talmage taught, "It is peculiar to the theology of the Latter-day Saints that we regard the body as an essential part of the soul. Read your dictionaries, the lexicons, and encyclopedias, and you will find that nowhere [in Christianity], outside of the Church of Jesus Christ, is the solemn and eternal truth taught that the soul of man is the body and the spirit combined."[9]

President Jeffrey R. Holland explained:

One of the "plain and precious" truths restored to this dispensation is that "the spirit *and* the body are the soul of man" (Doctrine and Covenants 88:15; emphasis added) and that when the spirit and body are separated, men and women "cannot receive a fulness of joy" (Doctrine and Covenants 93:34). Certainly that suggests something of the reason why obtaining a body is so fundamentally important to the plan of salvation in the first place, why sin of any kind is such a serious matter (namely because its automatic consequence is death, the separation of the spirit from the body and the separation of the spirit and the body from God), and why the resurrection of the body is so central to the great abiding and eternal triumph of Christ's atonement. We do not have to be a herd of demonically possessed swine charging down the Gadarene slopes toward the sea to understand that a body is *the* great prize of mortal life, and that even a pig's will do for those frenzied spirits that rebelled, and to this day remain dispossessed, in their first, unembodied estate.[10]

17 And the redemption of the soul is through him that quickeneth all things, in whose bosom it is decreed that the poor and the meek of the earth shall inherit it.

18 Therefore, it must needs be sanctified from all unrighteousness, that it may be prepared for the celestial glory;

19 For after it hath filled the measure of its creation, it shall be crowned with glory, even with the presence of God the Father;

20 That bodies who are of the celestial kingdom may possess it forever and ever; for, for this intent was it made and created, and for this intent are they sanctified.

21 And they who are not sanctified through the law which I have given unto you, even the law of Christ, must inherit another kingdom, even that of a terrestrial kingdom, or that of a telestial kingdom.

22 For he who is not able to abide the law of a celestial kingdom cannot abide a celestial glory.

23 And he who cannot abide the law of a terrestrial kingdom cannot abide a terrestrial glory.

24 And he who cannot abide the law of a telestial kingdom cannot abide a telestial glory; therefore he is not meet for a kingdom of glory. Therefore he must abide a kingdom which is not a kingdom of glory.

25 And again, verily I say unto you, the earth abideth the law of a celestial kingdom, for it filleth the measure of its creation, and transgresseth not the law—

26 Wherefore, it shall be sanctified; yea, notwithstanding it shall die, it shall be quickened again, and shall abide the power by which it is quickened, and the righteous shall inherit it.

The Savior reaffirms His promise given in the Sermon on the Mount and the sermon at the temple that the meek shall inherit the earth (see Matthew 5:5; 3 Nephi 12:5). This promise is not a metaphor; the earth itself is part of the plan of salvation and will eventually be resurrected (quickened) and become the celestial kingdom for those who lived here and qualified for its blessings. The work of Jesus Christ saves not only the men and women who live on earth but the entire ecosystem. As the Lord here declares, "the earth abideth the law of the celestial kingdom" (verse 25). How can a planet obey the celestial law? It obeys by simply fulfilling the measure of its creation.

Like us, the earth now exists in a fallen, telestial condition. In a vision, the ancient prophet Enoch "looked upon the earth; and he heard a voice from the bowels thereof, saying: Wo, wo is me, the mother of men; I am pained, I am weary, because of the wickedness of my children. When shall I rest, and be cleansed from the filthiness which is gone forth out of me?

When will my Creator sanctify me, that I may rest, and righteousness for a season abide upon my face?" (Moses 7:48). The earth longs to be cleansed and to achieve its full potential as a celestial kingdom.

The cleansing of the earth will take place in two stages. First, upon Christ's return, the earth "will be renewed and receive its paradisiacal glory" (Articles of Faith 1:10). Christ will sweep all things telestial off the earth and destroy every corruptible thing (see Doctrine and Covenants 101:24–25). After a millennium of peace and a "little season" (Doctrine and Covenants 29:22), the earth will die and be resurrected as a celestial kingdom. John saw "a new heaven and a new earth: for the first heaven and the first earth were passed away" (Revelation 21:1). An earlier revelation given to Joseph Smith declares that "all old things shall pass away, and all things shall become new, even the heaven and the earth, and all the fulness thereof, both men and beasts, the fowls of the air, and the fishes of the sea; And not one hair, neither mote, shall be lost, for it is the workmanship of mine hand" (Doctrine and Covenants 29:24–25).

> 27 For notwithstanding they die, they also shall rise again, a spiritual body.
>
> 28 They who are of a celestial spirit shall receive the same body which was a natural body; even ye shall receive your bodies, and your glory shall be that glory by which your bodies are quickened.
>
> 29 Ye who are quickened by a portion of the celestial glory shall then receive of the same, even a fulness.
>
> 30 And they who are quickened by a portion of the terrestrial glory shall then receive of the same, even a fulness.
>
> 31 And also they who are quickened by a portion of the telestial glory shall then receive of the same, even a fulness.

A *spiritual body* is not the same thing as a *spirit*, or immaterial body. Paul spoke of a person being "raised a spiritual body," adding that "there is a natural body, and there is a spiritual body" (1 Corinthians 15:44). In the context of this verse, a spiritual body is defined as a body that is not subject to corruption or death. Yet there are wide variances in the types of bodies given in the Resurrection. Speaking of resurrected bodies, Paul taught, "All flesh is not the same flesh: but there is one kind of flesh of men, another flesh of beasts, another of fishes, and another of birds. Also celestial bodies, and bodies terrestrial, *and bodies telestial;* but the glory of the celestial, one; and the terrestrial, another; *and the telestial, another.* There is one glory of the sun, and another glory of the moon, and another glory of the stars: for one star differeth from another star in glory" (1 Corinthians 15:39–41; italics denote the Joseph Smith Translation of verse 40).

The mortal body continuously goes through cycles of decay and renewal, but it reflects the body we receive in the Resurrection. At a conference held in April 1843, Joseph Smith responded to a remark by Elder Orson Pratt "that a man's body changes every seven years" by teaching, "There is no fundamental principle belonging to a human system that ever goes into another, in this world, or in the world to come; I care not what the theories of men are. We have the testimony that God will raise us up, and he has the power to do it, if any one supposes that any part of our bodies, that is, the fundamental parts thereof, ever goes into another body, he is mistaken."[11] Though Joseph Smith did not further elaborate on what he meant by the "fundamental principle" or the "fundamental parts," it seems safe to say that the resurrected you will still be you. It is true that the components of our bodies change over time, but our bodies in the Resurrection will be a glorified version of ourselves while retaining the fundamentals that make us who we really are.

> 32 And they who remain shall also be quickened; nevertheless, they shall return again to their own place, to enjoy that which they are willing to receive, because they were not willing to enjoy that which they might have received.
>
> 33 For what doth it profit a man if a gift is bestowed upon him, and he receive not the gift? Behold, he rejoices not in that which is given unto him, neither rejoices in him who is the giver of the gift.
>
> 34 And again, verily I say unto you, that which is governed by law is also preserved by law and perfected and sanctified by the same.
>
> 35 That which breaketh a law, and abideth not by law, but seeketh to become a law unto itself, and willeth to abide in sin, and altogether abideth in sin, cannot be sanctified by law, neither by mercy, justice, nor judgment. Therefore, they must remain filthy still.

"They who remain" are those who will not receive celestial, terrestrial, or telestial glory but will still be resurrected. They are called "sons of perdition" in other revelations (Doctrine and Covenants 76:32). These people will have their spirits reunited with their bodies but with no glory, remaining "filthy still" (verse 35). However, these individuals will have an advantage over the people who rebelled against God in premortality and did not receive a body (see Revelation 12:4; Doctrine and Covenants 29:36–38).

36 All kingdoms have a law given;

37 And there are many kingdoms; for there is no space in the which there is no kingdom; and there is no kingdom in which there is no space, either a greater or a lesser kingdom.

38 And unto every kingdom is given a law; and unto every law there are certain bounds also and conditions.

39 All beings who abide not in those conditions are not justified.

40 For intelligence cleaveth unto intelligence; wisdom receiveth wisdom; truth embraceth truth; virtue loveth virtue; light cleaveth unto light; mercy hath compassion on mercy and claimeth her own; justice continueth its course and claimeth its own; judgment goeth before the face of him who sitteth upon the throne and governeth and executeth all things.

41 He comprehendeth all things, and all things are before him, and all things are round about him; and he is above all things, and in all things, and is through all things, and is round about all things; and all things are by him, and of him, even God, forever and ever.

In a later discourse, Joseph Smith would explain, "There is a law, irrevocably decreed in heaven before the foundations of this world, upon which all blessings are predicated—And when we obtain any blessing from God, it is by obedience to that law upon which it is predicated" (Doctrine and Covenants 130:20–21). The same principle—that blessings, including the blessings of exaltation, come from our observance of the law—is taught here in verses 36–41. Each kingdom—celestial, terrestrial, and telestial—has different laws. In sacred texts, there is often a difference drawn between a *rule* and a *law.* The law of Moses, for example, contains hundreds of rules, or dos and don'ts, that together make up the law. The law is the entire collection of rules.

Accepting the law of the kingdom does not mean that a person perfectly obeys all the rules. The law of the celestial kingdom, perhaps best laid out in the sermons Jesus gave in Matthew 5–7 and 3 Nephi 12–14, is a demanding set of standards. To accept the celestial law does not mean, for instance, that you never get angry (see Matthew 5:22; 3 Nephi 12:22) or that you never experience feelings of lust (see Matthew 5:27; 3 Nephi 12:27). It simply means that we choose to use those rules as standards for governing our behavior and accept the consequences that come when we fail to live up to those standards. We determine our morality based on those standards and strive to live according to them. We first accept the grace of Christ and strive for forgiveness when we fall short.

One of the most beautiful teachings of this passage deals with the nature of God. While God loves us and wants us to live with Him in celestial glory, He does not force His laws upon us. All people possess the Light of Christ, which gives them a basic sense of morality. God then seeks to increase the light already within us by teaching true principles and allowing the Holy Ghost to influence us. When we choose to recognize good principles and follow them, our freedom grows. Though laws are sometimes seen as constricting, they help us gain greater freedom. The more we obey the laws of God, the greater our sanctification grows and the more likely it becomes that we will live in the celestial kingdom with God. However, if we choose to abide by a lesser law, God will reward us according to that law.

> 42 And again, verily I say unto you, he hath given a law unto all things, by which they move in their times and their seasons;
>
> 43 And their courses are fixed, even the courses of the heavens and the earth, which comprehend the earth and all the planets.
>
> 44 And they give light to each other in their times and in their seasons, in their minutes, in their hours, in their days, in their weeks, in their months, in their years—all these are one year with God, but not with man.
>
> 45 The earth rolls upon her wings, and the sun giveth his light by day, and the moon giveth her light by night, and the stars also give their light, as they roll upon their wings in their glory, in the midst of the power of God.

God is the great Lawgiver. Whether it is the moral laws that govern our daily interactions with each other, or the laws of physics that govern the movement of planets in their orbits, the source of these laws is God Himself. The order of the universe is one of the great proofs of the existence of God. When confronted by the anti-Christ Korihor, Alma argued, "All things denote there is a God; yea, even the earth, and all things that are upon the face of it, yea, and its motion, yea, and also all the planets which move in their regular form do witness that there is a Supreme Creator" (Alma 30:44).

However, we should not assume that the way the laws function for us here on earth is the way they function in all parts of God's creations. The formula given in verse 44, which equates all minutes, hours, weeks, months, and years as being "one year with God," contradicts other formulations of time given in the scriptures if it is taken literally (see Abraham 3:4; Facsimile 2:1; Moses 3:17; Abraham 5:13; Psalm 90:4; 2 Peter 3:8). The overall message of these verses appears to be that time works differently for God than it does for mortal men and women on earth. Rather than taking all of these statements literally, it is probably best to look to the statement of Alma the Younger that "all is as one day with God, and time only is measured unto men" (Alma 40:8).

46 Unto what shall I liken these kingdoms, that ye may understand?

47 Behold, all these are kingdoms, and any man who hath seen any or the least of these hath seen God moving in his majesty and power.

48 I say unto you, he hath seen him; nevertheless, he who came unto his own was not comprehended.

49 The light shineth in darkness, and the darkness comprehendeth it not; nevertheless, the day shall come when you shall comprehend even God, being quickened in him and by him.

50 Then shall ye know that ye have seen me, that I am, and that I am the true light that is in you, and that you are in me; otherwise ye could not abound.

Some might argue that God is incomprehensible to mortal minds, but both ancient and modern scripture argue to the contrary. The majesty and breadth of God's power and dominions might be incomprehensible to a mortal, but the character, attributes, and perfections of God are something that a mortal can and must comprehend in order to fully exercise faith in Him. Jesus taught, "And this is life eternal, that they might know thee the only true God, and Jesus Christ, whom thou hast sent" (John 17:3). Joseph Smith taught that "if men do not comprehend the character of God[,] they do not comprehend themselves."[12] God promises in verse 49 that at some future time (most likely after our resurrection), we will be able to comprehend everything about the nature of God.

Joseph Smith further expounded on this subject in an 1834 letter written to the Church:

> God has created man with a mind capable of instruction, and a faculty which may be enlarged in proportion to the heed and diligence given to the light communicated from heaven to the intellect; and that the nearer man approaches perfection, the more conspicuous are his views, & the greater his enjoyments, until he has overcome the evils of this life and lost every desire of sin; and like the ancients, arrives to that point of faith that he is wrapped in the glory and power of his Maker and is caught up to dwell with him. But we consider that this is a station to which no man ever arrived in a moment: he must have been instructed into the government and laws of that kingdom by proper degrees, till his mind was capable in some measure of comprehending the propriety, justice, equity, and consistency of the same.[13]

51 Behold, I will liken these kingdoms unto a man having a field, and he sent forth his servants into the field to dig in the field.

52 And he said unto the first: Go ye and labor in the field, and in the first hour I will come unto you, and ye shall behold the joy of my countenance.

53 And he said unto the second: Go ye also into the field, and in the second hour I will visit you with the joy of my countenance.

54 And also unto the third, saying: I will visit you;

55 And unto the fourth, and so on unto the twelfth.

56 And the lord of the field went unto the first in the first hour, and tarried with him all that hour, and he was made glad with the light of the countenance of his lord.

57 And then he withdrew from the first that he might visit the second also, and the third, and the fourth, and so on unto the twelfth.

58 And thus they all received the light of the countenance of their lord, every man in his hour, and in his time, and in his season—

59 Beginning at the first, and so on unto the last, and from the last unto the first, and from the first unto the last;

60 Every man in his own order, until his hour was finished, even according as his lord had commanded him, that his lord might be glorified in him, and he in his lord, that they all might be glorified.

61 Therefore, unto this parable I will liken all these kingdoms, and the inhabitants thereof—every kingdom in its hour, and in its time, and in its season, even according to the decree which God hath made.

One pair of commentators has labeled this passage "the parable of the multitude of kingdoms."[14] This passage, along with others in modern revelation, serves to illustrate that God is not just the God of the whole earth but the ruler of the universe. There are a multitude of worlds among the creations of God, and many are inhabited by the sons and daughters of God (see Doctrine and Covenants 76:24). When the Lord spoke unto Moses, He explained:

Worlds without number have I created; and I also created them for mine own purpose; and by the Son I created them, which is mine Only Begotten.
And the first man of all men have I called Adam, which is many.
But only an account of this earth, and the inhabitants thereof, give I unto you. For behold, there are many worlds that have passed away by the word of my power. And there are many that now stand, and innumerable are they unto man; but all things are numbered unto me, for they are mine and I know them. (Moses 1:33–35)

Each of these worlds undoubtedly has its own history and literature and hosts a multitude of cultures as complex and beautiful as the ones in our world. But the gospel is fundamentally the same no matter where it is taught, and the people of other worlds "are sav'd by the very same Saviour of ours; And, of course, are begotten God's daughters and sons, By the very same truths, and the very same pow'rs."[15] The gospel pattern remains the same—on all of these worlds, God calls prophets who teach and testify of the power of Jesus Christ to save. The work is much bigger in scope than we can conceive. However, the scriptures are clear that even though the work of Christ is infinite, on an individual level it is still intimate for each of us.

62 And again, verily I say unto you, my friends, I leave these sayings with you to ponder in your hearts, with this commandment which I give unto you, that ye shall call upon me while I am near—

63 Draw near unto me and I will draw near unto you; seek me diligently and ye shall find me; ask, and ye shall receive; knock, and it shall be opened unto you.

64 Whatsoever ye ask the Father in my name it shall be given unto you, that is expedient for you;

65 And if ye ask anything that is not expedient for you, it shall turn unto your condemnation.

66 Behold, that which you hear is as the voice of one crying in the wilderness—in the wilderness, because you cannot see him—my voice, because my voice is Spirit; my Spirit is truth; truth abideth and hath no end; and if it be in you it shall abound.

67 And if your eye be single to my glory, your whole bodies shall be filled with light, and there shall be no darkness in you; and that body which is filled with light comprehendeth all things.

68 Therefore, sanctify yourselves that your minds become single to God, and the days will come that you shall see him; for he will unveil his face unto you, and it shall be in his own time, and in his own way, and according to his own will.

69 Remember the great and last promise which I have made unto you; cast away your idle thoughts and your excess of laughter far from you.

70 Tarry ye, tarry ye in this place, and call a solemn assembly, even of those who are the first laborers in this last kingdom.

71 And let those whom they have warned in their traveling call on the Lord, and ponder the warning in their hearts which they have received, for a little season.

72 Behold, and lo, I will take care of your flocks, and will raise up elders and send unto them.

73 Behold, I will hasten my work in its time.

The Lord shifts here from teaching about the nature of the universe to addressing more earthly concerns among the Saints. The Lord promises that if they will sanctify themselves and make their minds single to the glory of God, "he will unveil his face unto [them]" (verse 68). He also commands them to call a "solemn assembly" (verse 70). Both of these commandments are linked to the construction of the first temple of the Church in Kirtland, Ohio.

Within two weeks of receiving this revelation, Joseph Smith wrote to the Saints in Missouri to tell them about the plans to build a temple in Kirtland. In a letter written on January 11, 1833, Joseph wrote to William W. Phelps to inform him "that the Lord commanded us in Kirtland to build an house of God, & establish a school for the Prophets, this is the word of the Lord to us."[16] A few years later, in a meeting with the newly called Quorum of the Twelve Apostles, Joseph instructed:

> We must have all things prepared and call our solemn assembly as the Lord has commanded us, that we may be able to accomplish his great work: and it must be done in God[']s own way, the house of the Lord must be prepared, and the solemn assembly called and organized in it according to the order of the house of God. . . .
>
> It is calculated to unite our hearts, that we may be one in feeling and sentiment and that our faith may be strong, so that Satan cannot over throw us, nor have any power over us,—the endowment you are so anxious about you cannot comprehend now, nor could Gabriel explain it to the understanding of your dark minds, but strive to be prepared in your hearts, be faithful in all things that when we meet in the solemn assembly that is such as God shall name out of all the official members, [we] will meet, and we must be clean every whit.[17]

The commandment to hold a solemn assembly and the promise that the Lord would unveil His face were both fulfilled during the events surrounding the dedication of the Kirtland Temple (see Doctrine and Covenants 109–110).

> 74 And I give unto you, who are the first laborers in this last kingdom, a commandment that you assemble yourselves together, and organize yourselves, and prepare yourselves, and sanctify yourselves; yea, purify your hearts, and cleanse your hands and your feet before me, that I may make you clean;
>
> 75 That I may testify unto your Father, and your God, and my God, that you are clean from the blood of this wicked generation; that I may fulfil this promise, this great and last promise, which I have made unto you, when I will.
>
> 76 Also, I give unto you a commandment that ye shall continue in prayer and fasting from this time forth.
>
> 77 And I give unto you a commandment that you shall teach one another the doctrine of the kingdom.
>
> 78 Teach ye diligently and my grace shall attend you, that you may be instructed more perfectly in theory, in principle, in doctrine, in the law of the gospel, in all things that pertain unto the kingdom of God, that are expedient for you to understand;
>
> 79 Of things both in heaven and in the earth, and under the earth; things which have been, things which are, things which must shortly come to pass; things which are at home, things which are abroad; the wars and the perplexities of the nations, and the judgments which are on the land; and a knowledge also of countries and of kingdoms—
>
> 80 That ye may be prepared in all things when I shall send you again to magnify the calling whereunto I have called you, and the mission with which I have commissioned you.

The commandment to "teach one another the doctrine of the kingdom" (verse 77) was given to the leading elders of the Church but has also been applied to the importance of education for Latter-day Saints. President Uchtdorf taught, "For members of the Church, education is not merely a good idea—it's a commandment."[18] The Lord instructs His disciples to gain learning on a number of subjects, both secular and spiritual. Disciples with educated minds are better prepared to "magnify" their callings (verse 80).

President Hinckley echoed the same message: "You need all the education you can get. Sacrifice a car, sacrifice anything that is needed to be sacrificed to qualify yourselves to do the work of the world." While education is a commandment and great blessing in our lives, there is no specific field or discipline held above any other. President Hinckley emphasized this when he taught, "The Lord wants you to educate your minds and hands, whatever your chosen field. Whether it be repairing refrigerators, or the work of a skilled surgeon, you must train yourselves. Seek for the best schooling available. Become a workman of integrity in the world that lies ahead of you. I repeat, you will bring honor to the Church and you will be generously blessed because of that training."[19]

> 81 Behold, I sent you out to testify and warn the people, and it becometh every man who hath been warned to warn his neighbor.
>
> 82 Therefore, they are left without excuse, and their sins are upon their own heads.
>
> 83 He that seeketh me early shall find me, and shall not be forsaken.
>
> 84 Therefore, tarry ye, and labor diligently, that you may be perfected in your ministry to go forth among the Gentiles for the last time, as many as the mouth of the Lord shall name, to bind up the law and seal up the testimony, and to prepare the saints for the hour of judgment which is to come;
>
> 85 That their souls may escape the wrath of God, the desolation of abomination which awaits the wicked, both in this world and in the world to come. Verily, I say unto you, let those who are not the first elders continue in the vineyard until the mouth of the Lord shall call them, for their time is not yet come; their garments are not clean from the blood of this generation.

The phrase "among the Gentiles" is a reference to all nations. The term *Gentile*, referring to any group of people to whom missionaries are sent forth to preach, is common in the Book of Mormon, which was written to "Jew and Gentile" (title page of the Book of Mormon; see also Doctrine and Covenants 109:60). One of the purposes of missionary work is to warn as many people as possible of the coming calamities linked to the Second Coming of the Savior.

Joseph Smith commented on this passage when he spoke to the Twelve Apostles in 1835. He taught, "When you are endowed and prepared to preach the gospel to all nations[,] kindred[s,] and tongues in their own languages[,] you must faithfully warn all and bind up the testimony and seal up the law (Doctrine and Covenants 88:84)[;] and the destroying angel will follow close at your heels and execute his tremendous mission upon the children of disobedience, and destroy the workers of iniquity, while the saints will be gathered out from among them and stand in holy places ready to meet the bride groom when he comes."[20]

> 86 Abide ye in the liberty wherewith ye are made free; entangle not yourselves in sin, but let your hands be clean, until the Lord comes.

> 87 For not many days hence and the earth shall tremble and reel to and fro as a drunken man; and the sun shall hide his face, and shall refuse to give light; and the moon shall be bathed in blood; and the stars shall become exceedingly angry, and shall cast themselves down as a fig that falleth from off a fig tree.

> 88 And after your testimony cometh wrath and indignation upon the people.

> 89 For after your testimony cometh the testimony of earthquakes, that shall cause groanings in the midst of her, and men shall fall upon the ground and shall not be able to stand.

> 90 And also cometh the testimony of the voice of thunderings, and the voice of lightnings, and the voice of tempests, and the voice of the waves of the sea heaving themselves beyond their bounds.

> 91 And all things shall be in commotion; and surely, men's hearts shall fail them; for fear shall come upon all people.

> 92 And angels shall fly through the midst of heaven, crying with a loud voice, sounding the trump of God, saying: Prepare ye, prepare ye, O inhabitants of the earth; for the judgment of our God is come. Behold, and lo, the Bridegroom cometh; go ye out to meet him.

> 93 And immediately there shall appear a great sign in heaven, and all people shall see it together.

94 And another angel shall sound his trump, saying: That great church, the mother of abominations, that made all nations drink of the wine of the wrath of her fornication, that persecuteth the saints of God, that shed their blood—she who sitteth upon many waters, and upon the islands of the sea—behold, she is the tares of the earth; she is bound in bundles; her bands are made strong, no man can loose them; therefore, she is ready to be burned. And he shall sound his trump both long and loud, and all nations shall hear it.

While the revelation given on Christmas Day, 1832 (Doctrine and Covenants 87), emphasized the man-made wars and calamities of the last days, this passage emphasizes upheavals within nature before the Second Coming. The description of the natural disasters here closely parallels the signs of the times given in chapters 7–22 of the book of Revelation. Doctrine and Covenants 77, the most valuable guide we have to understanding the book of Revelation, only explains the symbols of John's revelation up to chapter 11. However, in Doctrine and Covenants 88, verses 86–107 provide a guide to the second half of the book of Revelation. While it does not directly interpret the symbolism in the book of Revelation, this portion does further clarify and explain the second half of the book. The language used in this passage also parallels the signs of the times given in many other revelations (see Doctrine and Covenants 29:14; 43:18–25; 45:26, 42, 48; 133:22, 49; Joel 2:10, 31; 3:15–16; Matthew 24:29–31; Joseph Smith—Matthew 1:23–37; Revelation 11:13).

Accompanying the commotion of the earth is the rise of the great church Babylon, the mother of fornications. This church will persecute the Saints and gain power and influence among the children of men until the Savior intervenes. The "great sign" in verse 93 that appears in heaven is also referenced by the Savior (see Mathew 24:30; Luke 21:25–27).

In his time, the Prophet Joseph Smith cautioned against latching on to only a single sign or a small collection of signs and instead urged members to look at the signs collectively. When Hiram Redding, a resident of Ogle County, Illinois, claimed to have seen the sign of the Son of Man in heaven, Joseph Smith wrote back:

> I shall use my right, and declare, that notwithstanding Mr. Redding may
> have seen a wonderful appearance in the clouds, one morning about sun-
> rise, (which is nothing very uncommon in the winter season) he has not

seen the sign of the son of man, as foretold by Jesus; neither has any man, nor will any man, till after the sun shall have been darkened and the moon bathed in blood, for the Lord hath not shown me any such sign, and, as the prophet saith, so it must be: *Surely the Lord God will do nothing, but he revealeth his secret unto his servants the prophets.* (See Amos 3: 7). Therefore, hear this, O earth, the Lord will not come to reign over the righteous, in this world, in 1843, nor until every thing for the bridegroom is ready.[21]

95 And there shall be silence in heaven for the space of half an hour; and immediately after shall the curtain of heaven be unfolded, as a scroll is unfolded after it is rolled up, and the face of the Lord shall be unveiled;

96 And the saints that are upon the earth, who are alive, shall be quickened and be caught up to meet him.

97 And they who have slept in their graves shall come forth, for their graves shall be opened; and they also shall be caught up to meet him in the midst of the pillar of heaven—

98 They are Christ's, the first fruits, they who shall descend with him first, and they who are on the earth and in their graves, who are first caught up to meet him; and all this by the voice of the sounding of the trump of the angel of God.

99 And after this another angel shall sound, which is the second trump; and then cometh the redemption of those who are Christ's at his coming; who have received their part in that prison which is prepared for them, that they might receive the gospel, and be judged according to men in the flesh.

100 And again, another trump shall sound, which is the third trump; and then come the spirits of men who are to be judged, and are found under condemnation;

101 And these are the rest of the dead; and they live not again until the thousand years are ended, neither again, until the end of the earth.

102 And another trump shall sound, which is the fourth trump, saying: There are found among those who are to remain until that great and last day, even the end, who shall remain filthy still.

Concerning the "silence in heaven for the space of half an hour" that is mentioned in verse 95, Elder Orson Pratt said:

> Whether the half hour here spoke [*sic*] is according to our reckoning – thirty minutes, or whether it be according to the reckoning of the Lord[,] we do not know. We know that the word hour is used in some portions of the scriptures to represent quite a lengthy period of time. . . . During the period of silence all things are perfectly still; no angels flying during that half hour; no trumpets sounding; no noise in the heavens above; but immediately after this great silence the curtain of heaven shall be unfolded as a scroll is unfolded.[22]

Verses 96–102 describe in succession the multiple resurrections that will take place after the return of Christ to the earth. The "first fruits" of the Resurrection will be caught up to meet Christ as He descends from the heavens (see 2 Thessalonians 4:16–17). After they descend, the second trump shall sound, and those who accepted Christ in the world of spirits shall come forth from their graves as well. We consider both of these groups to be in the First Resurrection, or the resurrection of celestial and terrestrial beings. The third trump is then sounded for the spirits of those who "are found under condemnation," or telestial beings, who are not resurrected until the end of the Millennium (see verses 100–101). Finally, those who are "filthy still," or the sons of perdition, also receive their part in the Resurrection (see verse 102).

> 103 And another trump shall sound, which is the fifth trump, which is the fifth angel who committeth the everlasting gospel—flying through the midst of heaven, unto all nations, kindreds, tongues, and people;
>
> 104 And this shall be the sound of his trump, saying to all people, both in heaven and in earth, and that are under the earth—for every ear shall hear it, and every knee shall bow, and every tongue shall confess, while they hear the sound of the trump, saying: Fear God, and give glory to him who sitteth upon the throne, forever and ever; for the hour of his judgment is come.
>
> 105 And again, another angel shall sound his trump, which is the sixth angel, saying: She is fallen who made all nations drink of the wine of the wrath of her fornication; she is fallen, is fallen!

106 And again, another angel shall sound his trump, which is the seventh angel, saying: It is finished; it is finished! The Lamb of God hath overcome and trodden the wine-press alone, even the wine-press of the fierceness of the wrath of Almighty God.

107 And then shall the angels be crowned with the glory of his might, and the saints shall be filled with his glory, and receive their inheritance and be made equal with him.

At the sounding of the fifth trump, "every knee shall bow, and every tongue shall confess" the power of Jesus Christ (verse 104). All people will acknowledge Christ's victory, and those mortal men and women that remain on earth, both celestial and terrestrial beings, will see Christ as the King of kings and Lord of lords. This does not mean, however, that other religions will not exist on the earth at the beginning of the Millennium. On one occasion Brigham Young taught, "In the millennium men will have the privilege of being Presbyterians, Methodists, or Infidels, but they will not have the privilege of treating the name and character of Deity as they have done heretofore. No, but every knee shall bow and every tongue confess to the glory of God the Father that Jesus is the Christ."[23] All the mortals who remain will be judged according to the light and truth they have been given. But not all will choose to receive the fulness of the gospel, including all the ordinances necessary for exaltation (see Doctrine and Covenants 76:77).

The beautiful reunion of Christ with His people is described in more detail in a revelation God gave to Joseph Smith just a few months before (see Doctrine and Covenants 133:36–45).

108 And then shall the first angel again sound his trump in the ears of all living, and reveal the secret acts of men, and the mighty works of God in the first thousand years.

109 And then shall the second angel sound his trump, and reveal the secret acts of men, and the thoughts and intents of their hearts, and the mighty works of God in the second thousand years—

110 And so on, until the seventh angel shall sound his trump; and he shall stand forth upon the land and upon the sea, and swear in the name of him who sitteth upon the throne, that there shall be time no longer; and Satan shall be bound, that old

serpent, who is called the devil, and shall not be loosed for the space of a thousand years.

111 And then he shall be loosed for a little season, that he may gather together his armies.

112 And Michael, the seventh angel, even the archangel, shall gather together his armies, even the hosts of heaven.

113 And the devil shall gather together his armies; even the hosts of hell, and shall come up to battle against Michael and his armies.

114 And then cometh the battle of the great God; and the devil and his armies shall be cast away into their own place, that they shall not have power over the saints any more at all.

115 For Michael shall fight their battles, and shall overcome him who seeketh the throne of him who sitteth upon the throne, even the Lamb.

116 This is the glory of God, and the sanctified; and they shall not any more see death.

The seven angels described in verses 108–110 will then sound seven trumps, each representing one thousand years of the earth's existence (see Doctrine and Covenants 77:6–7). This process is described as a review of the history of men and women during each of the thousand-year periods, including "the secret acts of men, and the thoughts and intents of their hearts, and the mighty works of God" (verse 109). Not only will the future destiny of the earth and its people become clear but any fog surrounding humanity's past will be dispelled as well. At last we will have a true accounting of the history of the world (see Doctrine and Covenants 101:32–33).

Verse 110 also speaks of Satan's restrictions during the Millennium. Satan will be bound through the combined power of God and the righteousness of the people who will live in the Millennium. The Apostle John described the binding of Satan, writing, "I saw an angel come down from heaven, having the key of the bottomless pit and a great chain in his hand. And he laid hold on the dragon, that old serpent, which is the Devil, and Satan, and bound him a thousand years, And cast him into the bottomless pit, and shut him up, and set a seal upon him, that he should deceive the nations no more, till the thousand years should be fulfilled: and after that he must be loosed a little season" (Revelation 20:1–3).

The seal that binds Satan will be kept in place because of the righteousness of the men and women who will live in the Millennium. Nephi explained that "because of the righteousness of his [God's] people, Satan has no power; wherefore, he cannot be loosed for the space of many years; for he hath no power over the hearts of the people, for they dwell in righteousness, and the Holy One of Israel reigneth" (1 Nephi 22:26). The fact that Satan is loosed at the end of the thousand years implies that there may be some kind of apostasy at the end of the Millennium that allows Satan to gain power again for a brief space of time.

We do not know how long Satan will be unrestrained at the end of the Millennium. Some scriptural commentators have speculated that it may be another thousand years.[24] What is clear is that this is the final conflict, the last gasp of Satan's power. Michael, the great prince who holds the keys of salvation under the direction of Christ (see Doctrine and Covenants 78:16), will lead the charge against Satan and banish him once and for all from the earth. The earth will then become a celestial kingdom and our eternal home (see Doctrine and Covenants 88:16–31, 116).

> 117 Therefore, verily I say unto you, my friends, call your solemn assembly, as I have commanded you.
>
> 118 And as all have not faith, seek ye diligently and teach one another words of wisdom; yea, seek ye out of the best books words of wisdom; seek learning, even by study and also by faith.
>
> 119 Organize yourselves; prepare every needful thing; and establish a house, even a house of prayer, a house of fasting, a house of faith, a house of learning, a house of glory, a house of order, a house of God;
>
> 120 That your incomings may be in the name of the Lord; that your outgoings may be in the name of the Lord; that all your salutations may be in the name of the Lord, with uplifted hands unto the Most High.
>
> 121 Therefore, cease from all your light speeches, from all laughter, from all your lustful desires, from all your pride and light-mindedness, and from all your wicked doings.

122 Appoint among yourselves a teacher, and let not all be spokesmen at once; but let one speak at a time and let all listen unto his sayings, that when all have spoken that all may be edified of all, and that every man may have an equal privilege.

123 See that ye love one another; cease to be covetous; learn to impart one to another as the gospel requires.

124 Cease to be idle; cease to be unclean; cease to find fault one with another; cease to sleep longer than is needful; retire to thy bed early, that ye may not be weary; arise early, that your bodies and your minds may be invigorated.

125 And above all things, clothe yourselves with the bond of charity, as with a mantle, which is the bond of perfectness and peace.

126 Pray always, that ye may not faint, until I come. Behold, and lo, I will come quickly, and receive you unto myself. Amen.

In verses 117–119, the Lord repeats His command to call a solemn assembly and gives a direct commandment to build a house of prayer, fasting, faith, learning, glory, and order—in short, a house of God. The Saints fulfilled this commandment by constructing the house of the Lord in Kirtland, the first temple of this dispensation. In the months before and after the dedication of the Kirtland Temple, many members of the Church received instruction within its walls. A small group of men also received some of the preparatory ordinances of the temple. As outlined here, the Kirtland Temple was not only a place for ordinances and instruction but was also a multipurpose facility in which worship meetings, school, and other Church functions could be held. Every chapel, seminary building, university, and temple in the Church can trace its lineage back to this first house of the Lord built in Kirtland.

To prepare the Saints to receive a temple in their midst, the Lord outlines a program of behavior intended to ready them for this blessing. In keeping with instructions already given in other revelations, the Lord gives commandments for the Saints' spiritual health in parallel with ones regarding the Saints' temporal health. For example, the Lord gives a commandment to His disciples to have charity for each other and follows it with a commandment to receive the proper amount of rest. In all things, the spiritual and temporal are mingled together to create a holistic approach toward healthy living. The Lord commands His people to seek learning "even by study and also by faith" (verse 118). He indicates that the Saints should study the best works of literature, science, and art alongside the sacred books of scripture. Rather than becoming anti-intellectual, the Saints are commanded to embrace the best in all branches of learning.

> 127 And again, the order of the house prepared for the presidency of the school of the prophets, established for their instruction in all things that are expedient for them, even for all the officers of the church, or in other words, those who are called to the ministry in the church, beginning at the high priests, even down to the deacons—

> 128 And this shall be the order of the house of the presidency of the school: He that is appointed to be president, or teacher, shall be found standing in his place, in the house which shall be prepared for him.

> 129 Therefore, he shall be first in the house of God, in a place that the congregation in the house may hear his words carefully and distinctly, not with loud speech.

> 130 And when he cometh into the house of God, for he should be first in the house—behold, this is beautiful, that he may be an example—

> 131 Let him offer himself in prayer upon his knees before God, in token or remembrance of the everlasting covenant.

> 132 And when any shall come in after him, let the teacher arise, and, with uplifted hands to heaven, yea, even directly, salute his brother or brethren with these words:

> 133 Art thou a brother or brethren? I salute you in the name of the Lord Jesus Christ, in token or remembrance of the everlasting covenant, in which covenant I receive you to fellowship, in a determination that is fixed, immovable, and unchangeable, to be your friend and brother through the grace of God in the bonds of love, to walk in all the commandments of God blameless, in thanksgiving, forever and ever. Amen.

Doctrine and Covenants 88:127–41 consists of a separate revelation received a few days later on January 3, 1833. It was most likely combined with the first revelation because it commands Joseph Smith and his associates to set up a "school of the prophets" in the house of God (Doctrine and Covenants 88:136). The School of the Prophets would eventually meet in the Kirtland Temple, but the Saints began organizing it almost immediately after receiving this revelation. The School of the Prophets was the beginning of an educational structure that would eventually come to include all of the quorums and organizations affiliated with the Church, all of whom regularly meet in classes to receive instruction and inspiration.

Over the next few years, several different schools were organized in Kirtland and Missouri. The initial School of the Prophets met from January 23 to April 1, 1833, in an upper room of the Newel K. Whitney store in Kirtland. Joseph Smith presided over the school and selected Orson Hyde to be its teacher. This school consisted of a small group, probably never exceeding twenty-five people. Zebedee Coltrin, a member of the school, recalled that the teacher "saluted the brethren with upheld hands" as they entered and "they also answered with uplifted hands." Attending the school was a holy activity for those involved, with Coltrin remembering that "before going to school we washed ourselves and put on clean linen." Members of the school came fasting at sunrise and remained until around four o'clock in the evening.[25]

Dramatic spiritual manifestations occurred in the School of the Prophets. Zebedee Coltrin shared the following experience, which occurred in one of their meetings:

> At one of these meetings after the organization of the school . . . Joseph having given instructions, and while engaged in silent prayer, kneeling, with our hands uplifted[,] each one praying in silence, no one whispered above his breath, a personage walked through the room from east to west, and Joseph asked if we saw him. I saw him and suppose the others did[,] and Joseph answered[, "]that is Jesus, the Son of God, our elder brother.["] Afterward Joseph told us to resume our former position in prayer, which we did. Another person came through; he was surrounded as with a flame of fire. He [Brother Coltrin] experienced a sensation that it might destroy the tabernacle as it was of consuming fire of great brightness. The Prophet Joseph said this was the Father of our Lord Jesus Christ. I saw Him.[26]

When asked about the kind of clothing the Father had on, Brother Coltrin said:

I did not discover his clothing[,] for he was surrounded as with a flame of fire, which was so brilliant that I could not discover anything else but his person. I saw his hands, his legs, his feet, his eyes, nose, mouth, head and body in the shape and form of a perfect man. He sat in a chair as a man would sit in a chair, but this appearance was so grand and overwhelming that it seemed I should melt down in his presence, and the sensation was so powerful that it thrilled through my whole system and I felt it in the marrow of my bones. The Prophet Joseph said: ["]Brethren, now you are prepared to be the apostles of Jesus Christ, for you have seen both the Father and the Son and know that they exist and that they are two separate personages.["]²⁷

134 And he that is found unworthy of this salutation shall not have place among you; for ye shall not suffer that mine house shall be polluted by him.

135 And he that cometh in and is faithful before me, and is a brother, or if they be brethren, they shall salute the president or teacher with uplifted hands to heaven, with this same prayer and covenant, or by saying Amen, in token of the same.

136 Behold, verily, I say unto you, this is an ensample unto you for a salutation to one another in the house of God, in the school of the prophets.

137 And ye are called to do this by prayer and thanksgiving, as the Spirit shall give utterance in all your doings in the house of the Lord, in the school of the prophets, that it may become a sanctuary, a tabernacle of the Holy Spirit to your edification.

138 And ye shall not receive any among you into this school save he is clean from the blood of this generation;

139 And he shall be received by the ordinance of the washing of feet, for unto this end was the ordinance of the washing of feet instituted.

140 And again, the ordinance of washing feet is to be administered by the president, or presiding elder of the church.

141 It is to be commenced with prayer; and after partaking of bread and wine, he is to gird himself according to the pattern

given in the thirteenth chapter of John's testimony concerning me. Amen.

The Lord emphasized holiness in the School of the Prophets through the ordinance of the washing of the feet. This touching ordinance is described in some detail in the Gospel of John. After the Last Supper, Jesus "pour[ed] water into a basin, and began to wash the disciples' feet, and to wipe them with the towel wherewith he was girded." John recalled that Simon Peter at first resisted the ordinances, pleading, "Thou shalt never wash my feet." Jesus, emphasizing the importance of the act, answered Peter, "If I wash thee not, thou hast no part with me." In return, Simon Peter replied, "Lord, not my feet only, but also my hands and my head." After the ordinance was completed, the Savior instructed the Apostles, saying, "Know ye what I have done to you? Ye call me Master and Lord: and ye say well; for so I am. If I then, your Lord and Master, have washed your feet; ye also ought to wash one another's feet. For I have given you an example, that ye should do as I have done to you" (John 13:3–15).

Following the instructions given in verses 139–141 and the pattern set forth in the thirteenth chapter of John, the ordinance of the washing of the feet was carried out in the first meeting of the School of the Prophets on January 23, 1833. The minutes of that meeting described the act as follows:

Wednesday January 23rd. Meet agreeable to adjournment. Conference opened with Prayer by the President [Joseph Smith, Jr.] and after much speaking, praying, and singing, all done in tongues, [we] proceeded to washing hands, faces & feet in the name of the Lord as commanded of God, each one washing his own, after which the president girded himself with a towel and again washed the feet of all the Elders, wiping them with the towel. [After] his father present[ed] himself, the President asked of him [Joseph Smith, Sr.] a blessing before he would wash his feet, which he obtained by the laying on of his father's hands, pronouncing upon his head that he should continue in his Priest's office until Christ come.

At the close of which scene, Br. F[rederick] G. Williams, being moved upon by the Holy Ghost, washed the feet of the President as a token of his fixed determination to be with him in suffering or in rejoicing, in life or in death, and to be continually on his right hand, in which thing he was accepted. The President said after he had washed the feet of the Elders, "as I have done, so do ye; wash ye therefore one another's feet," pronouncing at the same time through the power of the Holy Ghost that the Elders were all clean from the blood of this generation, but that those among them who should sin willfully after they were thus cleansed and sealed up unto eternal life should be given over unto the buffetings of Satan until the day of redemption. Having continued all day in fasting and prayer before the Lord, at the close they partook of the Lord's supper, which was blessed by the president in the name of the Lord. All ate and drank and were filled, then [they] sang a hymn and went out.[28]

End Notes

1. Letter to William W. Phelps, 11 January 1833, 18, josephsmithpapers.org.
2. See Section VII, Doctrine and Covenants, 1835, 100, josephsmithpapers.org.
3. See Minutes, 27–28, December 1832, 3, josephsmithpapers.org. Those present at the conference included Joseph Smith, Sidney Rigdon, Orson Hyde, Joseph Smith Sr., Hyrum Smith, Samuel H. Smith, Newel K. Whitney, Frederick G. Williams, Ezra Thayer, and John Murdock.
4. Revelation Book 2, Index, 1, josephsmithpapers.org.
5. See "Historical Introduction," Revelation, 27–28 December 1832 [D&C 88:1–126], josephsmithpapers.org. See also "Historical Introduction," Revelation, 3 January 1833 [D&C 88:127–137], josephsmithpapers.org.
6. Discourse, between circa 26 June and circa 2 July 1839, as Reported by Wilford Woodruff, 33, josephsmithpapers.org.
7. James E. Talmage, *The Articles of Faith*, 12th ed. (1924), 488.
8. Joseph F. Smith, *Gospel Doctrine,* 5th ed., 1939, 67–68.
9. James E. Talmage, in Conference Report, Oct. 1913, 117.
10. Jeffrey R. Holland, "Of Souls, Symbols, and Sacraments" (Brigham Young University devotional, Jan. 12, 1988), 4, speeches.byu.edu.
11. Joseph Smith, in History, 1838–1856, volume D-1 [1 August 1842–1 July 1843], 1522, josephsmithpapers.org.
12. "Discourse, 7 April 1844, as Reported by Willard Richards," in Journal, December 1842–June 1844; Book 4, 1 March–22 June 1844, 67, josephsmithpapers.org.
13. Letter to the Church, circa February 1834, 135, josephsmithpapers.org.
14. Stephen E. Robinson and H. Dean Garrett, *A Commentary on the Doctrine and Covenants* (Salt Lake City, UT: Deseret Book, 2000), 3:51–61.
15. Poem to William W. Phelps, between circa 1 and circa 15 February 1843, 83, josephsmithpapers.org.
16. Letter to William W. Phelps, 11 January 1833, 19, josephsmithpapers.org.
17. Discourse, 12 November 1835, 33, josephsmithpapers.org.
18. Dieter F. Uchtdorf, "Two Principles for Any Economy," *Ensign* or *Liahona*, May 2009, 58.
19. Gordon B. Hinckley, "A Prophet's Counsel and Prayer for Youth," *Ensign*, Jan. 2001, 4.
20. Discourse, 12 November 1835, 35, josephsmithpapers.org.
21. Letter to the Editor, 28 February 1843, 113, josephsmithpapers.org.
22. Orson Pratt, in *Journal of Discourses,* 16:327–28.
23. Brigham Young, in *Journal of Discourses*, 12:274.

24. See Bruce R. McConkie, *The Millennial Messiah: The Second Coming of the Son of Man* (Salt Lake City, UT: Deseret Book, 1982), 22.
25. See Lyndon W. Cook, *The Revelations of the Prophet Joseph Smith: A Historical and Biographical Commentary of the Doctrine and Covenants* (Salt Lake City, UT: Deseret Book, 1985), 186–87.
26. "Remarks of Zebedee Coltrin," Minutes, Salt Lake City School of the Prophets, Oct. 3, 1883, in Cook, *The Revelations of the Prophet Joseph Smith,* 187–188.
27. "Remarks of Zebedee Coltrin," in Cook, *The Revelations of the Prophet Joseph Smith,* 187–188.
28. Minutes, 22–23 January 1833, 7–8, josephsmithpapers.org; spelling and punctuation modernized.

Doctrine and Covenants Section 89

A Word of Wisdom

Historical Context

IN THE UPPER FLOOR OF THE NEWEL K. WHITNEY STORE IN KIRTLAND, Ohio, the first School of the Prophets was held in a small room. In this school, local priesthood holders gathered to receive instruction in the principles of the gospel. While no contemporary sources have been located describing the circumstances under which Joseph Smith dictated this February 27, 1833 revelation, later accounts indicate that it was recorded in connection with the activities of the School of the Prophets. According to Brigham Young, heavy tobacco use—in the form of both smoking and chewing—among members of the school, combined with Emma Smith's and others' complaints about cleaning tobacco juice from the floor, led Joseph "to inquire of the Lord with regard to use of tobacco" and "to the conduct of the elders with this particular practice." He later said, "I think I am well acquainted with the circumstances which led to the giving of the Word of

Wisdom as any man in the Church, although I was not present at the time to witness them."[1]

In a discourse given in 1868, Brigham described the meetings of the School of the Prophets, saying, "When they assembled together in this room after breakfast, the first thing they did was to light their pipes, and while smoking, talk about the great things of the kingdom and spit all over the room, and as soon as the pipe was out of their mouths a large chew of tobacco would then be taken." The distraction of the smoke "and the complaints of his [Joseph's] wife," Brigham added, "made the Prophet think upon the matter, and he inquired of the Lord relating to the conduct of the Elders in using tobacco."[2] It was in these circumstances that one of the most unique and distinguishing traits of The Church of Jesus Christ of Latter-day Saints came into existence: the health code known as the Word of Wisdom.[3]

*V*erse-by-*V*erse *C*ommentary

> 1 A Word of Wisdom, for the benefit of the council of high priests, assembled in Kirtland, and the church, and also the saints in Zion—
>
> 2 To be sent greeting; not by commandment or constraint, but by revelation and the word of wisdom, showing forth the order and will of God in the temporal salvation of all saints in the last days—
>
> 3 Given for a principle with promise, adapted to the capacity of the weak and the weakest of all saints, who are or can be called saints.

The first three verses introduce the rest of the revelation. There has been some dispute over whether they should be considered part of the revelation itself. When the revelation was first published in the 1835 Doctrine and Covenants, these three verses were printed as part of the italicized section introduction, and not as part of the text of the revelation itself.[4] It remained this way until 1876 when, in a new edition of the Doctrine and Covenants produced under the direction of Brigham Young, these three verses were moved from the introduction into the revelation itself.[5] In the earliest copies of Doctrine and Covenants 89, the first three verses are included as part of the revelation.[6]

As these verses indicate, when the Word of Wisdom was originally given, it was not interpreted as a binding commandment for the Church. Observance of the Word of Wisdom varied during the lifetime of Joseph Smith. But over time, the leaders of the Church gradually elevated the Word of Wisdom in importance to today's expectation, which is completely abstaining from alcohol, tobacco, coffee, tea, and harmful drugs. President Joseph F. Smith explained why God implemented the Word of Wisdom in this measured, careful way. He taught, "The reason undoubtedly why the Word of Wisdom was given—as not by 'commandment or restraint' was that at that time, at least, if it had been given as a commandment[,] it would have brought every man, addicted to the use of these noxious things, under condemnation; so the Lord was merciful and gave them a chance to overcome, before He brought them under the law."[7]

In the decades following the death of Joseph Smith, the Word of Wisdom became increasingly important. For instance, at a September 1851 conference, Brigham Young motioned that "all the sisters who will leave off the use of tea, coffee, etc.[,] to manifest it by raising the right hand." He then motioned that "all the boys who were under ninety years of age who would covenant to leave off the use of tobacco, whisky, and all things mentioned in the Word of Wisdom, to manifest it in the same manner."[8] According to the conference minutes, the motions were carried out unanimously. In several sermons in the 1860s, Brigham spoke against the use of alcohol and tobacco, with his central focus on denouncing drunkenness. In 1870 he stated, "Tea Coffee whiskey & tobacco prepares the system for all diseases. . . . Those who say they Cannot keep the word of wisdom it shows they Cannot. . . . The word of wisdom if carried out would add to the lives of the rising generation 20 to 30 years."[9] Despite the fact that Brigham Young and other Church leaders regularly encouraged following the Word of Wisdom, only in cases of great excess, especially drunkenness, was any discipline taken. During this time, there was a wide range of interpretations about the Word of Wisdom.[10]

By the early twentieth century, abstinence was becoming more of the ideal. In the early 1900s water was substituted for sacramental wine, and in 1908 the First Presidency announced that Church members who did not live the Word of Wisdom would not be called to leadership positions in local units and quorums. In 1913 the First Presidency gave instructions to the president of the Salt Lake Stake to not recommend any young people for missionary service unless they lived the Word of Wisdom.[11] This trend continued under President Heber J. Grant, who favored a strict interpretation of the Word of Wisdom. In 1921, under the direction of President Grant, observing the Word of Wisdom became a requirement for receiving a temple recommend. President Grant clearly taught that the revelation was now to be considered a binding commandment, not merely as a guideline or a suggestion. On one occasion he wrote, "I have met any number of people who have said the Word of Wisdom is not a command from the Lord, that it is not given by the way of commandment. But the Word of Wisdom is the will of the Lord."[12] Since 1921, living the Word of Wisdom has become a standard expectation for active members of the Church.

> 4 Behold, verily, thus saith the Lord unto you: In consequence of evils and designs which do and will exist in the hearts of conspiring men in the last days, I have warned you, and forewarn you, by giving unto you this word of wisdom by revelation—

The Savior is very clear in this revelation that the Word of Wisdom is specifically crafted for the conditions found in the latter days. Throughout time, the Lord has often given His people health guidelines and changed these guidelines to meet the needs of the conditions they live in. In Moses's time, the Lord restricted what kind of animals, clean or unclean, the Israelites should eat (see Leviticus 11). While the logic behind some of these dietary laws seems obvious, the reasons for other laws are sometimes less clear. We are expected to act in faith to follow the Lord's commandments.

In verse 4 the Lord explains that He has given this law of health specifically in "consequence of evils and designs which *do* and *will* exist in the hearts of conspiring men in the last days" (emphasis added). Thus, this law is specifically tailored to help us counter the forces that might harm us in our time—and in the future. Some people deride the Word of Wisdom because in earlier dispensations, the Israelites, Nephites, and other peoples consumed wine, for instance. While the Bible counsels against the abuse of alcohol (see Proverbs 23:20), there is no provision in biblical health codes against the use of wine. The Savior and His disciples used wine at the Last Supper and drank it at the marriage feast. But the Word of Wisdom was not a commandment intended for earlier dispensations. The sacredness of the body and its health is a timeless teaching, and the Word of Wisdom should be considered a timely teaching for our time specifically.

Today members of the Church are not asked to abstain from the use of pork or products made from other animals that the Lord deemed unclean in the Old Testament. We are, however, asked to not use substances, such as wine, that the ancient Israelites could use in moderation. There are forces at work in the latter days that make these substances particularly dangerous for Latter-day Saints to use. In the revelation, God also declares that He gave the Word of Wisdom to counter evil designs that *will* exist in the future. In Joseph Smith's time, it was unthought of to consider as harmful some of the most pernicious substances the Word of Wisdom protects us against. We should consider the Word of Wisdom as the foundation of a living commandment that is constantly being adjusted by Church leaders to meet the needs of our time. It is possible that a century from now, the Lord will adapt the Word of Wisdom to meet the needs of that time, and so forth. We must look to the guidance of current prophets and apostles to know the conditions in which safety lies.

> 5 That inasmuch as any man drinketh wine or strong drink among you, behold it is not good, neither meet in the sight of your Father, only in assembling yourselves together to offer up your sacraments before him.
>
> 6 And, behold, this should be wine, yea, pure wine of the grape of the vine, of your own make.
>
> 7 And, again, strong drinks are not for the belly, but for the washing of your bodies.

In verse 5 the Lord prohibits the use of "wine or strong drink" except for uses in the sacrament. Throughout the nineteenth century, Latter-day Saints used wine in their sacrament services with only a few exceptions when wine was not available. This changed in the early twentieth century. Beginning on July 5, 1906, the First Presidency and the Quorum of the Twelve Apostles began using water instead of wine in the sacrament they administered to each other in their temple meetings. Local congregations followed this action shortly after, and the practice of using water for the sacrament soon became uniform throughout the Church (see Doctrine and Covenants 27:1–2).

Joseph Smith strongly believed in the truths of the Word of Wisdom, though he practiced a more relaxed application of the revelation than we observe in our day. Entries in journals tell of him consuming tea and wine and beer, sometimes in a more medicinal way as a relief in times of stress, but he did not consider a single drink as a violation of the commandment. In Carthage Jail, for example, Joseph and his friends felt "unusually dull or languid" and requested that wine be brought to the jail to raise their spirits.[13] Nevertheless, Joseph was strongly against drunkenness or the abuse of alcohol in any form. After hearing of a man freezing to death while under the influence of spirits, he lamented in his journal, "O my God[,] how long will this monster [of] intemperance find its victims on the earth."[14] On another occasion, he counseled, "There is no excuse for any man to drink and get drunk in the church of Christ."[15]

In the Church today, those who live the Word of Wisdom are expected to completely abstain from alcohol.[16] President Russell M. Nelson has commented, "The damaging effects of alcohol are so widely known, additional comment is hardly needed."[17]

> 8 And again, tobacco is not for the body, neither for the belly, and is not good for man, but is an herb for bruises and all sick cattle, to be used with judgment and skill.

Though the Word of Wisdom gradually went from being considered sound counsel to becoming a commandment, a few Latter-day Saints followed the revelation quite closely almost immediately. In the School of the Prophets, the men apparently determined to follow the revelation whenever they were attending those meetings. One writer, reminiscing about the School of the Prophets, recorded, "When the Word of Wisdom was first presented by the Prophet Joseph (as he came out of the translating room) and was read to the School, there were twenty out of the twenty-one who used tobacco[,] and they all immediately threw their tobacco and pipes into the fire."[18]

Recent archaeological excavations in Kirtland support these details. Near the Whitney Store in Kirtland was an ashery, another business operated by Newel K. Whitney. The ashery utilized ashes produced in the Kirtland area to manufacture potash, pearl ash, and other valuable commodities. It is likely that the ashes from the Newel K. Whitney Store ended up in this location. During an archaeological dig just south of the Kirtland ashery site, historian Mark Staker found several pipe fragments in 2000. It is possible that these fragments are remnants of the pipes thrown into the fireplace of the Whitney Store when the Word of Wisdom was first given. Staker and his team dated a layer above the pipe fragments to 1842. Though the fragments are difficult to date precisely, they are in a location that approximately aligns with the date the revelation was given. Given these factors, there is a good chance that some, if not all, of the pipe fragments came from the Whitney fireplace. One of the pipe stems has the name "Johnson" stamped on its side, which may indicate that the pipe belonged to Lyman Johnson, who was present at the time of the revelation. However, absolute certainty is impossible; there were many Johnsons in the area, and the stamp could also have been the name of the manufacturer.[19]

9 And again, hot drinks are not for the body or belly.

At the time this revelation was given, and to a certain extent even today, some members of the Church were confused over the meaning of "hot drinks" in the revelation. An editorial published on June 1, 1842 in the Church newspaper *Times and Seasons,* which was under Joseph Smith's editorial supervision, reads, "And again 'hot drinks are not for the body, or belly;' there are many who wonder what this can mean; whether it refers to tea, or coffee, or not. I say it does refer to tea, and coffee."[20] As with some other substances mentioned in the revelation, there was not a strict prohibition on coffee and tea when the Saints first received the revelation, and there is ample evidence that the Saints in Joseph Smith's time continued to drink coffee and tea. Sometimes the use of coffee or teas was occasionally for medicinal purposes, such as providing comfort to an exhausted traveler. Helen Mar Kimball Whitney, in an account written in 1881, remembered making tea from river water during her early stay in Nauvoo because the local water sources were contaminated.[21]

Even in our time, the Word of Wisdom continues to be adjusted through revelation to the leaders of the Church. An official statement on the Word of Wisdom made by Church leaders in August 2019 warned that any "substances that are destructive, habit-forming, or addictive should be avoided." The statement also explained that "Church leaders have clarified that several substances are prohibited by the Word of Wisdom, including vaping or e-cigarettes, green tea, and coffee-based products. They also have cautioned that substances such as marijuana and opioids should be used only for medicinal purposes as prescribed by a competent physician."[22] These changes demonstrate that the Word of Wisdom is a living revelation. The Lord still guides the prophets of our day as they interpret it, and Latter-day Saints should expect further revelation and clarification on this subject in the future.

10 And again, verily I say unto you, all wholesome herbs God hath ordained for the constitution, nature, and use of man—

11 Every herb in the season thereof, and every fruit in the season thereof; all these to be used with prudence and thanksgiving.

12 Yea, flesh also of beasts and of the fowls of the air, I, the Lord, have ordained for the use of man with thanksgiving; nevertheless they are to be used sparingly;

13 And it is pleasing unto me that they should not be used, only in times of winter, or of cold, or famine.

Not every part of the Word of Wisdom prohibits dangerous substances. A large part of the revelation encourages the Saints to use the Lord's bounty with good judgement and gratitude. Verses 10–17 of the revelation speak of substances that promote good health.

These verses are another illustration of how the Word of Wisdom is a living revelation. It is clear from other revelations in the Doctrine and Covenants that the Lord allows the eating of meat and the use of animal products. In a revelation given two years earlier, the Lord declared, "Whoso forbiddeth to abstain from meats, that man should not eat the same, is not ordained of God; For, behold, the beasts of the field and the fowls of the air, and that which cometh of the earth, is ordained for the use of man for food and for raiment, and that he might have in abundance" (Doctrine and Covenants 49:18–19).

The warning to eat meat "sparingly" might reference the fact that at the time the revelation was given, the typical adult in the United States consumed over a pound of meat every day.[23] Over time, this warning has been seen as good counsel but has not been emphasized by Church leaders in the same way that strong drinks, tobacco, tea, and coffee have been. The last time the excessive consumption of meat was mentioned by a prominent Church leader came in a fiery sermon delivered over the radio by Elder Joseph F. Merrill in 1945.[24] Since that time, Church leaders have generally refrained from providing counsel on this subject, and it is not typically mentioned as a part of the Word of Wisdom in temple recommend interviews or when missionaries teach this principle.

14 All grain is ordained for the use of man and of beasts, to be the staff of life, not only for man but for the beasts of the field,

and the fowls of heaven, and all wild animals that run or creep on the earth;

15 And these hath God made for the use of man only in times of famine and excess of hunger.

16 All grain is good for the food of man; as also the fruit of the vine; that which yieldeth fruit, whether in the ground or above the ground—

17 Nevertheless, wheat for man, and corn for the ox, and oats for the horse, and rye for the fowls and for swine, and for all beasts of the field, and barley for all useful animals, and for mild drinks, as also other grain.

18 And all saints who remember to keep and do these sayings, walking in obedience to the commandments, shall receive health in their navel and marrow to their bones;

19 And shall find wisdom and great treasures of knowledge, even hidden treasures;

20 And shall run and not be weary, and shall walk and not faint.

21 And I, the Lord, give unto them a promise, that the destroying angel shall pass by them, as the children of Israel, and not slay them. Amen.

The end of the revelation applies to not only the Word of Wisdom but also to all the commandments God has given us. While it is common for Latter-day Saints to highlight the physical blessings that come from abstaining from the substances prohibited by the Word of Wisdom, the Lord also promises spiritual blessings to those who hearken to this revelation. The provisions of the Word of Wisdom bring knowledge in addition to good health. We should also keep in mind that although we tend to think of the Word of Wisdom as a physical commandment, the Lord makes no distinction between physical commandments and spiritual commandments. In an earlier revelation to Joseph Smith, the Lord declared, "My commandments are spiritual; they are not natural nor temporal, neither carnal nor sensual" (Doctrine and Covenants 29:35).

Over time, many of the provisions of the Word of Wisdom, such as abstaining from tobacco and alcohol, have been demonstrated to have clear and measurable health benefits. The practical blessings of the Word of Wisdom are evident but are not the only reason to obey this law. We must remember that the most compelling reason to obey the Word of Wisdom is simply to show our faith in the Savior and our commitment to following the guidance given to His representatives in our day.

End Notes

1. Richard S. Van Wagoner, *The Complete Discourses of Brigham Young* (Salt Lake City, UT: The Smith-Pettit Foundation, 2009), 2:2532.
2. Wagoner, *The Complete Discourses of Brigham Young*, 2:2532.
3. See "Historical Introduction," Revelation, 27 February 1833 [D&C 89], josephsmithpapers.org.
4. See Doctrine and Covenants, 1835, 207, josephsmithpapers.org.
5. See Robert J. Woodford, "The Historical Development of the Doctrine and Covenants" (Provo, UT: Brigham Young University dissertation, 1974), 2:1171, 1175.
6. See Revelation, 27 February 1833 [D&C 89]; Revelation Book 2, 49, josephsmithpapers.org.
7. Joseph F. Smith, in Conference Report, Oct. 1913, 14.
8. "Minutes of the General Conference," Sept. 9, 1851, afternoon session; *Millennial Star*, Feb. 1, 1852, 14:35.
9. Wilford Woodruff, "Journal (October 22, 1865 – December 31, 1872," page 264 (June 23, 1870), Wilford Woodruff Papers, accessed Feb. 20, 2024, https://wilfordwoodruffpapers.org/documents/39f9b320-5b5a-4100-9d62-ca5507976bf1/page/807888e5-286a-447a-9f24-73ab3c4a6829.
10. See Paul H. Peterson and Ronald W. Walker, "Brigham Young's Word of Wisdom Legacy," *BYU Studies* 42, no. 3 (2003): 46–47.
11. See Stephen E. Robinson and H. Dean Garrett, *A Commentary on the Doctrine and Covenants* (Salt Lake City, UT: Deseret Book, 2000), 3:143.
12. *Messages of the First Presidency of The Church of Jesus Christ of Latter-day Saints, 1833-1964*, ed. James R. Clark (Salt Lake City, UT: Bookcraft, 1965), 5:301.
13. For a more specific accounting of Joseph Smith's observance of the Word of Wisdom, see "Historical Introduction," Revelation 27 February, 1833 [D&C 89], josephsmithpapers.org.
14. Journal, 1835–1836, 168, josephsmithpapers.org.
15. Discourse, 3 May 1844, 219, josephsmithpapers.org.
16. See *General Handbook: Serving in The Church of Jesus Christ of Latter-day Saints*, 38.7.14, Gospel Library.
17. Russell M. Nelson, "Joy Cometh in the Morning," *Ensign*, Nov. 1966, 69.
18. "3 October 1883," *School of the Prophets Salt Lake City meeting minutes, 1883*, page 56, Church History Catalog, accessed Feb. 20, 2024, https://catalog.churchofjesuschrist.org/record/45d6b218-478e-487e-b277-bc33b2b728f8/0.

19. See Mark L. Staker, "'Thou Art the Man:' Newell K. Whitney in Ohio," *BYU Studies* 42, no. 1 (2003): 107, figure 7.

20. *Times and Seasons,* 1 June 1842, 800, josephsmithpapers.org.

21. See "Historical Introduction," Revelation, 27 February 1833 [D&C 89], footnote 26, josephsmithpapers.org.

22. "Statement on the Word of Wisdom," Aug. 15, 2019, newsroom. ChurchofJesusChrist.org. See also "Vaping, Coffee, Tea, and Marijuana," *New Era*, Aug. 2019.

23. See "Historical Introduction," Revelation, 27 February 1833 [D&C 89], footnote 34, josephsmithpapers.org.

24. See Joseph F. Merrill, *The Truth-Seeker and Mormonism* (Whitefish, MT: Kessinger Publishing, 1946), 247.

Doctrine and Covenants Section 90

The Keys of This Last Kingdom

Historical Context

DOCTRINE AND COVENANTS 90 REPRESENTS ANOTHER SIGNIFICANT STEP toward organizing the presiding quorums of the Church, in this case the First Presidency. To understand this revelation, it is helpful to review the unfolding of leadership offices in the Church prior to this time. Joseph Smith and Oliver Cowdery received the authority necessary to lead the Church through the ministering of angelic beings. "Under the direction of the Father and the Son, heavenly messengers came to instruct Joseph and re-establish the Church of Jesus Christ. The resurrected John the Baptist restored the authority to baptize by immersion for the remission of sins. Three of the original twelve Apostles—Peter, James, and John—restored the apostleship and keys of priesthood authority."[1] From the time these heavenly messengers appeared to Joseph and Oliver, the necessary keys and powers to teach the gospel and perform the saving ordinances of the Church were in place, regardless of how the Church was organized administratively.

When the Church was organized on April 6, 1830, the revelation known as the "Articles and Covenants" affirmed that Joseph Smith and Oliver Cowdery were called of God and had been ordained as Apostles. Joseph was designated as the first elder of the Church and Oliver the second (see Doctrine and Covenants 20:2–3). These callings provided a temporary structure for them to minister through their authority and call additional leaders to assist in the work. On January 25, 1832, Joseph Smith was ordained as "President of the High Priesthood," following instructions given in November 1831 that "one be appointed" to that office (Doctrine and Covenants 107:65).[2] Several weeks later, on March 8, 1832, Joseph Smith called and ordained Sidney Rigdon and Jesse Gause to assist him as "counselors of the ministry of the presidency of the high Priesthood."[3] A few days later, on March 15, 1832, Joseph received another revelation in which God gave greater authority to the counselors in the presidency. The revelation also declared that Joseph Smith was "given the keys of the kingdom, which belong always unto the Presidency of the High Priesthood" (Doctrine and Covenants 81:2).

In the months that followed, Jesse Gause became estranged from the Church and was excommunicated on December 3, 1832. A month later, on January 5, 1833, Frederick G. Williams was called to replace Gause as a counselor and scribe. Doctrine and Covenants 90 elevated the role of the counselors, making them equal with Joseph Smith in "holding the keys of this last kingdom" (Doctrine and Covenants 90:3). Shortly after this revelation was given, official Church correspondence began referring to Joseph Smith, Sidney Rigdon, and Frederick G. Williams as the "Presidents of the High Priesthood."[4] By 1835 the three presidents were being referred to as the "first presidency" of the Church.[5]

In a later history, Joseph Smith wrote:

> Elder Rigdon expressed a desire that himself and Bro. F[rederick] G. Williams should be ordained to the office, to which they had been called, viz. that of Presidents of the high priesthood, and to be equal in holding the keys of the kingdom with Bro. Joseph Smith, Jun. according to the revelation given on the 8th of March. 1833. Accordingly I laid my hands on Brothers Sidney and Frederick, and ordained them to take part with me in holding the keys, of this last kingdom, and to assist in the presidency of the high priesthood, as my counselors; after which, I exhorted

the brethren to faithfulness, and diligence in keeping the commandments of God, and gave much instruction for the benefit of the saints, with a promise, that the pure in heart should see a heavenly vision; and, after remaining a short time in secret prayer, the promise was verified; for many present had the eyes of their understanding opened by the Spirit of God so as to behold many things.[6]

$\mathcal{V}$erse-by-$\mathcal{V}$erse $\mathcal{C}$ommentary

1 Thus saith the Lord, verily, verily I say unto you my son, thy sins are forgiven thee, according to thy petition, for thy prayers and the prayers of thy brethren have come up into my ears.

2 Therefore, thou art blessed from henceforth that bear the keys of the kingdom given unto you; which kingdom is coming forth for the last time.

3 Verily I say unto you, the keys of this kingdom shall never be taken from you, while thou art in the world, neither in the world to come;

4 Nevertheless, through you shall the oracles be given to another, yea, even unto the church.

5 And all they who receive the oracles of God, let them beware how they hold them lest they are accounted as a light thing, and are brought under condemnation thereby, and stumble and fall when the storms descend, and the winds blow, and the rains descend, and beat upon their house.

It is common in revelations for the Lord to recognize the human nature of His servants by forgiving them of their sins (see verse 1). The Lord also asserted Joseph Smith's leadership in these verses by affirming that the "keys of this kingdom shall never taken from you" (verse 3). These words offer an interesting comparison to earlier declarations of the Lord. In an 1830 revelation, the Lord said of Joseph Smith, "I have given him the keys of the mysteries, and the revelations which are sealed, until I shall appoint unto them another in his stead" (Doctrine and Covenants 28:7). In a revelation given a few months after the 1830 revelation, Joseph was told he held "the keys of the mystery of those things which have been sealed"—but only "if he abide in me, and if not, another will I plant in his stead" (Doctrine and Covenants 35:18). In a February 1831 revelation, Joseph was appointed to receive commandments and revelations for the Church, but with the same condition as the previous revelation: "if he abide in me" (Doctrine and Covenants 43:3). Finally, in a revelation given in September 1831, Joseph was told he held the "keys of the mysteries of the kingdom . . . inasmuch as he obeyeth mine ordinances" (Doctrine and Covenants 65:5).

In contrast to these earlier revelations, the Lord sets no conditions on Joseph in verses 1–5, indicating His increased trust in Joseph Smith fulfilling the role of prophet, seer, and revelator. Later the Lord gave Joseph an even greater assurance of trust when He declared, "Verily I seal upon you your exaltation, and prepare a throne for you in the kingdom of my Father, with Abraham your father" (Doctrine and Covenants 132:49). By comparing the verses in these revelations, it appears that even Joseph Smith went through a period of probation and testing as he grew into his prophetic calling. However, as indicated in section 90, he still holds the keys of this dispensation and acts as the presiding figure over all the prophets and apostles and other servants called in the last days.

> 6 And again, verily I say unto thy brethren, Sidney Rigdon and Frederick G. Williams, their sins are forgiven them also, and they are accounted as equal with thee in holding the keys of this last kingdom;
>
> 7 As also through your administration the keys of the school of the prophets, which I have commanded to be organized;

When Joseph ordained Sidney Rigdon and Frederick G. Williams, he gave them the keys necessary to operate the Church. The counselors in the First Presidency are "accounted as equal" and can act in the place of the President of the Church if necessary. President Hinckley served as a counselor in three First Presidencies, under Spencer W. Kimball, Ezra Taft Benson, and Howard W. Hunter. Near the end of their lives, it became increasingly difficult for Presidents Kimball, Benson, and Hunter to fulfill their duties because of health challenges. In these instances, President Hinckley assumed a greater role in the First Presidency to compensate.

When President Benson was in his ninety-fifth year and dealing with serious health issues, President Hinckley gave this assurance: "When the

President is ill or not able to function fully in all of the duties of his office, his two Counselors together comprise a Quorum of the First Presidency. They carry on with the day-to-day work of the Presidency."⁷ As long as the President of the Church is alive, the counselors in the First Presidency continue to lead the Church. But the promises made in verses 1–3 to Joseph Smith are different than the promises made to Sidney Rigdon and Frederick G. Williams in verse 6. Joseph was told that he would hold the keys of the kingdom in this world and the next. No such promise was given to his counselors.

In 1835 Joseph Smith taught, "Where I am not, there is no First Presidency."⁸ The counselors in the First Presidency are released upon the death of the President, and the leadership of the Church falls on the shoulders of the next highest quorum in the Church, the Quorum of the Twelve Apostles.

> 8 That thereby they may be perfected in their ministry for the salvation of Zion, and of the nations of Israel, and of the Gentiles, as many as will believe;
>
> 9 That through your administration they may receive the word, and through their administration the word may go forth unto the ends of the earth, unto the Gentiles first, and then, behold, and lo, they shall turn unto the Jews.
>
> 10 And then cometh the day when the arm of the Lord shall be revealed in power in convincing the nations, the heathen nations, the house of Joseph, of the gospel of their salvation.
>
> 11 For it shall come to pass in that day, that every man shall hear the fulness of the gospel in his own tongue, and in his own language, through those who are ordained unto this power, by the administration of the Comforter, shed forth upon them for the revelation of Jesus Christ.

These verses also affirm that the gospel of Jesus Christ transcends national and cultural boundaries, creating a new nation and a new culture. Nephi saw in a vision "that the Church of the Lamb, who were the Saints of God, were also upon all the face of the earth" (1 Nephi 14:12). John the Revelator saw in a vision that those redeemed by God came from "every kindred, and tongue, and people, and nation" and that these people became "kings and priests" unto God (Revelation 5:9–10). This does not downplay the importance and beauty of local customs and cultures. In section 90 the Lord declares "that every man shall hear the fulness of the gospel in his own tongue, and in his own language, through those who are ordained unto this power" (verse 11). While honoring the best in their local cultures, Latter-day Saints can also see themselves as part of a growing global family.

> 12 And now, verily I say unto you, I give unto you a commandment that you continue in the ministry and presidency.
>
> 13 And when you have finished the translation of the prophets, you shall from thenceforth preside over the affairs of the church and the school;
>
> 14 And from time to time, as shall be manifested by the Comforter, receive revelations to unfold the mysteries of the kingdom;
>
> 15 And set in order the churches, and study and learn, and become acquainted with all good books, and with languages, tongues, and people.
>
> 16 And this shall be your business and mission in all your lives, to preside in council, and set in order all the affairs of this church and kingdom.
>
> 17 Be not ashamed, neither confounded; but be admonished in all your high-mindedness and pride, for it bringeth a snare upon your souls.
>
> 18 Set in order your houses; keep slothfulness and uncleanness far from you.

The revelation shifts to provide counsel to Joseph Smith in his numerous prophetic duties. God counsels Joseph to complete his "translation of the prophets," which is most likely a reference to the books found at the end of the Old Testament. The day after receiving this revelation, Joseph inquired of the Lord about the Apocrypha, which was found directly after the twelve minor prophets found in his Bible. Verse 13 indicates that Joseph was drawing to the end of his most intensive period of biblical study, though he continued to work on his Bible translation sporadically throughout the rest of his lifetime.

The Lord also counseled him to continue to study and learn and "become acquainted with all good books, and with languages, tongues, and people" (verse 15). Joseph had an inquisitive mind and remained an enthusiastic student throughout the rest of his life. One scholar notes that "beginning in the mid-1830s and for the remainder of his life, [Joseph] studied Egyptian, Hebrew, Greek, and German" and that "while his skill with these languages was sometimes rudimentary, his exposure to each of them acted as steppingstones to additional scripture and distinct teachings about the nature of God, humanity, and the plan of salvation."[9] In a meeting of the Council of Fifty near the end of his life, Joseph counseled, "Every man ought to study geography, governments and languages, so that he may be able to go forth to any nation and before any multitude with eloquence."[10]

> 19 Now, verily I say unto you, let there be a place provided, as soon as it is possible, for the family of thy counselor and scribe, even Frederick G. Williams.
>
> 20 And let mine aged servant, Joseph Smith, Sen., continue with his family upon the place where he now lives; and let it not be sold until the mouth of the Lord shall name.
>
> 21 And let my counselor, even Sidney Rigdon, remain where he now resides until the mouth of the Lord shall name.
>
> 22 And let the bishop search diligently to obtain an agent, and let him be a man who has got riches in store—a man of God, and of strong faith—
>
> 23 That thereby he may be enabled to discharge every debt; that the storehouse of the Lord may not be brought into disrepute before the eyes of the people.
>
> 24 Search diligently, pray always, and be believing, and all things shall work together for your good, if ye walk uprightly and remember the covenant wherewith ye have covenanted one with another.
>
> 25 Let your families be small, especially mine aged servant Joseph Smith's, Sen., as pertaining to those who do not belong to your families;
>
> 26 That those things that are provided for you, to bring to pass my work, be not taken from you and given to those that are not worthy—

27 And thereby you be hindered in accomplishing those things which I have commanded you.

28 And again, verily I say unto you, it is my will that my hand-maid Vienna Jaques should receive money to bear her expenses, and go up unto the land of Zion;

29 And the residue of the money may be consecrated unto me, and she be rewarded in mine own due time.

30 Verily I say unto you, that it is meet in mine eyes that she should go up unto the land of Zion, and receive an inheritance from the hand of the bishop;

31 That she may settle down in peace inasmuch as she is faithful, and not be idle in her days from thenceforth.

32 And behold, verily I say unto you, that ye shall write this commandment, and say unto your brethren in Zion, in love greeting, that I have called you also to preside over Zion in mine own due time.

33 Therefore, let them cease wearying me concerning this matter.

34 Behold, I say unto you that your brethren in Zion begin to repent, and the angels rejoice over them.

35 Nevertheless, I am not well pleased with many things; and I am not well pleased with my servant William E. McLellin, neither with my servant Sidney Gilbert; and the bishop also, and others have many things to repent of.

36 But verily I say unto you, that I, the Lord, will contend with Zion, and plead with her strong ones, and chasten her until she overcomes and is clean before me.

37 For she shall not be removed out of her place. I, the Lord, have spoken it. Amen.

In the final part of the revelation, the Lord addresses the individual needs of several Church members, including the presidency of the high priesthood. A large part of this revelation provides direction and counsel to Vienna Jaques, a new convert who had traveled from Boston, Massachusetts, to Kirtland to meet with the Prophet. Vienna Jaques is one of the great heroic women of the early Restoration. Vienna was directed to consecrate her funds to the Church and to travel to Missouri to assist in building the city of Zion. She traveled to Missouri that summer, arriving in Zion in July 1833. However, shortly after her arrival, she lost most of her property when the Saints were driven from Jackson County by mob persecution. When Zion's Camp, a relief mission from Kirtland, arrived to assist the Saints, Vienna helped care for members of the camp who were stricken with cholera. Heber C. Kimball, a member of Zion's Camp, later wrote in his journal, "I received great kindness . . . from Sister Vienna Jaques, who administered to my wants and also to my brethren."[11]

Joseph Smith also expressed his gratitude for Vienna's sacrifice, writing a letter to her in September 1833 to thank her for her generosity. The letter is the earliest known communication Joseph Smith wrote to a woman other than his wife Emma Smith.[12] In the letter, Joseph described the following: "I have often felt a whispering since I received your letter like this: 'Joseph, thou art indebted to thy God for the offering of thy Sister Viana [Vienna Jaques], which proved a Savior of life as pertaining to thy pecuniary concern.'" He continued, "Therefore she should not be forgotten of thee, for the Lord hath done this, and thou shouldst remember her in all thy prayers and also by letter, for she oftentimes calleth on the Lord saying, 'O Lord, inspire thy Servant Joseph to communicate by letter some word to thine unworthy handmaid; canst thou not speak peaceably unto thine handmaid?'"[13]

Vienna eventually relocated to Nauvoo with her husband Daniel Shearer, a widower she married after meeting him in Missouri. While she was living in Nauvoo, Vienna served as one of the witnesses for what is likely the first baptism in this dispensation for a deceased person. The ordinance took place in the Mississippi River.[14] Later, after her marriage ended, she drove her own wagon across the plains at the age of sixty, arriving in the Salt Lake Valley in October 1847. She remained true and faithful to the gospel to the end of her life at ninety-six years of age. One tribute written to her at the time of her death reads, "She was true to her covenants and esteemed the restoration of the Gospel as a priceless treasure."[15]

End Notes

1. "The Restoration of the Fulness of the Gospel of Jesus Christ: A Bicentennial Proclamation to the World," Gospel Library.
2. See "Historical Introduction," Revelation, 25 January 1832-A [D&C 75:1–22], josephsmithpapers.org. See also Revelation 11 November 1831 B [D&C 107:65], josephsmithpapers.org.
3. Note, 8 March 1832, 10–11, josephsmithpapers.org.
4. See Minutes, 2 May 1833; Letter to the Church in Thompson, Ohio, 6 February 1833; and Letter to Church Leaders in Eugene, Indiana, 2 July 1833, josephsmithpapers.org.
5. See Revelation, 1 November 1831–A [D&C 68], in "Revelations," *The Evening and the Morning Star,* Oct. 1832 (June 1835), 73. See also Doctrine and Covenants 68:15.
6. Joseph Smith, in History, 1838–1856, volume A-1 [23 December 1805–30 August 1834], 281, josephsmithpapers.org. See also "Historical Introduction," Revelation, 8 March 1833 [D&C 90], josephsmithpapers.org.
7. Gordon B. Hinckley, "God Is at the Helm," *Ensign,* May 1994, 54.
8. Joseph Smith, in History, 1838–1856, volume B-1 [1 September 1834–2 November 1838], 691, josephsmithpapers.org.
9. Petra Javadi-Evans, "'Knowledge Saves a Man': Joseph Smith's Devotion to Learning," in *Know Brother Joseph: New Perspectives on Joseph Smith's Life & Character* (Salt Lake City, UT: Deseret Book, 2021), 78.
10. Council of Fifty, Minutes, March 1844–January 1846; Volume 1, 10 March 1844–1 March 1845, 107–8, josephsmithpapers.org.
11. Heber C. Kimball, "Extracts from H. C. Kimball's Journal," *Times and Seasons,* Mar. 15, 1845, 839–40.
12. See "Historical Introduction," Letter to Vienna Jaques, 4 September 1833, josephsmithpapers.org.
13. Letter to Vienna Jaques, 4 September 1833, 1, josephsmithpapers.org; spelling and punctuation modernized.
14. See Anthony Sweat, *Repicturing the Restoration: New Art to Expand Our Understanding* (Provo, UT: Religious Studies Center, 2020), 152.
15. Susan Easton Black, *Who's Who in the Doctrine & Covenants* (Salt Lake City, UT: Bookcraft, 1997), 147.

$\mathcal{D}$octrine and $\mathcal{C}$ovenants
Section 91
Concerning the Apocrypha

$\mathcal{H}$istorical $\mathcal{C}$ontext

IN THE SPRING OF 1833 JOSEPH SMITH CONTINUED HIS PROJECT OF TRANS-
lating the Bible. A month earlier, Joseph noted in his minute book, "This
day completed the translation and the reviewing of the New testament and
sealed up no more to be broken till it goes to Zion."[1] It seems that after he
completed his work on the New Testament, Joseph Smith returned to his
translation of the Old Testament. The day before he received Doctrine and
Covenants 91, Joseph Smith obtained a different revelation that outlined
several responsibilities to carry out "when you have finished the translation
of the prophets" (Doctrine and Covenants 90:13). It appears that after God
gave him this commandment, Joseph desired to know if the books popularly
known as "the Apocrypha" should be translated as well.

Even while the Book of Mormon was being printed, Joseph Smith and
his associates had begun plans to complete a translation of the Bible. They

intended to correct many of the errors that had crept into the text and put back many of the plain and precious truths that had been lost. On October 8, 1829, Oliver Cowdery purchased a large King James Bible from the Grandin Press, the printers of the Book of Mormon. This Bible, which is currently in the custody of the Community of Christ, is helpful in understanding why Joseph and his associates had questions about the Apocrypha. The Bible that Cowdery purchased is a large, pulpit-style edition containing the Old and New Testaments along with the Apocrypha. It is nine inches wide, eleven inches long, and about two and a half inches thick, and it weighs just under five pounds. On the inside cover in the large handwriting of Oliver Cowdery is the following inscription: "The Book of the Jews and the property of Joseph Smith Junior and Oliver Cowdery, bought October 3, 1829 at Egbert B. Grandin's Book Store, Palmyra, Wayne County, New York. Price $3.75. Holiness to the Lord."[2] It is believed that this Bible served as the primary study text for Joseph Smith's inspired translation of the Bible.

The Apocrypha consists of a collection of books that were not found in Hebrew collections of sacred writings but were included in the Greek version of the Old Testament commonly known as the Septuagint. The Roman Catholic and Eastern Orthodox Christians include the Apocrypha in their Old Testament and consider it to contain inspired writings of God. When Martin Luther translated the Bible in 1534, he moved the books of the Apocrypha to the end of the Old Testament, writing that they were "not held equal to the Holy Scriptures, and yet are profitable and good to read."[3] Most Protestant Christians have followed Luther's lead and generally exclude the Apocrypha from their Old Testament.

As he began his translation of the Bible, Joseph Smith showed more willingness to accept books like the Apocrypha into the scriptural canon. The coming forth of the Book of Mormon demonstrated that scripture could be found outside of the typical Christian canon. Reflecting on his own project to translate the Bible, Joseph later wrote, "Much conjecture and conversation frequently occurred among the saints, concerning the books mentioned and referred to, in various places in the Old and New testaments, which were now nowhere to be found. The common remark was, they are 'lost books'; but it seems the apostolic churches had some of these writings, as Jude mentions or quotes the prophecy of Enoch the seventh from Adam."[4]

Given his openness to the concept of additional scripture, it was natural for Joseph Smith to inquire about the Apocrypha and whether it needed to be translated. In his own history, the Prophet wrote simply, "Having come to that portion of the Ancient writings called the Apocrypha I received the following [Doctrine and Covenants 91]."[5]

$\mathcal{V}$erse-by-$\mathcal{V}$erse $\mathcal{C}$ommentary

> 1 Verily, thus saith the Lord unto you concerning the Apocrypha—There are many things contained therein that are true, and it is mostly translated correctly;
>
> 2 There are many things contained therein that are not true, which are interpolations by the hands of men.
>
> 3 Verily, I say unto you, that it is not needful that the Apocrypha should be translated.

The Bible Joseph Smith used for his translation project contained a section designated as "Apocrypha" that contained 1 & 2 Esdras, Tobit, Judith, the Wisdom of Solomon, the Wisdom of Jesus, the Son of Sirach, Baruch, the Song of the Three Holy Children, Susanna, Bel and the Dragon, The Prayer of Manasses, and 1 & 2 Maccabees.[6] The name *Apocrypha* is derived from a Greek term which means "hidden" or "concealed."[7] The name should be distinguished from the term *apocryphal*, which is often used to describe other works of ancient origin like the Dead Sea Scrolls, the Nag Hammadi library, or apocryphal books of the New Testament. The revelation in section 91 only addresses the specific books found in the Greek Septuagint that are not in the Hebrew Bible, or the upper-case *Apocrypha* that is accepted by Catholic Christians but generally not by Protestant Christians.[8]

In general, the Lord speaks positively about the Apocrypha in verse 1, saying that "there are many things therein that are true, and it is mostly translated correctly." However, it was not necessary for the Prophet to translate it (see verse 3). The instructions given in Doctrine and Covenants 91 should not be applied to all apocryphal works, which vary widely in their claims to authenticity and their usefulness. This revelation is useful in cautioning Latter-day Saints to not put too much stock in books outside of the scriptural canon established by the Lord's authorized servants. These books can be useful and enlightening, but they do not carry the same weight as the canonical books. The Apocrypha's truths must be measured against the Church's scriptural canon before they are accepted. The word *canon* itself is of Greek origin and denotes "a rod for testing straightness" (Bible Dictionary, "canon"). The "standard works" are what we must use to test the truth of other writings, particularly those that claim to also be of ancient origin.

> 4 Therefore, whoso readeth it, let him understand, for the Spirit manifesteth truth;
>
> 5 And whoso is enlightened by the Spirit shall obtain benefit therefrom;
>
> 6 And whoso receiveth not by the Spirit, cannot be benefited. Therefore it is not needful that it should be translated. Amen.

The principles in these last verses not only apply to the Apocrypha but also could be applied generally to any book. We must approach any work of scripture, literature, film, or music with the enlightenment of the Spirit, seeking to obtain the benefits that we can from them. Reading, viewing, or hearing obscene and degrading works would give us little benefit. However, there are sublime works in all branches of the human effort that uplift and greatly benefit us. The Lord continually admonished the Saints to not only seek out the best books (see Doctrine and Covenants 88:118, 90:15) but also to seek after all good things.

Joseph Smith encapsulated this philosophy when he wrote, "If there is anything virtuous, lovely, or of good report or praiseworthy, we seek after these things" (Articles of Faith 1:13). As disciples of Jesus Christ, we have an obligation to seek out the things of most benefit. Many of these come from our brothers and sisters of other faiths, cultures, and backgrounds. With the Spirit as our guide, we should embrace all things of benefit as we seek to make the world a better place.

SECTION 91

End Notes

1. Minute Book 1, 8, josephsmithpapers.org.
2. See "Historical Introduction," Bible Used for Bible Revision, josephsmithpapers.org.
3. Bruce Metzger, *An Introduction to the Apocrypha* (New York: Oxford University Press, 1957), 183, quoted in "Historical Introduction," Revelation, 9 March 1833 [D&C 91], footnote 4, josephsmithpapers.org.
4. Joseph Smith, in History, 1838–1856, volume A-1 [23 December 1805–30 August 1834], 80–81, josephsmithpapers.org.
5. Joseph Smith, in History, 1838–1856, volume A-1 [23 December 1805–30 August 1834], 279–280, josephsmithpapers.org. See also "Historical Introduction," Revelation, 9 March 1833 [D&C 91], josephsmithpapers.org.
6. See Bible Used for Bible Revision, Apocrypha, 1–99, josephsmithpapers.org.
7. "Historical Introduction," Revelation, 9 March 1833 [D&C 91], josephsmithpapers.org.
8. See Stephen E. Robinson and H. Dean Garrett, *A Commentary on the Doctrine and Covenants* (Salt Lake City, UT: Deseret Book, 2000), 3:167.

$\mathcal{D}$octrine and $\mathcal{C}$ovenants
Section 92
Be a Lively Member

$\mathcal{H}$istorical $\mathcal{C}$ontext

WHEN FREDERICK G. WILLIAMS WAS BROUGHT INTO THE PRESIDENCY OF the high priesthood on March 8, 1833 (see Doctrine and Covenants 90), several other responsibilities came along with his new calling. One of these involved a group of Church leaders that Joseph Smith had organized a year earlier. This group formed the "United Firm" (referred to in this section as the "united order"), a governing financial council that oversaw several crucial projects for the Church. The United Firm was responsible for "regulating and establishing the affairs of the storehouse for the poor of my people" (Doctrine and Covenants 78:3); holding Church properties in trust; operating general stores in Independence, Missouri, and Kirtland, Ohio; and overseeing the publication of scripture. They also supervised city planning and the construction of church buildings, including the Kirtland Temple. Earlier members of the United Firm were Joseph Smith, Oliver

Cowdery, Sidney Gilbert, Martin Harris, Edward Partridge, William W. Phelps, Sidney Rigdon, John Whitmer, and Newel K. Whitney. Frederick G. Williams was the first new member of the firm since its organization a year earlier.

In the spring of 1833 the plans for building the city of Zion and the temple in Kirtland were accelerating, and Frederick G. Williams eventually became deeply involved in both projects. Both the plat of the city of Zion and the design for the temple were recorded in Williams's handwriting and sent to Missouri later that summer.[1] Williams also copied the revelation found in section 92 by his own hand into Joseph Smith's letter book.[2]

*V*erse-by-*V*erse *C*ommentary

> 1 Verily, thus saith the Lord, I give unto the united order, organized agreeable to the commandment previously given, a revelation and commandment concerning my servant Frederick G. Williams, that ye shall receive him into the order. What I say unto one I say unto all.
>
> 2 And again, I say unto you my servant Frederick G. Williams, you shall be a lively member in this order; and inasmuch as you are faithful in keeping all former commandments you shall be blessed forever. Amen.

The "commandment previously given" (verse 1) is found in Doctrine and Covenants 78:11 and asks the members of the united order to "organize yourselves by a bond or everlasting covenant that cannot be broken" (Doctrine and Covenants 78:13). In a part of this revelation, Frederick G. Williams was asked to be a "lively" member of the order. One of the synonyms for *lively* in the language of the time was active. The word *active* is often used in the Church today to distinguish someone who participates in the Church from someone who is simply on the membership roll but has little or no functioning role in the Church. There are a number of reasons why people fall into inactivity or struggle to participate. Such individuals need our love and encouragement, not our judgement.

To be lively members of the Church, we should view our Church membership as an outlet in which we each offer up our best rather than demanding something in return for our participation. Daniel Becerra, a professor of ancient scripture at Brigham Young University, has likened these two attitudes to a restaurant and a potluck dinner. Some people treat the Church like a restaurant, going in with expectations of being served. These people commonly complain, "I get nothing out of it." Participation in the Church is a more enriching experience if we treat it like a potluck dinner. We need to go in asking "What am I bringing to bless and serve others?"[3] When the Lord asked Frederick G. Williams to be a lively member of the united order, it was a simple way of asking him to contribute and be proactive in his service. The Lord expects the same of each of us—to be a lively member of the Church.

End Notes

1. See "Source Note," Plat of the City of Zion, circa Early June–25 June 1833, josephsmithpapers.org; and "Source Note," Plan of the House of the Lord, between 1 and 25 June 1833, josephsmithpapers.org.
2. See "Historical Introduction," Revelation, 15 March 1833 [D&C 92], josephsmithpapers.org.
3. Daniel Becerra, "Surprised by Christ," Y Religion (podcast), Feb. 2021, https://rsc.byu.edu/media/y-religion/25.

Doctrine and Covenants Section 93

How and What We Worship

Historical Context

WE KNOW VERY LITTLE ABOUT THE CONTEXT OF DOCTRINE AND COVENANTS 93. Joseph Smith himself only provided a one-line introduction to the revelation in his history, writing, "On the 6th [May 1833] I received the following."[1] Because of the revelation's similarities to the first chapter of the Gospel of John, it might be easy to assume that it came in relation to Joseph's translation of the Bible. However, records kept by the Prophet and his scribes show that they completed work on the New Testament over three months earlier, in February 1833.[2] In addition, the changes made to the Gospel of John in this revelation do not match the changes Joseph made as part of his new translation of the Bible.

A small insight into the context of the revelation comes from Bishop Newel K. Whitney, who is mentioned in the revelation. On the back of the earliest surviving copy of the revelation, he wrote, "Revelation to Joseph,

Sidney [Rigdon], Frederick [G. Williams] and Newel [K. Whitney] by chastisement and also relative to the Father and Son."[3] Probably the best motivation for this revelation comes from the Savior Himself, who states in the text, "I give unto you these sayings that you may understand and know how to worship, and know what you worship, that you may come unto the Father in my name, and in due time receive of his fulness" (Doctrine and Covenants 93:20). Contained within this revelation are not only profound insights into how we worship the Father and the Son but also some of the weightiest statements made about the natures of God, Jesus Christ, and the sons and daughters of God themselves.

Verse-by-Verse Commentary

1 Verily, thus saith the Lord: It shall come to pass that every soul who forsaketh his sins and cometh unto me, and calleth on my name, and obeyeth my voice, and keepeth my commandments, shall see my face and know that I am;

2 And that I am the true light that lighteth every man that cometh into the world;

3 And that I am in the Father, and the Father in me, and the Father and I are one—

4 The Father because he gave me of his fulness, and the Son because I was in the world and made flesh my tabernacle, and dwelt among the sons of men.

5 I was in the world and received of my Father, and the works of him were plainly manifest.

This brief set of verses, particularly verse 1, is one of the most comprehensive yet simple descriptions of the gospel of Jesus Christ. Previous to this time, the Savior had already made several promises to prominent Church leaders that they might see His face (see Doctrine and Covenants 50:45; 67:10, 14; 76:116–118; 88:68), but in verse 1 the promise is made to "every soul" that follows five simple and logically progressive steps to enter into the presence of the Savior. These promises can be applied not only after our death and resurrection but also in this life, including the promise to truly know Christ through receiving the Second Comforter (see Doctrine and Covenants 88:3–4; 68:12).[4]

The five steps provided in verse 1 are to (1) forsake your sins, (2) come unto Jesus Christ, (3) call upon the name of Jesus Christ, (4) obey the voice of Christ, and (5) keep the commandments. This simple sequence gives all men and women the straightforward instructions they need to enter the presence of God. The Savior also explains two advantages that every man and woman who seeks this path already possesses to help them along the way. First, we have "true light," or the Light of Christ, which gives an intrinsic sense of right and wrong to every person born into this world (see Moroni 7:16; Doctrine and Covenants 84:46–54; 88:5–13). Second, we have the example of Jesus Christ, who gained a body of flesh, received of the fulness of the Father, and demonstrated the works of the Father (see 2 Nephi 31:7). These two guides—the Light of Christ within us and the example of Jesus Christ's life—prepare our path to eternal life.

> 6 And John saw and bore record of the fulness of my glory, and the fulness of John's record is hereafter to be revealed.
>
> 7 And he bore record, saying: I saw his glory, that he was in the beginning, before the world was;
>
> 8 Therefore, in the beginning the Word was, for he was the Word, even the messenger of salvation—
>
> 9 The light and the Redeemer of the world; the Spirit of truth, who came into the world, because the world was made by him, and in him was the life of men and the light of men.
>
> 10 The worlds were made by him; men were made by him; all things were made by him, and through him, and of him.
>
> 11 And I, John, bear record that I beheld his glory, as the glory of the Only Begotten of the Father, full of grace and truth, even the Spirit of truth, which came and dwelt in the flesh, and dwelt among us.

Because of the similarities between the first chapter of the Gospel of John and the opening of Doctrine and Covenants 93, it is easy to assume that the record referred to in verse 6 is the Gospel written by John. However, a close examination of the text shows that the record referred to here is a record kept and recorded by John the Baptist (see Doctrine and Covenants

93:15). Several prominent Latter-day Saint scriptural commentators, including Orson Pratt, John Taylor, Sidney B. Sperry, and Bruce R. McConkie, have interpreted this verse in a similar way.[5] Bruce R. McConkie urged his readers to carefully compare these verses with Matthew 3:16–17 to identify the writer of this passage.

Identifying John the Baptist as the author of this passage connects well with the Savior's tribute to him: "Among them that are born of women there hath not risen a greater than John the Baptist" (Matthew 11:11). What made John the Baptist truly great was his role as a testator of Jesus Christ. In the Baptist's words recorded in Doctrine and Covenants 93 and in his words recorded in the New Testament, John was first and foremost a witness of Jesus Christ. John was given the singular honor of performing the baptism of the Savior of the world. But he never cared to shine a light on himself. Instead, he wisely noted the true source of light, the Messiah (see verse 9). To his own devoted band of followers, John testified, "I am not the Christ, but I am sent before him. . . . He must increase, but I must decrease" (John 3:28–30). These unselfish acts of devotion to Jesus Christ and his unfailing witness of Jesus Christ to the day of his martyrdom set John the Baptist apart as one of the greatest among all the prophets who ever lived.

John's work as a witness of Jesus Christ continues into our time. He was among the first angels to appear in this dispensation to restore "the authority to baptize by immersion for the remission of sins."[6] We look forward to the time when we can receive the fulness of the record written by John the Baptist (see Doctrine and Covenants 93:18).

> 12 And I, John, saw that he received not of the fulness at the first, but received grace for grace;
>
> 13 And he received not of the fulness at first, but continued from grace to grace, until he received a fulness;
>
> 14 And thus he was called the Son of God, because he received not of the fulness at the first.
>
> 15 And I, John, bear record, and lo, the heavens were opened, and the Holy Ghost descended upon him in the form of a dove, and sat upon him, and there came a voice out of heaven saying: This is my beloved Son.
>
> 16 And I, John, bear record that he received a fulness of the glory of the Father;

17 And he received all power, both in heaven and on earth, and the glory of the Father was with him, for he dwelt in him.

18 And it shall come to pass, that if you are faithful you shall receive the fulness of the record of John.

One of the most frustrating aspects of the records of the Savior's mortal ministry is that they share relatively little about it. The time from the Savior's baptism to His Resurrection is recorded in detail in the four New Testament Gospels, but there is little information about His life before that time. Matthew and Luke provide the most information, yet even they remain closely fixated on the story of Mary and Joseph and the nativity of the Savior (see Matthew 1–2; Luke 1; 2:1–41). Luke provides a brief glimpse into the childhood of Christ when he tells the story of Jesus being found in the temple sitting with a group of wise men who were "hearing [Jesus] and asking him questions" (Joseph Smith Translation, Luke 2:46 [in Luke 2:46, footnote *c*]). Luke then summarizes the rest of the Savior's childhood by simply recording, "And Jesus increased in wisdom and stature, and in favour with God and man" (Luke 2:52).

Because we lack knowledge about the early life of Jesus Christ, a number of folk legends have arisen surrounding what He was like as a child. One beloved Christian hymn speaks of the night of his birth, saying, "The cattle are lowing, the poor baby wakes, but little Lord Jesus, no crying he makes."[7] In reality, the Savior probably cried the night he was born. While we may not know many of the details about the Savior's youth, the record of John the Baptist provides some doctrinal background that the Savior "received not of the fulness at first, but received grace for grace" (verse 12). The underlying lesson here is clear. The Savior came to earth and passed through the veil, losing all the knowledge and power He had previously held as Jehovah, God of the Old Testament. Paul taught, "Let this mind be in you, which was also in Christ Jesus: Who, being in the form of God, thought it not robbery to be equal with God: But made himself of no reputation, and took upon him the form of a servant, and was made in the likeness of men: And being found in fashion as a man, he humbled himself, and became obedient unto death, even the death of the cross" (Philippians 2:5–8).

Jesus never asked any man or woman to do anything He was not willing to do Himself. Because all men and women lose the memory of their premortal stature when they come to earth, so did He. Lorenzo Snow taught:

When Jesus lay in the manger, a helpless infant, He knew not that He was the Son of God, and that formerly He created the earth. When the edict of Herod was issued, He knew nothing of it; He had not power to save Himself; and His father and mother had to take Him and fly into Egypt to preserve Him from the effects of that edict. Well, He grew up to manhood, and during His progress it was revealed unto Him who He was, and for what purpose He was in the world. The glory and power He possessed before He came into the world was made known unto Him.[8]

> 19 I give unto you these sayings that you may understand and know how to worship, and know what you worship, that you may come unto the Father in my name, and in due time receive of his fulness.
>
> 20 For if you keep my commandments you shall receive of his fulness, and be glorified in me as I am in the Father; therefore, I say unto you, you shall receive grace for grace.

In these short verses, the Savior describes the purpose of the revelation: "that you may understand and know how to worship, and know what you worship" (verse 19). Addressing the first part of this statement, we must ask ourselves what *worship* really consists of. Elder Bruce R. McConkie taught, "Perfect worship is emulation. We honor those whom we imitate. The most perfect way to worship is to be holy as Jehovah is holy. It is to be pure as Christ is pure. It is to do the things that enable us to become like the Father. The course is one of obedience."[9] In church worship services, for instance, we ask young men to prepare, bless, and pass the sacrament, actions that Christ Himself first demonstrated. These simple acts of imitation, only a few minutes of every week, are intended to help us worship through direct imitation.

In connection with His statement that He wants us to know *what* we worship, the Savior begins to describe the sons and daughters of God by using the words that John the Baptist used to describe Him. By teaching that men and women must also receive "grace for grace," the Savior is teaching that humanity is an embryonic form of divinity and that all men and women have the potential to become like God. However, this teaching ran contrary to the prominent Christian thinking of the day—that Christ was both fully human and fully divine, a philosophy which most Christians have followed since the Council of Chalcedon in AD 451.[10]

Beginning here, the next few verses (see verses 21–35) lead the reader through a sequence of truths that explain the true nature of all people and their relationship to God. Elder Tad R. Callister summarized these truths when he taught:

> The difference between man and God is significant—but it is one of degree, not kind. It is the difference between an acorn and an oak tree, a rosebud and a rose, a son and a father. In truth, every man is a potential god in embryo, in fulfillment of that eternal law that like begets like. . . . Why is it so critical to have a correct vision of this divine destiny of godliness of which the scriptures and other witnesses so clearly testify? Because with increased vision comes increased motivation.[11]

> 21 And now, verily I say unto you, I was in the beginning with the Father, and am the Firstborn;

> 22 And all those who are begotten through me are partakers of the glory of the same, and are the church of the Firstborn.

> 23 Ye were also in the beginning with the Father; that which is Spirit, even the Spirit of truth;

After telling us that we must also receive grace for grace, Jesus makes a second connection, related to our premortal existence, between men and women, the Savior, and the Father. Jesus teaches that He was in the beginning with the Father and is the Firstborn. A 1909 declaration of the First Presidency clarifies the status of Jesus as the Firstborn, teaching, "Jesus . . . is the firstborn among all the sons of God—the first begotten in the spirit, and the only begotten in the flesh. He is our elder brother, and we, like Him, are in the image of God."[12] The status of Jesus as "the firstborn of every creature" was also taught by Paul in his letter to the Colossians (Colossians 1:15).

Jesus, however, asserts not only that He was in the beginning with God but also that *we* were in the beginning with God. This is the first place in the Doctrine and Covenants in which the Lord clearly teaches of the premortal existence of men and women. In an earlier revelation given to Joseph Smith during his translation of the book of Genesis, the Lord declared, "I am God; I made the world, and men before they were in the flesh" (Moses 6:51). But in stating that all people were also in the beginning with God, the Savior is referring to the eternal, uncreated characteristics of all men and women. Contrary to Christian perceptions of the day, which generally taught that human beings were created *ex nihilo*, or out of nothing, there is an eternal and everlasting part of every person. This is the revelation's second great doctrinal contribution: the difference between humans and God is one of degree, not one of kind. It is the difference between a majestic oak tree and an acorn.

> 24 And truth is knowledge of things as they are, and as they were, and as they are to come;
>
> 25 And whatsoever is more or less than this is the spirit of that wicked one who was a liar from the beginning.
>
> 26 The Spirit of truth is of God. I am the Spirit of truth, and John bore record of me, saying: He received a fulness of truth, yea, even of all truth;
>
> 27 And no man receiveth a fulness unless he keepeth his commandments.
>
> 28 He that keepeth his commandments receiveth truth and light, until he is glorified in truth and knoweth all things.

In the hours leading up to His death on the cross, Jesus was asked by Pontius Pilate, "What is truth?" (John 18:38). The Gospel of John does not record an answer from the Savior, but the answer is found in this revelation. The Savior declares, "Truth is knowledge of things as they are, and as they were, and as they are to come" (verse 24). In our time there are many who would suggest that all truth is relative, subject to the perceptions of the person who is viewing it. In contrast to this idea, verse 24 teaches that there is an objective truth of things as they are, were, and are to come. While we sometimes preoccupy ourselves with the question of what is coming, the questions of how things were in the past and how things actually are in the present are both important as well. At times the most difficult task is not to know the past or the future but to know the reality of what the truth is in the present.

President Uchtdorf once quoted the John Godrey Saxe poem "The Blind Men and the Elephant" to illustrate the danger of approaching the truth in the wrong way. The poem begins,

> Six men of Indostan
> To learning much inclined,
> Who went to see the Elephant
> (Though all of them were blind),

That each by observation
Might satisfy his mind.

Elder Uchtdorf added:

In the poem each of the six travelers takes hold of a different part of the elephant and then describes to the others what he has discovered. One of the men finds the elephant's leg and describes it as being round and rough like a tree. Another feels the tusk and describes the elephant as a spear. A third grabs the tail and insists that an elephant is like a rope. A fourth discovers the trunk and insists that the elephant is like a large snake. Each is describing truth. And because his truth comes from personal experience, each insists that he knows what he knows.

The poem concludes:

And so these men of Indostan
Disputed loud and long,
Each in his own opinion
Exceeding stiff and strong,
Though each was partly in the right,
And all were in the wrong![13]

As with the blind men in the poem, we make a mistake when we assume to know the whole objective truth—in reality, we may only know part of it. The Father and the Son, however, see and view the whole truth, which exists objectively in Their sight. We must trust that They see the entire picture and guide us so that we can know what the truth is in relation to the past, present, and future.

> 29 Man was also in the beginning with God. Intelligence, or the light of truth, was not created or made, neither indeed can be.
>
> 30 All truth is independent in that sphere in which God has placed it, to act for itself, as all intelligence also; otherwise there is no existence.
>
> 31 Behold, here is the agency of man, and here is the condemnation of man; because that which was from the beginning is plainly manifest unto them, and they receive not the light.
>
> 32 And every man whose spirit receiveth not the light is under condemnation.

In verses 30–32 the Savior explains how men and women can be coeternal with God and still be His children. The eternal element of man is labeled here as "intelligence." This revelation establishes two things about the nature of intelligence. First, it cannot be created or made (see verse 29). Second, intelligence is free to act in the sphere in which God has placed it—or, written more simply, all intelligence has agency (see verse 30). Beyond these two things, there is little that we know about intelligence. Joseph Fielding Smith warned about the dangers of taking our limited knowledge on this subject too far: "Some of our writers have endeavored to explain what an intelligence is, but to do so is futile, for we have never been given any insight into this matter beyond what the Lord has fragmentarily revealed. We know, however, that there is something called intelligence which always existed. It is the real eternal part of man, which was not created nor made. This intelligence combined with the spirit constitutes a spiritual identity or individual."[14]

This revelation about the eternal nature of intelligence and agency has widespread philosophical consequences. Consider, for instance, the problem of evil. Those who question the existence of God often use the existence of evil and suffering in the world as evidence that there is no overseer to the universe. When people of faith point out that men and women have agency and at times use it unwisely, leading to evil, those who question might respond, "Why did God make men and women as the kind of beings who could do evil things?"

Doctrine and Covenants 93 presents the answer to this question regarding the capacity of men and women to engage in acts of evil. There is a part of men and women, here called intelligence, that God did not create. Intelligence has always existed and has always had agency. Thus, men and women are responsible for their own decisions and have always been. This addresses not only the problem of evil but also the nature of free will and predeterminism. Truman G. Madsen, a professor of philosophy, phrased the issue this way: "Q. If man is totally the creation of God, how can he be anything or do anything that he was not divinely pre-caused to do? A. Man is not totally the creation of God. 'Intelligence was not created or made, neither indeed can be. . . . Behold, here is the agency of man.'"[15]

The intelligence part of our beings that was not created by God does not lessen our relationship with Him. God took intelligence, provided it with a body of spirit, and then arranged for the eternal progression of those who follow Him. In this sense, the relationship between God and His children closely mirrors the relationship between earthly parents and children.

Parents do not love their children less because they know they existed before they came into their home. Knowing the eternal nature of each child makes our connection to our Father in Heaven even more profound.

> 33 For man is spirit. The elements are eternal, and spirit and element, inseparably connected, receive a fulness of joy;
>
> 34 And when separated, man cannot receive a fulness of joy.
>
> 35 The elements are the tabernacle of God; yea, man is the tabernacle of God, even temples; and whatsoever temple is defiled, God shall destroy that temple.

The Prophet Joseph Smith taught, "Anything created cannot be eternal. Air, earth, water, all these had their existence in an elementary state from eternity."[16] He would later teach that "there is no such thing as immaterial matter. All spirit is matter but is more fine or pure and can only be discerned by purer eyes. We cannot see it, but when our bodies are purified, we shall see that it is all matter."[17]

Asserting that spirit and matter are forms of the same thing, and that both are eternal, ran contrary to the popular theology of the day. Historically, most Christian religions taught that God created all things *ex nihilo,* or out of nothing, and that only spiritual things are eternal in nature—they thought that all physical things are only transitory. These ideas, rooted in Greek philosophy, set up the physical world as a prison that spirits are trapped within.[18] In contrast to this view, the revelations given in the Doctrine and Covenants establish that both spirit and matter are eternal. People obtain a fulness of joy when these two elements are brought together and find their true, eternal form. In contrast to the tenet that God is a being without bodily parts or passions, we know that God lives in a physical body. All people are created in His image and have the potential to truly become like Him if they only choose to follow His plan.

> 36 The glory of God is intelligence, or, in other words, light and truth.
>
> 37 Light and truth forsake that evil one.

In the revelations given to Joseph Smith, terms such as *intelligence, light, truth, spirit,* and *glory* are often used interchangeably. The phrase "the glory of God is intelligence" is often used to highlight the importance of learning. While education is important in this life, some kinds of knowledge are more useful than others. John A. Widtsoe suggested that the gospel meaning of *intelligence* is more profound than just the acquisition of facts. He taught, "The intelligent man is he who seeks knowledge and uses it in accordance with the plan of the Lord for human good. . . . When men follow the light their knowledge will always be used as well. Intelligence, then, becomes another name for wisdom. In the language of mathematics we may say that knowledge, plus the proper use of knowledge, equals intelligence, or wisdom. In this sense intelligence becomes the goal of the successful life."[19]

> 38 Every spirit of man was innocent in the beginning; and God having redeemed man from the fall, men became again, in their infant state, innocent before God.
>
> 39 And that wicked one cometh and taketh away light and truth, through disobedience, from the children of men, and because of the tradition of their fathers.
>
> 40 But I have commanded you to bring up your children in light and truth.

These verses answer one more important philosophical question: Are men and women good or evil by nature? The revelation declares that all people are innocent at the time of their birth and do not have a predisposition toward evil. The choices people make cause them to move toward becoming good or evil, but every person begins life with a new start. Whatever sins or transgressions people may have committed during premortal life, they have a new beginning with a lifetime of new possibilities laid before them when they come to earth. The Lord acknowledges that some are born into better and some into worse environments. The traditions of their fathers can at times blur the sense of morality given to individuals through the Light of Christ. However, the default setting for mortality is innocence. Men and women are not inherently evil but are sometimes led into making bad choices by the wicked one, and these choices may subsequently cause them to lose the light and truth that is their birthright.

Truman G. Madsen phrases it this way: "Q. How can man be a divine creation, and yet be 'totally depraved'? A. Man is not totally depraved. 'Every spirit of man was innocent in the beginning; and God having redeemed them from the fall, men became again, in their infant state, innocent before God.'"[20] This truth does not deny the presence of genuine evil in the world but is saying that the evil is unnatural. Evil comes when a person's agency is distorted to work against the greater good and the will of God.

41 But verily I say unto you, my servant Frederick G. Williams, you have continued under this condemnation;

42 You have not taught your children light and truth, according to the commandments; and that wicked one hath power, as yet, over you, and this is the cause of your affliction.

43 And now a commandment I give unto you—if you will be delivered you shall set in order your own house, for there are many things that are not right in your house.

44 Verily, I say unto my servant Sidney Rigdon, that in some things he hath not kept the commandments concerning his children; therefore, first set in order thy house.

45 Verily, I say unto my servant Joseph Smith, Jun., or in other words, I will call you friends, for you are my friends, and ye shall have an inheritance with me—

46 I called you servants for the world's sake, and ye are their servants for my sake—

47 And now, verily I say unto Joseph Smith, Jun.—You have not kept the commandments, and must needs stand rebuked before the Lord;

48 Your family must needs repent and forsake some things, and give more earnest heed unto your sayings, or be removed out of their place.

49 What I say unto one I say unto all; pray always lest that wicked one have power in you, and remove you out of your place.

50 My servant Newel K. Whitney also, a bishop of my church, hath need to be chastened, and set in order his family, and see that they are more diligent and concerned at home, and pray always, or they shall be removed out of their place.

51 Now, I say unto you, my friends, let my servant Sidney Rigdon go on his journey, and make haste, and also proclaim the acceptable year of the Lord, and the gospel of salvation, as I shall

give him utterance; and by your prayer of faith with one consent I will uphold him.

52 And let my servants Joseph Smith, Jun., and Frederick G. Williams make haste also, and it shall be given them even according to the prayer of faith; and inasmuch as you keep my sayings you shall not be confounded in this world, nor in the world to come.

53 And, verily I say unto you, that it is my will that you should hasten to translate my scriptures, and to obtain a knowledge of history, and of countries, and of kingdoms, of laws of God and man, and all this for the salvation of Zion. Amen.

The last few verses of the revelation may seem to be a departure from the profound doctrinal declarations of the revelation, but thematically they are linked. The truths taught in this section inform the Saints of the sacred nature of all people. In this last part of the revelation, the members of the First Presidency and Bishop Whitney are reproved for not focusing on their families. As a later prophet of the Church would teach, "No other success can compensate for failure in the home."[21] In the measure of eternity, the role we play in our homes is more significant than the callings we hold in the Church, even the calling of being a prophet.

Out of all the grand roles and powers of God that are discussed in the revelations, the most significant role He holds is to nurture and help His children along their path to eternal life. Fatherhood is an inseparable element of how Latter-day Saints conceive, think of, and conceptualize the nature of God. President Oaks taught, "Our theology begins with heavenly parents. Our highest aspiration is to be like them. Under the merciful plan of the Father, all of this is possible through the atonement of the Only Begotten of the Father, our Lord and Savior, Jesus Christ. As earthly parents we participate in the gospel plan by providing mortal bodies for the spirit children of God. The fulness of eternal salvation is a family matter."[22] While not all will be parents in this life, nurturing and helping other people become better aids us significantly in understanding God and becoming like Him. We are learning the nature of godhood when we act as fathers, mothers, teachers, or mentors to other people.

End Notes

1. Joseph Smith, in History, 1838–1856, volume A-1 [23 December 1805–30 August 1834], 291, josephsmithpapers.org.
2. See Minute Book 1, 8, josephsmithpapers.org.
3. "Historical Introduction," Revelation, 6 May 1833, josephsmithpapers.org. There is also some evidence that this copy of the revelation may be the original copy of the revelation.
4. See Stephen E. Robinson and H. Dean Garrett, *A Commentary on the Doctrine and Covenants* (Salt Lake City, UT: Deseret Book, 2000), 3:173–74.
5. See *Journal of Discourses,* 16:58; John Taylor, *Mediation and Atonement* (Salt Lake City, UT: Stevens & Wallis, 1950), 55; Sidney B. Sperry, *Doctrine and Covenants Compendium* (Salt Lake City, UT: Bookcraft, 1960), 472–73; Bruce R. McConkie, *Doctrinal New Testament Commentary* (Salt Lake City, UT: Deseret Book, 1973), 1:70–71.
6. "The Restoration of the Fulness of the Gospel of Jesus Christ: A Bicentennial Proclamation to the World," Gospel Library.
7. "Away in a Manger," *Hymns,* no. 206.
8. Lorenzo Snow, in Conference Report, Apr. 1901, 3.
9. Bruce R. McConkie, *The Promised Messiah: The First Coming of Christ* (Salt Lake City, UT: Deseret Book, 1978), 568.
10. See "Historical Introduction," Revelation, 6 May 1833 [D&C 93], footnote 8, josephsmithpapers.org.
11. Tad R. Callister, "Our Identity and Our Destiny" (Education Week devotional, Aug. 14, 2012), 9, speeches.byu.edu.
12. *Messages of the First Presidency of The Church of Jesus Christ of Latter-day Saints, 1833-1964,* ed. James R. Clark (Salt Lake City, UT: Bookcraft, 1965), 4:203.
13. Dieter F. Uchtdorf, "What is Truth?" (Church Educational System fireside for young adults, Jan. 13, 2013), 1, speeches.byu.edu.
14. Joseph Fielding Smith, *The Progress of Man* (Salt Lake City, UT: Deseret News Press, 1964), 11.
15. Truman G. Madsen, *Joseph Smith the Prophet* (Salt Lake City, UT: Bookcraft, 1989), 140–41. See also David L. Paulsen, "Joseph Smith and the Problem of Evil" (Brigham Young University forum, Sept. 21, 1999), speeches.byu.edu.
16. Discourse, between circa 26 June and circa 4 August 1839–A, as Reported by William Clayton, 13, josephsmithpapers.org.

17. See Doctrine and Covenants 131:7–8. See also Discourse, 17 May 1843–B, as Reported by William Clayton, 18, josephsmithpapers.org; punctuation modernized.

18. See Robinson and Garrett, *A Commentary on the Doctrine and Covenants,* 3:173–74.

19. John A. Widtsoe, in Conference Report, Apr. 1938, 50.

20. Truman G. Madsen, *Joseph Smith the Prophet,* 140–141.

21. David O. McKay, in Conference Report, Apr. 1935, 116.

22. Dallin H. Oaks, "Apostasy and Restoration," *Ensign,* May 1995, 87.

Doctrine and Covenants Section 94

My Glory Shall Be There

Historical Context

IN THE SUMMER OF 1833 THE CONSTRUCTION OF THE TEMPLE IN KIRTLAND, Ohio, was beginning to gain momentum. Around this time, Church leaders in Kirtland also sent architectural plans to Church members in Zion to build another house of the Lord in Independence, Missouri. Along with these plans, they sent along the plat for the city of Zion.[1] The temple was located at the center of the city of Zion—just as it was in Kirtland. The Lord refers to Kirtland in this revelation as "the city of the stake of Zion" (Doctrine and Covenants 94:2).

Framing this revelation in his history, Joseph Smith wrote, "A conference of high priests assembled in Kirtland, to take into consideration the necessity of building a school-house, for the accommodation of the elders, who should come together to receive instruction preparatory for their missions and ministry, according to a revelation on that subject, given March

195

8th. 1833 [Doctrine and Covenants 90]."[2] This revelation instructed Church leaders to lay out a plan for building Kirtland up to be "the city of the stake of Zion." It also gave instructions to build two additional buildings: a house for the presidency and a house for the printing of the scriptures (see Doctrine and Covenants 94:3, 10). A third building designated in an earlier revelation (see Doctrine and Covenants 88:119) was intended to serve as a home to the "school of the prophets" (Doctrine and Covenants 90:7) and became the Kirtland Temple, where the Savior, as well as Moses, Elias, and Elijah, appeared to give priesthood keys to Joseph Smith and Oliver Cowdery (see Doctrine and Covenants 110).

This revelation was incorrectly dated to May 6, 1833, when it was first given a date in the 1876 edition of the Doctrine and Covenants. From the evidence that is available, this section appears to have been received on the same day as section 97. When the revelation was originally recorded in Revelation Book 2, it was given its own heading and date, recorded as "Kirtland 2nd August 1833."[3] However, when it was later recorded into Revelation Book 1, it was included as part of a letter written to Church leaders in Jackson County that is dated August 6, 1833.[4] When the 1835 edition of the Doctrine and Covenants was published, this revelation was apparently mistakenly inserted after Doctrine and Covenants 93 with a heading that read "revelation given the same date." This wording gave the impression that the revelation was received on May 6, 1833, the same date that section 93 was received.[5] This mistake in the revelation's date continued until the 2013 edition of the Doctrine and Covenants when historians from the Joseph Smith Papers were able to correct the date.[6]

*V*erse-by-*V*erse *C*ommentary

1 And again, verily I say unto you, my friends, a commandment I give unto you, that ye shall commence a work of laying out and preparing a beginning and foundation of the city of the stake of Zion, here in the land of Kirtland, beginning at my house.

2 And behold, it must be done according to the pattern which I have given unto you.

3 And let the first lot on the south be consecrated unto me for the building of a house for the presidency, for the work of the presidency, in obtaining revelations; and for the work of the ministry of the presidency, in all things pertaining to the church and kingdom.

4 Verily I say unto you, that it shall be built fifty-five by sixty-five feet in the width thereof and in the length thereof, in the inner court.

5 And there shall be a lower court and a higher court, according to the pattern which shall be given unto you hereafter.

Christ intends for the city of Zion, which was planned for Jackson County, Missouri, to be the eventual seat of the Church in the latter days. However, this revelation and others demonstrate that Christ also wanted the Saints to build additional cities before the Second Coming. The instructions sent to the Saints in Missouri even specified that after the first city of Zion was finished, they should "lay off another in the same way and so fill up the world in these last days and let every man live in the City for this is the City of Zion."[7] The Lord refers to Kirtland as "the city of the stake of Zion" (verse 1). In a revelation given several years later, the Lord declared that the Saints would gather "together upon the land of Zion, and upon her stakes," which act "for a defense, and refuge from the storm" (Doctrine and Covenants 115:6).

At the center of the city of Zion, the Saints planned to build a complex of twenty-four temples, each dedicated to different offices of the priesthood.[8] In the heart of Kirtland, a smaller complex was to be built. Next to the Kirtland Temple, which is referred to in verse 1 simply as "my house," the Saints were commanded to build a house for the First Presidency. This house was to be similar in size to the Kirtland Temple (see Doctrine and Covenants 95:15) and would have functioned as an administrative center in which the presidency of the Church could labor. At the time this revelation was given, the presidency of the high priesthood, later called the First Presidency, were the only general officers of the Church. The offices of Apostle, Seventy, Presiding Bishopric, and others were revealed later (see Doctrine and Covenants 107). The command to build this structure reflects the priorities of the Lord. Next to His own house, a place that would provide the means for His prophets to carry out their work was also of great importance.

6 And it shall be dedicated unto the Lord from the foundation thereof, according to the order of the priesthood, according to the pattern which shall be given unto you hereafter.

7 And it shall be wholly dedicated unto the Lord for the work of the presidency.

8 And ye shall not suffer any unclean thing to come in unto it; and my glory shall be there, and my presence shall be there.

9 But if there shall come into it any unclean thing, my glory shall not be there; and my presence shall not come into it.

These verses set the pattern of dedicating all Church buildings, whether they are temples, chapels, schools, or any other manner of structure, "according to the order of the priesthood" (verse 6). Later, when the cornerstones for the Nauvoo Temple were put into place, Joseph Smith explained in more detail what the "order of the priesthood" meant in regard to laying out the foundation of temples:

> If the strict order of the Priesthood, were carried out in the building of Temples. The first stone will be laid at the South East Corner by the First Presidency of the Church; the South West Corner should be laid next, the Third or N.W. Corner next, and the fourth or N.E. corner the last. The first presidency should lay the S.E. Corner stone, and dictate who are the proper persons to lay the other Corner Stones. If a Temple is built at a distance, and the First Presidency are not present, then the Quorum of the Twelve Apostles are the persons to dictate the order for that Temple; and in the absence of the Twelve Apostles, then the Presidency of the Stake, will lay the South East Corner Stone; the Melchisedeck [sic] Priesthood laying the Corner Stones at the East side of the Temple; and the Lesser Priesthood, those on the West side.[9]

Rather than reading too much into the meaning of these details, we can simply note the importance of temples and the need to involve prophets and apostles in every phase of their creation. Every temple is dedicated and re-dedicated under the direction of the First Presidency and the Twelve. In our time of temple building, the rapid growth in the number of temples means that at times the First Presidency delegates the responsibility of dedicating temples to members of the Quorum of the Twelve. For instance, from 1998 to 2000, more temples were dedicated than in the previous 167 years. In an unprecedented event on November 14, 1999, President Hinckley dedicated the Halifax Nova Scotia Temple on the same day that President Packer dedicated the Regina Saskatchewan Temple.[10] In all cases, the structures built by the Church, whatever their purpose, are dedicated to the work of the Lord.

Even a home can be considered a sacred space that is in need of dedicating. In the Church handbook published in 2020, dedicating a home was listed as a priesthood ordinance. The handbook states, "Church members may have their homes dedicated by the authority of the Melchizedek Priesthood. Homes do not need to be owned or free of debt to be dedicated. Unlike Church buildings, homes are not consecrated to the Lord."[11] If there is no Melchizedek Priesthood holder in the home, a family can also invite a close friend, relative, or ministering brother to perform the dedication.

> 10 And again, verily I say unto you, the second lot on the south shall be dedicated unto me for the building of a house unto me, for the work of the printing of the translation of my scriptures, and all things whatsoever I shall command you.
>
> 11 And it shall be fifty-five by sixty-five feet in the width thereof and the length thereof, in the inner court; and there shall be a lower and a higher court.
>
> 12 And this house shall be wholly dedicated unto the Lord from the foundation thereof, for the work of the printing, in all things whatsoever I shall command you, to be holy, undefiled, according to the pattern in all things as it shall be given unto you.

The design of the "city of the stake of Zion" at Kirtland also reflected another important priority: the printing of the scriptures. Joseph Smith completed his translation of the Bible in July 1833, though he tinkered with it throughout the remainder of his life. The Lord designated the printing office in Kirtland for printing this new translation.[12] Though the printing office was intended to be the same size as the temple, a few months after this revelation was given, work began on a smaller printing office (thirty by thirty-eight feet). The building, completed in November 1834, was put to immediate use by the Saints in Kirtland. The first story housed the School of the Prophets, and the upper story housed the printing press. Other rooms in the building were used as offices for the First Presidency and other Church functions.[13]

In 1837–38 a serious apostasy occurred in Kirtland, and Joseph Smith was forced to flee. Some of Joseph's enemies sought to use the printing office and its materials to set up an organization opposed to the work of the Prophet. To defy the apostates, who intended to seize the printing office, the building was set on fire by Lyman Sherman, a Church member who remained loyal to Joseph Smith (see Doctrine and Covenants 108). The printing office and its equipment were completely destroyed in the fire.[14]

> 13 And on the third lot shall my servant Hyrum Smith receive his inheritance.
>
> 14 And on the first and second lots on the north shall my servants Reynolds Cahoon and Jared Carter receive their inheritances—
>
> 15 That they may do the work which I have appointed unto them, to be a committee to build mine houses, according to the commandment, which I, the Lord God, have given unto you.
>
> 16 These two houses are not to be built until I give unto you a commandment concerning them.
>
> 17 And now I give unto you no more at this time. Amen.

Construction of the Kirtland Temple drained the already-limited resources of the Saints, and they were unable to build the house of the Presidency (see Doctrine and Covenants 94:3) and the house for printing scriptures (see Doctrine and Covenants 94:10). A smaller building housed both functions until it was destroyed in 1838. However, the three priorities associated with these houses are reflected in the later cities of Zion built by the Saints. At Church headquarters today there is a house of the Lord (the Salt Lake Temple), a house for the Presidency (the Church Administration Building), and a house for printing scriptures (the Church Office Building). Each of these buildings has evolved beyond its original intended use in the stake of Zion in Kirtland. The house of the Lord now houses the sacred ordinances made possible by the keys given in the Kirtland Temple. The Church Administration Building currently houses the offices of not only the First Presidency but also the Quorum of the Twelve Apostles and many other General Officers of the Church. Finally, not just in the Church Office Building but in many facilities around the world, the scriptures are printed, filmed, and sent forth to the world in ways not dreamt of by the Kirtland Saints.

End Notes

1. See Plan of the House of the Lord, between 1 and 25 June 1833, josephsmithpapers.org; and Plat of the City of Zion, circa Early June–25 June 1833, josephsmithpapers.org.
2. Joseph Smith, in History, 1838–1856, volume A-1 [23 December 1805–30 August 1834], 291, josephsmithpapers.org. The Prophet's history, written several years after this revelation was given, gives the incorrect date for this revelation as May 6, 1833. According to available evidence, the revelation was most likely received later that summer on August 2, 1833.
3. Revelation Book 2, 64, josephsmithpapers.org.
4. See Letter to Church Leaders in Jackson County, Missouri, 6 August 1833, josephsmithpapers.org.
5. See Doctrine and Covenants, 1835, 213, josephsmithpapers.org.
6. See "Historical Introduction," Revelation, 2 August 1833–B [D&C 94], josephsmithpapers.org.
7. Letterbook 1, 40, josephsmithpapers.org.
8. See Plat of the City of Zion, circa Early June–25 June 1833, josephsmithpapers.org.
9. Joseph Smith, in History, 1838–1856, volume C-1 [2 November 1838–31 July 1842], 1186, josephsmithpapers.org.
10. See "Temple Chronology," Temples of the Church of Jesus Christ of Latter-day Saints, accessed Apr. 21, 2021, https://churchofjesuschristtemples.org/temples/chronology/.
11. *General Handbook: Serving in The Church of Jesus Christ of Latter-day Saints*, 18.15, Gospel Library.
12. See Letter to Church Leaders in Jackson County, Missouri, 6 August 1833, 3, josephsmithpapers.org.
13. See Lyndon W. Cook, *The Revelations of the Prophet Joseph Smith: A Historical and Biographical Commentary of the Doctrine and Covenants* (Salt Lake City, UT: Deseret Book, 1985), 196–97.
14. See Lyndon W. Cook, "Lyman Sherman—Man of God, Would-Be Apostle," *BYU Studies* 19, no. 1 (Fall 1978): 123.

Doctrine and Covenants Section 95

Whom I Love I Also Chasten

Historical Context

JOSEPH SMITH RECEIVED THIS REVELATION SEVERAL MONTHS AFTER THE
Lord gave a command to organize a "school of the prophets" (Doctrine and
Covenants 88:11–27) and to "establish a house, even a house of prayer, a
house of fasting, a house of faith, a house of learning, a house of glory, a house
of order, a house of God" (Doctrine and Covenants 88:119). Emphasizing
the importance of fulfilling these commandments, Joseph Smith wrote to
William W. Phelps shortly after section 88 was received, telling him:

> You will see that the Lord commanded us in Kirtland to build an house
> of God, & establish a school for the Prophets, this is the word of the Lord
> to us, and we must—yea[,] the Lord helping us[,] we will obey, as on
> conditions of our obedience, he has promised us great things, yea[,] even
> a visit from the heavens to honor us with his own presence, we greatly fear
> before the Lord lest we should fail of this great honor which our master

proposes to confer on us, we are seeking for humility & great faith lest we be ashamed in his presence.[1]

A few months later on May 4, 1833, a conference of high priests held a discussion about the "necessity of building a school house for the purpose of accommodating the elders who should come in to receive their education for the ministry."[2] At this conference Hyrum Smith, Jared Carter, and Reynolds Cahoon were appointed to a committee for procuring donations from Church members to raise funds to build the "school house," which eventually became the Kirtland Temple. About a month later on June 1, 1833, this committee wrote a letter to the entire Church, asking the following:

> That they make every possible exertion to aid temporally as well as spiritually in this great work that the Lord is bringing about and is about to accomplish. And unless we fulfil this command, vis. establish an house and prepare all things necessary whereby the Elders may gather into a school called the School of the prophets and receive that instruction that the Lord designs they should receive, we may all despair of obtaining the great blessing that God has promised to the faithful of the Church of Christ. Therefore, it is as important as our salvation that we obey this above-mentioned command as well as all of the commandments of the Lord.[3]

Section 95 was received the same day that the committee's letter was sent out. It chastens the Saints for neglecting the commandment to build the house of the Lord. In Joseph Smith's later history he introduced the revelation by writing, "Great preparations were making to commence a house for the Lord; and, notwithstanding the church was poor, yet, our unity, harmony and charity abounded to strengthen us to do the commandments of the Lord. . . . The building of the House of the Lord in Kirtland continued to increase its interest in the hearts of the brethren, and the building committee issued the following circular to the different branches of the Church. . . . The same day I received the following [Doctrine and Covenants 94]."[4]

Verse-by-Verse Commentary

1 Verily, thus saith the Lord unto you whom I love, and whom I love I also chasten that their sins may be forgiven, for with the

chastisement I prepare a way for their deliverance in all things out of temptation, and I have loved you—

2 Wherefore, ye must needs be chastened and stand rebuked before my face;

3 For ye have sinned against me a very grievous sin, in that ye have not considered the great commandment in all things, that I have given unto you concerning the building of mine house;

4 For the preparation wherewith I design to prepare mine apostles to prune my vineyard for the last time, that I may bring to pass my strange act, that I may pour out my Spirit upon all flesh—

5 But behold, verily I say unto you, that there are many who have been ordained among you, whom I have called but few of them are chosen.

6 They who are not chosen have sinned a very grievous sin, in that they are walking in darkness at noon-day.

The Lord chastens the Saints for their slothfulness in beginning the work of building the house of the Lord in Kirtland. In March 1833 Levi Hancock captured in his journal some of the frustration felt by Church leaders due to the Saints' lack of initiative to build the temple. He wrote that the Church members in Kirtland "had no place to worship in." Hancock noted that "Jared Carter went around with a subscription paper to get signers. I signed two dollars. He made up a little over thirty and presented it to Joseph—the Lord would not accept it and gave a command to build a temple."[5]

According to Lucy Mack Smith, the Saints in Kirtland also equivocated regarding the importance of the structure they were building. She recorded the following:

A council was called and Joseph requested the brethren[,] each one[,] to rise and give his views. After they were through he would give his opinion [on what] they all spoke. Some thought that it would be better to build a frame [house]. Others said that a frame was too costly kind [sic] of a house, and the majority concluded upon the putting up a log house and made their calculations about what they could do towards building it. Joseph rose and reminded them that they were not making a house for themselves or any other man but a house for God. Joseph then declared, "Shall we brethren build a house for our God of logs? No, brethren, I have a better plan than that[;] I have the plan of the house of the Lord given by himself." . . . [Joseph] then gave them the plan in full of the house of the Lord at Kirtland with which[,] when the brethren heard[,] they were highly delighted.[6]

The use of *apostle* in verse 4 most likely reflects the general meaning of the term as "one sent forth," since the first Quorum of the Twelve was called nearly two years after section 95 was received. However, the Lord emphasizes the importance of the temple in "bring[ing] to pass my strange act, that I may pour out my Spirit upon all flesh" (verse 4). The priesthood keys given to Joseph Smith in the Kirtland Temple continue to play a key role in the work of the Church around the world.

> 7 And for this cause I gave unto you a commandment that you should call your solemn assembly, that your fastings and your mourning might come up into the ears of the Lord of Sabaoth, which is by interpretation, the creator of the first day, the beginning and the end.
>
> 8 Yea, verily I say unto you, I gave unto you a commandment that you should build a house, in the which house I design to endow those whom I have chosen with power from on high;
>
> 9 For this is the promise of the Father unto you; therefore I command you to tarry, even as mine apostles at Jerusalem.
>
> 10 Nevertheless, my servants sinned a very grievous sin; and contentions arose in the school of the prophets; which was very grievous unto me, saith your Lord; therefore I sent them forth to be chastened.

In many of the documents linked to this time, the house of the Lord is referred to as a school or a schoolhouse.[7] When it was completed, the Kirtland Temple was used as a multipurpose structure not only for education but also for administration and for worship. Here the Lord emphasizes the endowment that He will give to the Saints within the Kirtland Temple. While this endowment was different than the later ordinance revealed in Nauvoo that is practiced in temples today, the Kirtland endowment ceremony was a vital source of strength to those who participated in it. In a larger sense, the spiritual outpouring that accompanied the dedication of the

Kirtland Temple served as an endowment of sorts to the entire community of Saints in Kirtland.

Elder Orson Pratt, a participant in both the Kirtland endowment ceremony and the Pentecostal season during the temple's dedication, later recalled, "God was there, his angels were there, the Holy Ghost was in the midst of the people . . . and they were filled from the crown of their heads to the soles of their feet with the power and inspiration of the Holy Ghost."[8]

> 11 Verily I say unto you, it is my will that you should build a house. If you keep my commandments you shall have power to build it.
>
> 12 If you keep not my commandments, the love of the Father shall not continue with you, therefore you shall walk in darkness.
>
> 13 Now here is wisdom, and the mind of the Lord—let the house be built, not after the manner of the world, for I give not unto you that ye shall live after the manner of the world;
>
> 14 Therefore, let it be built after the manner which I shall show unto three of you, whom ye shall appoint and ordain unto this power.
>
> 15 And the size thereof shall be fifty and five feet in width, and let it be sixty-five feet in length, in the inner court thereof.
>
> 16 And let the lower part of the inner court be dedicated unto me for your sacrament offering, and for your preaching, and your fasting, and your praying, and the offering up of your most holy desires unto me, saith your Lord.
>
> 17 And let the higher part of the inner court be dedicated unto me for the school of mine apostles, saith Son Ahman; or, in other words, Alphus; or, in other words, Omegus; even Jesus Christ your Lord. Amen.

In contrast to the suggestions of some Church members to build the temple as a frame house or even a log cabin, the Lord declares that the temple shall "be built after the manner which I shall show unto three of you, whom ye shall appoint and ordain unto this power" (verse 14). The Lord fulfilled this promise when He gave a remarkable vision on June 3 or 4 to Joseph Smith, Sidney Rigdon, and Frederick G. Williams. Williams described this vision to laborers at the temple: "Carpenter Rolph said, 'Doctor [Williams], what do you think of the house?' [Williams] answered, 'It looks to me like the pattern precisely.'" Williams then related the following:

> Joseph [Smith] received the word of the Lord for him to take his two counselors, Williams and Rigdon, and come before the Lord, and He would show them the plan or model of the house to be built. We went upon our knees, called on the Lord, and the building appeared within viewing distance, I being the first to discover it. Then we all viewed it together. After we had taken a good look at the exterior, the building seemed to come right over us, and the makeup of the Hall seemed to coincide with that I there saw to a minutiae.[9]

Orson Pratt also confirmed the visionary origins of the Kirtland Temple's design. In a discourse given in 1871, Elder Pratt declared, "When the Lord commanded this people to build a house in the land of Kirtland, he gave them the pattern by vision from heaven, and commanded them to build that house according to that pattern and order; to have the architecture, not in accordance with architecture devised by men, but to have everything constructed in that house according to the heavenly pattern that he by his voice had inspired to his servants."[10]

End Notes

1. Letter to William W. Phelps, 11 January 1833, 19, josephsmithpapers.org.
2. Minutes, 4 May 1833, 20, josephsmithpapers.org.
3. Letter Book 1, 36–37, josephsmithpapers.org; punctuation modernized.
4. Joseph Smith, in History, 1838–1856, volume A-1 [23 December 1805–30 August 1834], 296–299, josephsmithpapers.org. See also "Historical Introduction," Revelation, 1 June 1833 [D&C 95], josephsmithpapers. org.
5. Robert J. Woodford, "The Historical Development of the Doctrine and Covenants" (Provo, UT: Brigham Young University dissertation, 1974), 2:1222.
6. "Book 14," Lucy Mack Smith, History, 1844–1845, 1, josephsmithpapers.org.
7. See, for example, Minutes, 4 May 1833, 20, josephsmithpapers.org.
8. Orson Pratt, "Remarks," *Deseret News,* Jan. 12, 1876, 788.
9. Elwin C. Robinson, *The First Mormon Temple: Design, Construction, and Historic Context of the Kirtland Temple* (Provo, UT: Brigham Young University Press, 1997), 8.
10. Orson Pratt, in *Journal of Discourses,* 14:273.

$\mathcal{D}$octrine and $\mathcal{C}$ovenants Section 96

For the Strength of Zion

$\mathcal{H}$istorical $\mathcal{C}$ontext

AT A CONFERENCE OF HIGH PRIESTS HELD AT NEWEL K. WHITNEY'S STORE in Kirtland, Ohio, on March 23, 1833, those in attendance discussed acquiring more land to accommodate Church growth in the Kirtland area. Several farms were considered during the meeting, the largest of which was the Peter French farm of 103 acres. It was reported that "Peter French would sell his farm for five thousand dollars" during the meeting.[1]

A few months later, some still disagreed about who should be put in charge of the Church-purchased properties, and another conference was held. The minutes of the conference state, "A conference of high Priests met in Kirtland on the 4th of June 1833—in the translating room and took into consideration how the French farm should be disposed of[;] the council could not agree who should take the charge of it but all agreed to enquire of the lord[;] accordingly we received a revelation which decided that [Brother]

N[ewel] K Whitney should take the charge thereof and also that Brother John Johnson be admitted as a member of the united firm[;] accordingly[,] he was ordained unto the high Priesthood and admitted."[2]

The Church purchased the farm, and over the next few years it became the site of many houses and community buildings, including a new schoolhouse and the Kirtland Temple.[3]

Verse-by-Verse Commentary

1 Behold, I say unto you, here is wisdom, whereby ye may know how to act concerning this matter, for it is expedient in me that this stake that I have set for the strength of Zion should be made strong.

2 Therefore, let my servant Newel K. Whitney take charge of the place which is named among you, upon which I design to build mine holy house.

3 And again, let it be divided into lots, according to wisdom, for the benefit of those who seek inheritances, as it shall be determined in council among you.

4 Therefore, take heed that ye see to this matter, and that portion that is necessary to benefit mine order, for the purpose of bringing forth my word to the children of men.

5 For behold, verily I say unto you, this is the most expedient in me, that my word should go forth unto the children of men, for the purpose of subduing the hearts of the children of men for your good. Even so. Amen.

During this time, there were only two stakes in the Church, one in Ohio and one in Missouri. Edward Partridge was appointed to serve as the bishop in Missouri (see Doctrine and Covenants 58:14–17) while Newel K. Whitney served as the bishop in Ohio (see Doctrine and Covenants 72:7–8). Bishop Whitney's assignment to take charge of the land mentioned in verses 2 and 3 is an early indication of the role that the Presiding Bishopric would eventually fill within the Church. The role of the Presiding Bishopric is further explained in Doctrine and Covenants 107, which teaches that "the office of the bishop is in administering in all temporal things" (Doctrine and Covenants 107:68).

Today the Presiding Bishopric takes the lead in overseeing the temporal affairs of the Church, including the construction of temples. Some of the roles filled by the Presiding Bishop include "involvement in receiving, distributing, and accounting for member tithes, offerings, and contributions; administration of programs to assist the poor and needy; design, construction, and maintenance of places of worship; and auditing and transferring records of membership. Men chosen to be Presiding Bishops have been recognized for their business and management skills as well as their religious commitment."[4]

> 6 And again, verily I say unto you, it is wisdom and expedient in me, that my servant John Johnson whose offering I have accepted, and whose prayers I have heard, unto whom I give a promise of eternal life inasmuch as he keepeth my commandments from henceforth—
>
> 7 For he is a descendant of Joseph and a partaker of the blessings of the promise made unto his fathers—
>
> 8 Verily I say unto you, it is expedient in me that he should become a member of the order, that he may assist in bringing forth my word unto the children of men.
>
> 9 Therefore ye shall ordain him unto this blessing, and he shall seek diligently to take away incumbrances that are upon the house named among you, that he may dwell therein. Even so. Amen.

John Johnson is highlighted here for his faithfulness, and Joseph Smith is directed to make Johnson part of the United Firm, or united order. Because of his generosity, Johnson was already a key figure in several important events in Church history. The conference that discussed publishing Joseph Smith's revelations was held at his home in Hiram, Ohio. Joseph Smith and Sidney Rigdon spent much of the winter of 1831–32 staying with Johnson's family and working on the new translation of the Bible. In the Johnson home in February 1832, Joseph and Sidney saw their vision of the three degrees of glory. Later Joseph and Sidney were tarred and feathered by an angry mob that dragged the Prophet from the Johnson home. During the attack, Johnson, armed only with a club, bravely rushed into the midst of the mob that was accosting Sidney. In the melee Johnson was knocked down and broke his collarbone. He was later given a blessing by David Whitmer and recovered.[5]

Johnson later relocated to Kirtland and opened an inn near the Newel K. Whitney store. In the inn he displayed the mummies and papyri purchased from Michael Chandler that were associated with the book of Abraham. Two of Johnson's sons, Luke and Lyman, were chosen as members of the original Quorum of the Twelve Apostles. Johnson also served as a member of the Kirtland high council when it was formed in February 1834.

Unfortunately, Johnson and his sons became disaffected from the Church during the Kirtland apostasy of 1837–38. He withdrew from the Church, dying in Kirtland in 1843. Lyman Johnson, an Apostle, also withdrew from the Church during this time and never returned. One son from the Johnson family, Luke, did return to the Church, though he was never placed back into the Quorum of the Twelve. John Johnson's wife, Elsa, withdrew from Church fellowship in 1838 but lived close to her daughter Emily, who continued to worship with the Saints who remained in Kirtland. After Emily's death in 1855, Elsa and her remaining sons traveled from Kirtland to Iowa. Elsa died in Iowa while traveling to the West. The oldest daughter of the Johnsons, also named Elsa, remained in the Church and passed away in Nauvoo. Another daughter, Nancy Marinda Hyde, remained in the Church, traveling to Salt Lake City where she remained stalwart in the Church until her passing in 1886.[6]

End Notes

1. French Farm, Kirtland Township, Ohio, josephsmithpapers.org.

2. Minutes, 4 June 1833, 13, josephsmithpapers.org. See also History, 1838–1856, volume A-1 [23 December 1805–30 August 1834], 301, josephsmithpapers.org.

3. See "Historical Introduction," Revelation, 4 June 1833 [D&C 96], josephsmithpapers.org.

4. "Presiding Bishopric," last modified July 13, 2023, newsroom. ChurchofJesusChrist.org.

5. See Mark Staker, *Hearken, O Ye People: The Historical Setting of Joseph Smith's Ohio Revelations* (Sandy, UT: Greg Kofford Books, 2010), 352–53.

6. See Susan Easton Black, *Who's Who in the Doctrine & Covenants* (Salt Lake City, UT: Bookcraft, 1997), 152–53; "Biography: Johnson, John," Joseph Smith Papers, accessed Feb. 19, 2023, https://www.josephsmithpapers. org/person/john-johnson; Lyndon W. Cook, *The Revelations of the Prophet Joseph Smith: A Historical and Biographical Commentary of the Doctrine and Covenants* (Salt Lake City, UT: Deseret Book, 1985), 199; "Biography: Hyde, Marinda Nancy Johnson," Joseph Smith Papers, accessed Feb. 19, 2023, https://www.josephsmithpapers.org/person/ marinda-nancy-johnson-hyde; Curtis Ashton, "Kirtland through the Eyes of the John and Elsa Johnson Family," Church History, Mar. 4, 2019.

$\mathcal{D}$octrine and $\mathcal{C}$ovenants
Section 97
Zion Is the Pure in Heart

$\mathcal{H}$istorical $\mathcal{C}$ontext

PARLEY P. PRATT REPORTED THAT BY THE SUMMER OF 1833, "IMMIGRATION had poured into [Jackson County, Missouri] in great numbers; and the Church in that county now numbered upwards of one thousand souls."[1] In July 1833 two letters, one from Oliver Cowdery and one from the "brethren composing the school," arrived in Kirtland. Neither of these letters remains today. From the context of the letters, it appears that the Saints in Missouri desired for Joseph Smith to ask the Lord for revelation concerning the school in Zion. In response, Joseph and other Church leaders inquired and received this revelation, which was sent to the members of the Church in Missouri as part of a larger letter that also contained two more revelations, now Doctrine and Covenants 94 and 98.

The revelation in section 97 follows up on earlier plans sent to the members of the Church in Zion instructing them to build a temple and begin laying plans for the city of Zion.[2] This revelation contains strong warnings that if the Saints did not heed these commandments and begin work on the temple, they might face severe trials. The Lord warns, "The ax is laid at the root of the trees; and every tree that bringeth forth not good fruit shall be hewn down and cast into the fire" (Doctrine and Covenants 97:7).

At the time this revelation was given, the leaders of the Church in Kirtland did not know that violence against the Saints had already broken out in Missouri. On July 20, 1833, an armed mob sanctioned by state Lieutenant Governor Lilburn W. Boggs sent a demand to Church members to leave Jackson County. The mob ransacked the home of William W. Phelps and destroyed the unbound copies of the Book of Commandments, an early version of the Doctrine and Covenants, that were in the Church's printing office inside the Phelps's home. The mob also threw the printing press from the upper window of the home. John Whitmer, or some other Church employee, managed to save the manuscript revelation books, and Phelps, along with a handful of Church members, saved some of the printed copies of the revelations.[3] During the confusion, Mary Elizabeth Rollins and her sister Caroline also ran in, snatched a few unbound copies of the revelations, and hid in a nearby cornfield to escape the mob.[4]

The mob also plundered the store owned by Sidney Gilbert and then tarred and feathered Bishop Edward Partridge and Charles Allen. The damage only ceased when Church leaders, under threat of more violence from the mob, signed an agreement for all Saints to leave Jackson County by January 1, 1834. Seeking help, the Saints in Missouri dispatched Oliver Cowdery to travel to Ohio to seek assistance.[5] It is possible that Joseph Smith may have known of the trouble brewing in Jackson County from a letter, now lost, that Oliver Cowdery wrote to him on July 9. However, given the communications of the time, it is impossible that Joseph could have known that the storm had broken in its full fury upon the Saints in Missouri by August 6, when Joseph sent the letter containing Doctrine and Covenants 94, 97, and 98 to the Saints in Zion. The warnings in this revelation take on a more poignant tone, knowing that the Lord was aware of the danger facing the Saints in Missouri.[6]

Verse-by-Verse Commentary

1 Verily I say unto you my friends, I speak unto you with my voice, even the voice of my Spirit, that I may show unto you my will concerning your brethren in the land of Zion, many of whom are truly humble and are seeking diligently to learn wisdom and to find truth.

2 Verily, verily I say unto you, blessed are such, for they shall obtain; for I, the Lord, show mercy unto all the meek, and upon all whomsoever I will, that I may be justified when I shall bring them unto judgment.

While this revelation generally reproves the Saints in Missouri, the Lord does begin the revelation by proclaiming that many of them are truly humble and are seeking to "learn wisdom and find truth" (verse 1). Among the Missouri Saints who should be commended for their integrity in the face of persecution were two of the three witnesses of the Book of Mormon, Oliver Cowdery and David Whitmer. William McLellin, who was in Jackson County during the persecutions, later recounted:

> In 1833, when the mobbing reigned triumphant in Jackson Co., [Missouri], I and O[liver] fled from our homes, for fear of personal violence. . . . They offered eighty dollars reward for any one who would deliver Cowdery or McLellin in Independence. . . . I slipped down into the Whitmer's settlement, and there in the lonely woods I met with David Whitmer and Oliver Cowdery. I said to them, "Brethren, I have never seen an open vision in my life, but you men say you have, and therefore you positively know. Now you know that our lives are in danger every hour, if the mob can only catch us. Tell me in the fear of God, is that book of Mormon true?" Cowdery looked at me with solemnity depicted in his face, and said, "Brother William, God sent his holy angel to declare the truth of the translation to us, and therefore we know. And though the mob kill us, yet we must die declaring its truth." David said, "Oliver has told you the solemn truth, for we could not be deceived. I most truly declare to you its truth!!" Said I, "boys, I believe you. I can see no object for you to tell me falsehood now, when our lives are endangered."[7]

During this time, McLellin also recorded a mob attack on Hiram Page, one of the eight witnesses of the Book of Mormon. He wrote:

While the mob was raging in Jackson Co., [Missouri,] in 1833 some young men ran down Hiram Page in the woods, one of the eight witnesses, and commenced beating and pounding him with whips and clubs. He begged, but there was no mercy. They said he was a damned Mormon, and they meant to beat him to death! But finally one of them said to him, "If you will deny that damned book, we will let you go." Said he, "How can I deny what I know to be true?" Then they pounded him again. When they thought he was about to breathe his last, they said to him, "Now what do you think of your God, and when he don't save you?" "Well," said he, "I believe in God"—"Well," said one of the most intelligent among them, "I believe the damned fool will stick to it though we kill him. Let us let him go." But his life was nearly run out. He was confined to his bed for a length of time. So much for a man who knows for himself. Knowledge is beyond faith or doubt. It is positive certainty.[8]

While the Saints in Missouri were reproved by the Lord for their transgressions (see Doctrine and Covenants 101:1–8), it is important to remember that many were faithful to their testimonies. The persecutions in Missouri came about through a mixture of the Saints' transgressions and the bigotry and intolerance of the original settlers of Jackson County who saw the infusion of the Saints into the region as a threat to their political power.

Citing the sources of the outside opposition to the Saints, Parley P. Pratt later wrote, "The portion of the inhabitants of Jackson County which did not belong to the Church, became jealous of our growing influence and numbers. Political demagogues were afraid we should rule the county; and religious priests and bigots felt we were powerful rivals, and about to excel all other societies in the state in numbers, and in power and influence. These feelings, and the false statements and influences growing out of them, gave rise to the organization of a company of outlaws, whose avowed object was to drive the Church of the Saints from the county."[9]

> 3 Behold, I say unto you, concerning the school in Zion, I, the Lord, am well pleased that there should be a school in Zion, and also with my servant Parley P. Pratt, for he abideth in me.
>
> 4 And inasmuch as he continueth to abide in me he shall continue to preside over the school in the land of Zion until I shall give unto him other commandments.

5 And I will bless him with a multiplicity of blessings, in expounding all scriptures and mysteries to the edification of the school, and of the church in Zion.

6 And to the residue of the school, I, the Lord, am willing to show mercy; nevertheless, there are those that must needs be chastened, and their works shall be made known.

During this same time, Parley P. Pratt helped set up a School of the Elders (Prophets) among the Saints in Missouri in accordance with instructions given in Doctrine and Covenants 88. Parley later recorded:

> This class, to the number of about sixty, met for instruction once a week. The place of meeting was in the open air, under some tall trees, in a retired place in the wilderness, where we prayed, preached and prophesied, and exercised ourselves in the gifts of the Holy Spirit. Here great blessings were poured out, and many great and marvelous things were manifested and taught. The Lord gave me great wisdom, and enabled me to teach and edify the Elders, and comfort and encourage them in their preparations for the work which lay before us. I was also much edified and strengthened. To attend this school I had to travel on foot, and sometimes with bare feet at that, about six miles. This I did once a week, besides visiting and preaching in five or six branches a week.[10]

The School of the Elders that Parley P. Pratt conducted was another example of the good that was happening among the Saints in Zion. Though the Lord reproved and chastened some of the members of the school, Parley was commended for his work. God promised him a "multiplicity of blessings, in expounding all scriptures and mysteries to the edification of the school" (verse 5). This promise can broadly apply to all those who teach in the Church, whether they teach adults, youth, or children. Multiple passages in the Doctrine and Covenants highlight the importance of teaching (see Doctrine and Covenants 42:12; 68:25; 88:77; 93:42), and in a larger sense, every member of the Church is a teacher. In the New Testament, Paul placed the role of teachers behind only prophets and apostles (see 1 Corinthians 12:28).[11]

7 The ax is laid at the root of the trees; and every tree that bringeth not forth good fruit shall be hewn down and cast into the fire. I, the Lord, have spoken it.

8 Verily I say unto you, all among them who know their hearts are honest, and are broken, and their spirits contrite, and are willing to observe their covenants by sacrifice—yea, every sacrifice which I, the Lord, shall command—they are accepted of me.

9 For I, the Lord, will cause them to bring forth as a very fruitful tree which is planted in a goodly land, by a pure stream, that yieldeth much precious fruit.

After commending the humble and the faithful in Zion, the Lord turns to the most immediate and ominous part of His message in this section: Zion is in danger. The wording used in verses 7–9 closely parallels the warnings given by John the Baptist in the New Testament (see Matthew 3:10; Luke 3:9) and Alma the Younger in the Book of Mormon (see Alma 5:52). Alma and John both present their warnings in the shadow of the coming of the true Messiah, and in Alma's case, the great wars with the Lamanites contained in the latter part of the book of Alma.

In this case, the ax had already begun to cut into the tree, and the Saints were in the midst of serious opposition already. The Lord provides this warning with an accompanying chance to repent if the Saints will unite and begin their work on the temple in Zion. Parley P. Pratt later noted with some sorrow, "This revelation [Doctrine and Covenants 97] was not complied with by the leaders and Church in Missouri, as a whole; notwithstanding many were humble and faithful. Therefore, the threatened judgment was poured out to the uttermost, as the history of the five following years (1833–38) will show."[12]

10 Verily I say unto you, that it is my will that a house should be built unto me in the land of Zion, like unto the pattern which I have given you.

11 Yea, let it be built speedily, by the tithing of my people.

12 Behold, this is the tithing and the sacrifice which I, the Lord, require at their hands, that there may be a house built unto me for the salvation of Zion—

13 For a place of thanksgiving for all saints, and for a place of instruction for all those who are called to the work of the ministry in all their several callings and offices;

14 That they may be perfected in the understanding of their ministry, in theory, in principle, and in doctrine, in all things pertaining to the kingdom of God on the earth, the keys of which kingdom have been conferred upon you.

15 And inasmuch as my people build a house unto me in the name of the Lord, and do not suffer any unclean thing to come into it, that it be not defiled, my glory shall rest upon it;

16 Yea, and my presence shall be there, for I will come into it, and all the pure in heart that shall come into it shall see God.

17 But if it be defiled I will not come into it, and my glory shall not be there; for I will not come into unholy temples.

Plans for the city of Zion sent in June, August, and November 1833 all included a complex of twenty-four temples at the heart of the city.[13] However, the Saints had to begin building the complex with one structure, and plans were sent to the Saints in Missouri for this first temple in June and August 1833. This temple's plans resembled the Kirtland Temple in many ways. The interior of the temple would have featured a large congregational meeting space with twelve pulpits representing different offices within the greater and the lesser priesthood at each end of the room.[14]

The plans were sent to the Missouri Saints in early June 1833, but they took no action before the mob attacks began on the Saints the following month. If the Saints in Missouri had complied with these revelations, the city may have been built (see Doctrine and Covenants 95:18, 25–26). However, the Saints failed to comply, and the Lord, accepting the offerings and sacrifices of the Saints as sufficient to demonstrate repentance for their failure to build the first temple in Missouri, later removed the commandment to build the city (see Doctrine and Covenants 124:49–51).

18 And, now, behold, if Zion do these things she shall prosper, and spread herself and become very glorious, very great, and very terrible.

19 And the nations of the earth shall honor her, and shall say: Surely Zion is the city of our God, and surely Zion cannot fall, neither be moved out of her place, for God is there, and the hand of the Lord is there;

20 And he hath sworn by the power of his might to be her salvation and her high tower.

21 Therefore, verily, thus saith the Lord, let Zion rejoice, for this is Zion—the pure in heart; therefore, let Zion rejoice, while all the wicked shall mourn.

Even though the land for the city of Zion and its accompanying temples was identified by revelation, the land itself was not the most important component of the city. Ultimately, a city consists of people. Take away the material things, and if the people are united, the city remains. When the city of Enoch was taken up into heaven (see Moses 7:69), we assume a large hole was not left in the ground. Likewise, when Melchizedek and the city of Salem were taken up by God (see Joseph Smith Translation, Genesis 14:34 [in the Bible appendix]), the land where the later city of Jerusalem was built remained. Zion is a people.

However, the land that the Lord designates as Zion is important. The Lord later decrees that "Zion shall not be moved out of her place, notwithstanding her children are scattered" (Doctrine and Covenants 101:17). The Saints will yet return to Missouri and build the city of Zion in its foreordained place. In verse 21 the Lord reminds the Saints that even though they possessed the land of Zion at the time of the revelation, they had not built the city. All the Saints are to build the city in their hearts before the physical city can come into being. In this sense, the city of Zion will be built throughout the world, in all the communities in which the pure in heart dwell, particularly among the Latter-day Saints.

22 For behold, and lo, vengeance cometh speedily upon the ungodly as the whirlwind; and who shall escape it?

23 The Lord's scourge shall pass over by night and by day, and the report thereof shall vex all people; yea, it shall not be stayed until the Lord come;

24 For the indignation of the Lord is kindled against their abominations and all their wicked works.

25 Nevertheless, Zion shall escape if she observe to do all things whatsoever I have commanded her.

26 But if she observe not to do whatsoever I have commanded her, I will visit her according to all her works, with sore afflic-

tion, with pestilence, with plague, with sword, with vengeance, with devouring fire.

27 Nevertheless, let it be read this once to her ears, that I, the Lord, have accepted of her offering; and if she sin no more none of these things shall come upon her;

28 And I will bless her with blessings, and multiply a multiplicity of blessings upon her, and upon her generations forever and ever, saith the Lord your God. Amen.

When initial persecutions erupted in Jackson County, no one could have conceived how long and difficult the road would be to redeem Zion. Almost two centuries later, we are still looking toward building the New Jerusalem. A few months before the persecutions against the Saints in Missouri began, Joseph Smith wrote to them, desperately seeking for them to repent before the window of opportunity to build the city of Zion closed. In January 1833, seven months before the mob attacks began in force, Joseph wrote:

The Lord will have a place from whence his word will go forth in these last days in purity, for if Zion, will not purify herself so as to be approved of in all things[,] in his sight he will seek—another people[,] for his work will go on until Israel is gathered, and they who will not hear his voice must expect to feel his wrath. Let me say to you, seek to purify yourselves, and also all the inhabitants of Zion, lest the Lord's anger be kindled to fierceness.

Repent, repent, is the voice of God, to Zion, and yet strange as it may appear, yet it is true[,] mankind will persist in self-justification until all their iniquity is exposed and their character past being redeemed, and that which is treasured up in their hearts be exposed to the gaze of mankind, I say to you—(& what I say to you, I say to all) hear the warning voice of God lest Zion fall, and the Lord swear in his wrath. . . . The brethren in Kirtland pray for you unceasingly, for knowing the terrors of the Lord, they greatly fear for you. . . . All we can say by way of conclusion is, if the fountain of our tears are [*sic*] not dried up[,] we will still weep for Zion, this from your brother who trembles greatly for Zion—and for the wrath of heaven which awaits her if she repent not.[15]

End Notes

1. Parley P. Pratt, *Autobiography of Parley P. Pratt (Revised and Enhanced)* (Salt Lake City, UT: Deseret Book, 2000), 112–13.

2. See Plan of the House of the Lord, between 1 and 25 June 1833, josephsmithpapers.org; and Plat of the City of Zion, circa Early June–25 June 1833, josephsmithpapers.org.

3. See Bruce Van Orden, *We'll Sing and We'll Shout: The Life and Times of W. W. Phelps* (Salt Lake City, UT: Deseret Book, 2018), 100–102.

4. See "Autobiography of Mary E. Lightner," *The Utah Genealogical and Historical Magazine* 17 (July 1926): 193–205.

5. See B. H. Roberts, *The Missouri Persecutions* (Salt Lake City, UT: Bookcraft, 1965), 90.

6. See Stephen E. Robinson and H. Dean Garrett, *A Commentary on the Doctrine and Covenants* (Salt Lake City, UT: Deseret Book, 2000), 3:217–18. See also "Historical Introduction," Revelation, 2 August 1833–A [D&C 97], josephsmithpapers.org.

7. *William E. McLellin's Lost Manuscript*, ed. Mitchell K. Schaefer (Salt Lake City, UT: Eborn Books, 2012), 166–67; spelling and punctuation modernized, emphasis in original.

8. *William E. McLellin's Lost Manuscript*, 166–67; spelling and punctuation modernized, emphasis in original.

9. Parley P. Pratt, *Autobiography of Parley P. Pratt*, 116.

10. Parley P. Pratt, *Autobiography of Parley P. Pratt*, 113.

11. See Joseph Fielding McConkie and Craig J. Ostler, *Revelations of the Restoration* (Salt Lake City, UT: Deseret Book, 2000), 702.

12. Parley P. Pratt, *Autobiography of Parley P. Pratt*, 115–16.

13. See Plat of the City of Zion, circa Early June–25 June 1833; Revised Plat of the City of Zion, circa Early August 1833; and Proposal for Zion's City Center from Edward Partridge, circa Late September 1833, josephsmithpapers.org.

14. See Plan of the House of the Lord, between 1 and 25 June 1833, josephsmithpapers.org.

15. Letter to William W. Phelps, 11 January 1833, 19, josephsmithpapers.org.

Doctrine and Covenants Section 98

Renounce War and Proclaim Peace

Historical Context

THIS REVELATION CAME JUST OVER TWO WEEKS AFTER THE CHURCH PRINTing office was destroyed in Jackson County, Missouri. Joseph Smith knew about the increasing tensions in Missouri, but it is practically impossible that he knew just how bad things had become. On July 9, 1833, Oliver Cowdery wrote a letter—no longer in existence—explaining the worsening relations between the Saints and their neighbors in Jackson County. Oliver likely expressed concerns over growing violence in Missouri. These concerns prompted Joseph Smith to write back to Oliver in a letter dated August 6, 1833. The August 6, 1833, letter contained the revelations that were later canonized as Doctrine and Covenants 94, 97, and 98.[1] On July 15, 1833, shortly after Oliver sent his letter, a hostile group in Jackson County issued a manifesto declaring their intent to remove the Saints from the county "peaceably if we can, forcibly if we must."[2]

Although the Lord addresses the Kirtland Saints specifically in verses 19–21 and reproves them for their transgressions, it is likely that the instructions contained in Joseph's letter were intended not only for the Saints in Missouri but also for the members of the Church in Kirtland as well. During this time, opposition to the Church was intensifying in the area around Kirtland. In late June 1833 a bishop's court excommunicated Doctor Philastus Hurlbut, who then became a bitter enemy of the Church. In a different letter written a few days after this revelation, Joseph Smith wrote to leaders in Jackson County, telling them, "We are suffering great persecution on account of one man by the name of Doctor Hurlburt[,] who has been expelled from the church for lewd and adulterous conduct, and to spite us he is lying in a wonderful manner and the people are running after him and giving him money to brake [*sic*] down Mormonism[,] which much endangers our lives at present."[3]

With both Church centers coming under increasing opposition, the Lord provided counsel about how the Saints should respond to their enemies. Oliver Cowdery arrived in Kirtland, having traveled from Missouri, two days after this revelation was sent to the Saints in Zion. Oliver's arrival brought to light the full extent of the persecutions in Missouri. After hearing Oliver's report, Joseph Smith immediately dispatched Elders Orson Hyde and John Gould to provide assistance and support to the Saints in Missouri.[4] The difficulties surrounding the Saints in Missouri set off a chain of events that would occupy the Prophet's time for the next year as he labored to help the Saints gain redress and return to their homes in Jackson County.[5]

Verse-by-Verse Commentary

1 Verily I say unto you my friends, fear not, let your hearts be comforted; yea, rejoice evermore, and in everything give thanks;

2 Waiting patiently on the Lord, for your prayers have entered into the ears of the Lord of Sabaoth, and are recorded with this seal and testament—the Lord hath sworn and decreed that they shall be granted.

3 Therefore, he giveth this promise unto you, with an immutable covenant that they shall be fulfilled; and all things wherewith

you have been afflicted shall work together for your good, and to my name's glory, saith the Lord.

It is noteworthy that the first commandment the Lord gives to the Saints at this particularly trying time is "in everything give thanks" (verse 1). Even in the midst of our most severe trials, gratitude helps alleviate the pain and sorrow that we feel. When Job found himself in the midst of the most severe trials imaginable—so severe that his wife urged him to "curse God, and die"—Job responded, "Shall we receive good at the hand of God, and shall we not receive evil?" (Job 2:9–10). God later compared Joseph Smith to Job (see Doctrine and Covenants 121:10) and told Joseph that his adversity and afflictions would be "but a small moment" (Doctrine and Covenants 121:7). When we are confronted with challenges like the Saints were during this time, there are still things in our lives to be grateful for. Focusing on the good in our lives can help us gain the strength to overcome our current trials.

Secondly, the Lord urges the Saints to be patient in waiting for the Lord to answer their prayers. In the panicked moment of our trials, we often want an instant response from the Lord, but this type of response is not typically how the Lord works. When our prayers appear unanswered, President Holland offered this counsel: "Some blessings come soon, some come late, and some don't come until heaven. But for those who embrace the gospel of Jesus Christ, *they come*. It will be all right in the end. Trust God and believe in good things to come."[6]

> 4 And now, verily I say unto you concerning the laws of the land, it is my will that my people should observe to do all things whatsoever I command them.
>
> 5 And that law of the land which is constitutional, supporting that principle of freedom in maintaining rights and privileges, belongs to all mankind, and is justifiable before me.
>
> 6 Therefore, I, the Lord, justify you, and your brethren of my church, in befriending that law which is the constitutional law of the land;
>
> 7 And as pertaining to law of man, whatsoever is more or less than this, cometh of evil.
>
> 8 I, the Lord God, make you free, therefore ye are free indeed; and the law also maketh you free.

The historical context of the phrase "the constitutional law of the land" (verse 6) refers to the laws and constitution of the United States of America at the time this revelation was given (1833). In a larger sense, Latter-day Saints in all countries "believe in being subject to kings, presidents, rulers, and magistrates, in obeying, honoring, and sustaining the law" (Articles of Faith 1:12). Joseph Smith taught that "the constitution of the United States is a glorious standard[;] it is founded in the wisdom of God. It is a heavenly banner[;] it is to all those who are privileged with the sweets of its liberty like the cooling shades and refreshing waters of a great rock in a thirsty and a weary land. It is like a great tree under whose branches men from every clime can be shielded from the burning rays of an inclement sun."[7]

Joseph Smith's sentiments regarding the Constitution do not mean, however, that the Constitution of the United States—or of any other country—is perfect and without flaw. President Oaks taught, "Our belief that the United States Constitution was divinely inspired does not mean that divine revelation dictated every word and phrase, such as the provisions allocating the number of representatives from each state or the minimum age of each. The Constitution was not 'a fully grown document,' said President J. Reuben Clark. 'On the contrary,' he explained, 'we believe it must grow and develop to meet the changing needs of an advancing world.'"[8] For example, the US Constitution allowed for legal slavery at the time Doctrine and Covenants 98 was given. But a revelation given only a few months later to Joseph Smith declared, "It is not right that any man should be in bondage one to another" (Doctrine and Covenants 101:79). The Thirteenth Amendment to the US Constitution, ratified in 1865, later outlawed slavery.

> 9 Nevertheless, when the wicked rule the people mourn.
>
> 10 Wherefore, honest men and wise men should be sought for diligently, and good men and wise men ye should observe to uphold; otherwise whatsoever is less than these cometh of evil.

While the Church does not endorse specific candidates or political parties, it does urge its members to participate in the political process and seek out honest, wise, and good men and women to lead their communities and countries. In the Book of Mormon, King Mosiah warned, "For behold, how much iniquity doth one wicked king cause to be committed, yea, and what great destruction!" (Mosiah 29:17). President Oaks taught that it is important for Saints to be involved in the political process of their homelands: "In the United States and in other democracies, political influence is exercised by running for office (which we encourage), by voting, by financial support, by membership and service in political parties, and by ongoing communications to officials, parties, and candidates. To function well, a democracy needs all of these, but a conscientious citizen does not need to provide all of them."[9]

In verse 10 the Lord also urges the Saints to diligently seek for good leaders. This counsel suggests that staying informed on current issues, candidates, and political movements is important. President Oaks also counseled, "There are many political issues, and no party, platform, or individual candidate can satisfy all personal preferences. Each citizen must therefore decide which issues are most important to him or her at any particular time. Then members should seek inspiration on how to exercise their influence according to their individual priorities. This process will not be easy. It may require changing party support or candidate choices, even from election to election."[10]

> 11 And I give unto you a commandment, that ye shall forsake all evil and cleave unto all good, that ye shall live by every word which proceedeth forth out of the mouth of God.
>
> 12 For he will give unto the faithful line upon line, precept upon precept; and I will try you and prove you herewith.
>
> 13 And whoso layeth down his life in my cause, for my name's sake, shall find it again, even life eternal.
>
> 14 Therefore, be not afraid of your enemies, for I have decreed in my heart, saith the Lord, that I will prove you in all things, whether you will abide in my covenant, even unto death, that you may be found worthy.
>
> 15 For if ye will not abide in my covenant ye are not worthy of me.

One of the most frustrating conditions in times of trial is the feeling of helplessness. We often feel helpless because we do not have all the information regarding our situation or we cannot see all of the variables at play. The Lord in verse 12 points out that by design, He gives us information "line upon line, precept on precept." This pattern of gaining information is part of the test we face in this life. It is impossible to fully know everything that we want to know in mortality. We may not be able to discern the motives of our antagonists, the cause of our sufferings, or the outcome of the events surrounding us. This lack of knowledge compels us to act in faith and trust God. There is a reason that faith in Jesus Christ is the *first* principle of the gospel: we cannot know or control everything, so we *must* trust in God.

The great and final unknowable factor in this life is death and what happens after it. But regarding this mystery that all men and women must face, the Savior provides an assurance that death is not the end. The Savior assures the Saints that if they are asked to lay down their life for His cause, there will be a place prepared for them (see Doctrine and Covenants 98:14, 18). For those who die while sincerely engaged in a noble cause, death is not the end of their existence but a gateway into eternal life. Being faithful to the gospel does not come with an assurance that you will be free from trials, but it does allow you to make choices about what your future state after this life will be.

> 16 Therefore, renounce war and proclaim peace, and seek diligently to turn the hearts of the children to their fathers, and the hearts of the fathers to the children;
>
> 17 And again, the hearts of the Jews unto the prophets, and the prophets unto the Jews; lest I come and smite the whole earth with a curse, and all flesh be consumed before me.
>
> 18 Let not your hearts be troubled; for in my Father's house are many mansions, and I have prepared a place for you; and where my Father and I am, there ye shall be also.

Though the Saints were victims of unjust persecution, they were not free from transgressions (see Doctrine and Covenants 101:1–2). Many among the Saints may have felt justified in answering violence with violence. However, the Lord asks the Saints in verse 16 to seek a higher road, leave violent measures behind, and settle their conflicts peacefully.

The Lord makes an interesting allusion in these verses to Malachi's prophecy about the return of Elijah and the turning of "the hearts of the children to the fathers, and the hearts of the fathers to the children" (Doctrine and Covenants 98:16; Malachi 4:5–6). In 1833 the Saints' understanding of the importance of temple work was only in its infancy. The Lord may be alluding here to the vital work of temple building and proxy ordinances for the dead that He intended to be carried out by the Latter-day Saints. The most important work of the last days is not found in violence but in the peaceful work of connecting the roots and branches of humanity through the ordinances of the Lord's house.

In the immediate context of section 98, finding peaceful solutions to challenges rather than incurring further violence was the Saints' goal. However, the work carried out in temples allows the entire human family, long mired in violence and conflict, to at last be peacefully connected through the sacred covenants of the gospel of Jesus Christ.

> 19 Behold, I, the Lord, am not well pleased with many who are in the church at Kirtland;
>
> 20 For they do not forsake their sins, and their wicked ways, the pride of their hearts, and their covetousness, and all their detestable things, and observe the words of wisdom and eternal life which I have given unto them.
>
> 21 Verily I say unto you, that I, the Lord, will chasten them and will do whatsoever I list, if they do not repent and observe all things whatsoever I have said unto them.
>
> 22 And again I say unto you, if ye observe to do whatsoever I command you, I, the Lord, will turn away all wrath and indignation from you, and the gates of hell shall not prevail against you.

Though section 98 is primarily thought to have been intended for the Saints in Missouri who were facing expulsion from their homes, in verses 19–21 the Lord also reproves the Saints in Kirtland for their transgressions. At this time, there were only around 150 members of the Church in Kirtland, which was not nearly as many members as those in Missouri. The challenges the Kirtland Saints faced were different in nature from the Saints in Missouri, yet the Lord's warning is the same: the wording used in verses 19–22 closely mirrors the warning given to the Saints in Missouri only a few days prior (see Doctrine and Covenants 97:24–27). As with the Saints in Missouri, the Lord was speaking to the Kirtland Saints as a group. There were many individuals among the Saints in Kirtland keeping the commandments.

When we see another person or group amid difficulties, we can sometimes assume that their trials are brought on by their own faults. This small group of verses is a simple reminder that if we are not suffering, we should not take others' suffering as evidence of our superiority. Our trials may yet await. It is important that we do not measure our own righteousness against the misfortune or suffering of others. Instead, we should approach the Lord as individuals, asking what we can do to follow His will in our own circumstances.

> 23 Now, I speak unto you concerning your families—if men will smite you, or your families, once, and ye bear it patiently and revile not against them, neither seek revenge, ye shall be rewarded;

> 24 But if ye bear it not patiently, it shall be accounted unto you as being meted out as a just measure unto you.

> 25 And again, if your enemy shall smite you the second time, and you revile not against your enemy, and bear it patiently, your reward shall be an hundred-fold.

> 26 And again, if he shall smite you the third time, and ye bear it patiently, your reward shall be doubled unto you four-fold;

> 27 And these three testimonies shall stand against your enemy if he repent not, and shall not be blotted out.

> 28 And now, verily I say unto you, if that enemy shall escape my vengeance, that he be not brought into judgment before me, then ye shall see to it that ye warn him in my name, that he come no more upon you, neither upon your family, even your children's children unto the third and fourth generation.

> 29 And then, if he shall come upon you or your children, or your children's children unto the third and fourth generation, I have delivered thine enemy into thine hands;

> 30 And then if thou wilt spare him, thou shalt be rewarded for thy righteousness; and also thy children and thy children's children unto the third and fourth generation.

> 31 Nevertheless, thine enemy is in thine hands; and if thou rewardest him according to his works thou art justified; if he has sought thy life, and thy life is endangered by him, thine enemy is in thine hands and thou art justified.

The Lord's law of retribution as given to ancient prophets is reiterated in verses 23–31. The Saints must first seek peace with their enemies and act in self-defense, not in aggression. They are asked to bear their trials patiently and seek nonviolent solutions to conflict. One figure who exemplified this approach was Bishop Edward Partridge, the leader of the Saints in Zion. On July 20, 1833, the day that a mob ransacked and destroyed the Church printing office, Bishop Partridge and Charles Allen were dragged by the mob to the public square near the courthouse in Independence. Bishop Partridge later related the events that followed:

> I was stripped of my hat, coat and vest, and daubed with tar from head to foot, and then had a quantity of feathers put upon me; and all this because I would not agree to leave the county, and my home where I had lived two years.
>
> Before tarring and feathering me, I was permitted to speak. I told them that the saints had had to suffer persecution in all ages of the world. That I had done nothing which ought to offend anyone. That if they abused me they would abuse an innocent person. That I was willing to suffer for the sake of Christ; but to leave the country I was not then willing to consent to it. By this time the multitude made so much noise that I could not be heard: some were cursing and swearing, saying call upon your Jesus, &c, &c; others were equally noisy in trying to still the rest, that they might be enabled to hear what I was saying.
>
> Until after I had spoken, I knew not what they intended to do with me, whether to kill me, to whip me, or what else I knew not. I bore my abuse with so much resignation and meekness, that it appeared to astound the multitude, who permitted me to retire in silence, many looking very solemn, their sympathies having been touched as I thought; and, as to myself, I was so filled with the Spirit and Love of God, that I had no hatred towards my persecutors, or anyone else.[11]

Bishop Partridge's actions under these circumstances demonstrate the validity of the Lord's counsel to the Saints. His meekness in the face of unjust persecution undoubtedly saved his life and may have spared the Saints even worse suffering than what they had already endured.

> 32 Behold, this is the law I gave unto my servant Nephi, and thy fathers, Joseph, and Jacob, and Isaac, and Abraham, and all mine ancient prophets and apostles.
>
> 33 And again, this is the law that I gave unto mine ancients, that they should not go out unto battle against any nation, kindred, tongue, or people, save I, the Lord, commanded them.

34 And if any nation, tongue, or people should proclaim war against them, they should first lift a standard of peace unto that people, nation, or tongue;

35 And if that people did not accept the offering of peace, neither the second nor the third time, they should bring these testimonies before the Lord;

36 Then I, the Lord, would give unto them a commandment, and justify them in going out to battle against that nation, tongue, or people.

37 And I, the Lord, would fight their battles, and their children's battles, and their children's children's, until they had avenged themselves on all their enemies, to the third and fourth generation.

38 Behold, this is an ensample unto all people, saith the Lord your God, for justification before me.

These verses provide the Lord's teaching on war. War can be justified given the conditions provided in verses 32–38. During a period of global war, the First Presidency (which at the time consisted of Heber J. Grant, J. Reuben Clark, and David O. McKay) issued a statement on war that reads as follows: "The Church is and must be against war. The Church itself cannot wage war, unless and until the Lord shall issue new commands. It cannot regard war as a righteous means of settling international disputes; these should and could be settled—the nations agreeing—by peaceful negotiation and adjustment."[12] While righteous men in the scriptures, such as Gideon, Captain Moroni, or Mormon, were skilled commanders and generals, they were also men of peace who fought for the right reasons. Speaking of the righteous Nephites, the Book of Mormon declares, "They were sorry to take up arms against the Lamanites, because they did not delight in the shedding of blood; yea, and this was not all—they were sorry to be the means of sending so many of their brethren out of this world into an eternal world, unprepared to meet their God" (Alma 48:23).

Speaking in the April 1942 general conference in the midst of the Second World War, President David O. McKay outlined several principles surrounding the waging of just war: "There are, however, two conditions which may justify a truly Christian man to enter—mind you, I say enter, not begin—a war: (1) An attempt to dominate and to deprive another of his free agency, and, (2) Loyalty to his country. Possibly there is a third, viz., Defense of a weak nation that is being unjustly crushed by a strong, ruthless one." President McKay added:

> Paramount among these reasons, of course, is the defense of man's freedom. An attempt to rob man of his free agency caused dissension even in heaven. . . . To deprive an intelligent human being of his free agency is to commit the crime of the ages. . . . So fundamental in man's eternal progress is his inherent right to choose, that the Lord would defend it even at the price of war. Without freedom of thought, freedom of choice, freedom of action within lawful bounds, man cannot progress. . . . The greatest responsibility of the state is to guard the lives, and to protect the property and rights of its citizens; and if the state is obligated to protect its citizens from lawlessness within its boundaries, it is equally obligated to protect them from lawless encroachments from without—whether the attacking criminals be individuals or nations.[13]

> 39 And again, verily I say unto you, if after thine enemy has come upon thee the first time, he repent and come unto thee praying thy forgiveness, thou shalt forgive him, and shalt hold it no more as a testimony against thine enemy—

> 40 And so on unto the second and third time; and as oft as thine enemy repenteth of the trespass wherewith he has trespassed against thee, thou shalt forgive him, until seventy times seven.

> 41 And if he trespass against thee and repent not the first time, nevertheless thou shalt forgive him.

> 42 And if he trespass against thee the second time, and repent not, nevertheless thou shalt forgive him.

> 43 And if he trespass against thee the third time, and repent not, thou shalt also forgive him.

> 44 But if he trespass against thee the fourth time thou shalt not forgive him, but shalt bring these testimonies before the Lord; and they shall not be blotted out until he repent and reward thee four-fold in all things wherewith he has trespassed against thee.

> 45 And if he do this, thou shalt forgive him with all thine heart; and if he do not this, I, the Lord, will avenge thee of thine enemy an hundred-fold;

46 And upon his children, and upon his children's children of all them that hate me, unto the third and fourth generation.

47 But if the children shall repent, or the children's children, and turn to the Lord their God, with all their hearts and with all their might, mind, and strength, and restore four-fold for all their trespasses wherewith they have trespassed, or wherewith their fathers have trespassed, or their fathers' fathers, then thine indignation shall be turned away;

48 And vengeance shall no more come upon them, saith the Lord thy God, and their trespasses shall never be brought any more as a testimony before the Lord against them. Amen.

Even in the midst of the terrible persecutions facing the Saints in Missouri, the Savior asked the Saints to seek a path of reconciliation and forgiveness toward their enemies. Several years later, when contentions erupted between the Saints and their neighbors in Clay County, Missouri, Joseph Smith and other Church leaders provided similar counsel, writing:

> We are sorry that this disturbance has broken out—we do not consider it our fault. You are better acquainted with circumstances than we are, and of course have been directed in wisdom. . . . We advise that you be not the first aggressors—give no occasion, and if the people will let you dispose of your property, settle your affairs, and go in peace, go. . . . You know our feelings relative to not giving the first offence, and also of protecting your wives and little ones in case a mob should seek their lives. . . . Be wise, let prudence dictate all your counsels, preserve peace with all men, if possible, stand by the constitution of your country, observe its principles, and above all, show yourselves men of God, worthy citizens, and we doubt not, community ere long, will do you justice, and rise in indignation against those who are the instigators of your suffering and affliction.[14]

Forgiveness, even for those who hurt us the deepest, is always the better course than retribution. We should also note that the Lord's promise to avenge wrongs upon the third and fourth generations of those who are wicked is conditional as well. We believe that men and women will be punished for their own sins and not for those of their fathers (see Articles of Faith 1:2). It is true that grudges and sins are often passed from one generation to another, but we have an obligation to help heal these wounds, not perpetuate them. Justice must be left in the hands of the Lord.

End Notes

1. See Letter to Church Leaders in Jackson County, Missouri, 6 August 1833, josephsmithpapers.org.

2. Letter to Church Leaders in Jackson County, Missouri, 18 August 1833, 2, josephsmithpapers.org.

3. Letter to Church Leaders in Jackson County, Missouri, 18 August 1833, 3, josephsmithpapers.org.

4. See History, 1838–1856, volume A-1 [23 December 1805–30 August 1834], 344, josephsmithpapers.org.

5. See "Historical Introduction," Revelation, 6 August 1833 [D&C 98], josephsmithpapers.org.

6. Jeffrey R. Holland, "An High Priest of Good Things to Come," *Ensign*, Nov. 1999, 38.

7. Letter to Edward Partridge and the Church, circa 22 March 1839, 8–9, josephsmithpapers.org.

8. Dallin H. Oaks, "Defending Our Divinely Inspired Constitution," *Ensign* or *Liahona*, May 2021, 106.

9. Dallin H. Oaks, "Defending Our Divinely Inspired Constitution," 108.

10. Dallin H. Oaks, "Defending Our Divinely Inspired Constitution," 108.

11. History, 1838–1856, volume A-1 [23 December 1805–30 August 1834], 327–28, josephsmithpapers.org; emphasis in original.

12. First Presidency Statement, in Conference Report, Apr. 1942, 94.

13. David O. McKay, in Conference Report, Apr. 1942, 72–73.

14. Letter to William W. Phelps and Others, 25 July 1836, 359, josephsmithpapers.org.

$\mathcal{D}$octrine and $\mathcal{C}$ovenants
Section 99
Go Up Also unto the Goodly Land

$\mathcal{H}$istorical $\mathcal{C}$ontext

THIS REVELATION WAS GIVEN TO JOHN MURDOCK IN LATE AUGUST 1832. John Murdock was among the first people converted to the Church in the Kirtland area when Oliver Cowdery and the missionaries to the Lamanites arrived in the area in November 1830, and later John served as one of the first missionaries in the region. On April 30, 1831, John suffered a terrible loss when his wife, Julia, died just a few hours after giving birth to twins, a boy and a girl. The same day, Emma Smith also gave birth to twins who both passed away. A widower with three other children to care for, John asked Joseph and Emma to adopt the twins, which they gladly did. Joseph and Emma named the female twin Julia after the twins' mother, and they named the male twin Joseph. The infant Joseph died ten months later as a result of exposure suffered during a mob attack on Joseph Smith at the John

Johnson home, but Julia eventually became the first Smith child to live to adulthood.[1]

After John received the revelation in section 99, he left on a mission to the East while his three children traveled to Missouri. John recorded the following regarding this revelation: "I then continued with the church preaching to them and strengthening them and regaining my health till the month of Aug. [1832] when I received the Revelation [Doctrine and Covenants 99], at which time I immediately commended to arrange my business and provide for my children and sent them up [to] the Bishop in Zion, which I did by the hand of Bro. Caleb Baldwin in Sept [1832]. I have [sic] him ten Dollars a head for carrying up my three eldest children [Orrice C., John R., and Phebe C.]."[2] It was two years before John was reunited with his children, a moment that only happened when John arrived in Missouri as a member of Zion's Camp.[3]

Revelation Book 1, Revelation Book 2, and John Murdock's own journal date the revelation found in section 99 to August 1832, as does every published version of the revelation until the 1876 Doctrine and Covenants.[4] Because of an error in the 1876 edition of the Doctrine and Covenants, the revelation's date was listed as August 1833. The error remained until it was corrected in the 2013 edition of the Doctrine and Covenants. In proper chronological order, this revelation was received after section 83 but before section 84 of the Doctrine and Covenants.[5]

*V*erse-by-*V*erse *C*ommentary

1 Behold, thus saith the Lord unto my servant John Murdock—thou art called to go into the eastern countries from house to house, from village to village, and from city to city, to proclaim mine everlasting gospel unto the inhabitants thereof, in the midst of persecution and wickedness.

2 And who receiveth you receiveth me; and you shall have power to declare my word in the demonstration of my Holy Spirit.

3 And who receiveth you as a little child, receiveth my kingdom; and blessed are they, for they shall obtain mercy.

4 And whoso rejecteth you shall be rejected of my Father and his house; and you shall cleanse your feet in the secret places by the way for a testimony against them.

5 And behold, and lo, I come quickly to judgment, to convince all of their ungodly deeds which they have committed against me, as it is written of me in the volume of the book.

6 And now, verily I say unto you, that it is not expedient that you should go until your children are provided for, and sent up kindly unto the bishop of Zion.

7 And after a few years, if thou desirest of me, thou mayest go up also unto the goodly land, to possess thine inheritance;

8 Otherwise thou shalt continue proclaiming my gospel until thou be taken. Amen.

In section 99 John Murdock is called to serve as a missionary but is instructed first to provide for his children and arrange for them to travel to Zion. The situation with John's children was complex at the time this revelation was given. The family caring for his oldest son, Orrice, had left the Church, and they insisted that John should pay them for keeping Orrice. The family looking after his next son, John, had moved to Missouri, and the family caring for his daughter Phebe told John they would "keep her no longer" and also demanded payment. John's other daughter, Julia, was healthy and well in the care of Joseph and Emma Smith, but his last son, Joseph, was gone. "My little son Joseph was dead," John painfully recorded. "When the Prophet was hauled out of bed by the mob in Hiram, the child having the measles lay in bed with him . . . at that time they stripped the cloth off the child. He took cold and died." Writing of the mob responsible for his son's death, John simply wrote, "They are in the Lord's hands."[6]

John spent two months in Kirtland making arrangements for his children before fulfilling his call to serve in the Eastern states. His children traveled to Zion with Caleb Baldwin, and there they were placed in the care of Edward Partridge, the bishop of the Church in Missouri. It was two years before John was reunited with them. When John arrived in Missouri as part of Zion's Camp, he was told that his daughter Phebe, then just six years old, was deathly ill with cholera. "I had seen all my children in good health," he later wrote, "but the destroyer commenced his work."[7] John continued, "I immediately went and took care of her until July 6th [1834] when the Spirit left the body just at the break of day, being 6 years 3 months and 27 days old."[8] John's two older sons lived to adulthood and served with distinction in the Church.

Doctrine and Covenants 99 also contains a promise from the Savior to John: "Whoso receiveth you receiveth me" (verse 2). John had become a very real witness of Jesus Christ only a few months earlier. During the meetings of the School of the Prophets in the spring of 1833, John recorded a vision in his journal:

> In one of these meetings the prophet told us if we could humble ourselves before God, and exercise strong faith, we should see the face of the Lord. And about midday the visions of my mind were opened, and the eyes of my understanding were enlightened and I saw the form of a man [the Savior] most lovely. The visage of his face was sound and fair as the sun. His hair a bright silver gray, curled in the most majestic form. His eyes a keen, penetrating blue, and the skin of his neck a most beautiful white. And he was covered from the neck to the feet with a loose garment, pure white, whiter than any garment I have ever before seen. His countenance was most penetrating, and yet most lovely. And while I was endeavoring to comprehend the whole personage from head to feet, it slipped from me and the vision was closed up. But it left on my mind the impression of love for months that I never felt before to that degree.[9]

John Murdock remained a witness of Jesus Christ throughout the remainder of his life. After serving as one of the first missionaries to Australia, he eventually settled in Utah. He died as a patriarch of the Church and is buried in Beaver, Utah.

End Notes

1. See Susan Easton Black, *Who's Who in the Doctrine & Covenants* (Salt Lake City, UT: Bookcraft, 1997), 202.

2. Lyndon W. Cook, *The Revelations of the Prophet Joseph Smith: A Historical and Biographical Commentary of the Doctrine and Covenants* (Salt Lake City, UT: Deseret Book, 1985), 201–3.

3. See Lisa Olsen Tait, "I Quit Other Business: Early Missionaries," in *Revelations in Context* (2016), 87–89.

4. See Revelation Book 1, 148, josephsmithpapers.org; Revelation Book 2, 19, josephsmithpapers.org; *John Murdock journal and autobiography, circa 1830-1867*, Church History Catalog, accessed Feb. 20, 2024, https://catalog.churchofjesuschrist.org/record/e8018e8a-058f-4a05-844b-357b250c1d0d/0.

5. See "Historical Introduction," Revelation, 29 August 1832 [D&C 99], josephsmithpapers.org.

6. Tait, "I Quit Other Business," 88.

7. Tait, "I Quit Other Business," 88.

8. John Murdock Journal, 25, L. Tom Perry Special Collections, Harold B. Lee Library, Brigham Young University, Provo, Utah.

9. John Murdock Journal, 13.

Doctrine and Covenants Section 100

A Word Concerning Zion

Historical Context

IN SPITE OF THE CHALLENGES FACING THE CHURCH IN MISSOURI AND IN Ohio, missionary efforts continued and the Church grew. In September 1833, Freeman and Huldah Nickerson, new converts of just a few months, visited Joseph Smith and Sidney Rigdon in Kirtland and invited them to travel to Perrysburg, New York, to preach to several of their relatives. Perrysburg was a week's journey away from Kirtland, and Joseph began to feel anxiety over leaving his family. His feelings might have been caused by Doctor Philastus Hurlbut, an excommunicated member of the Church who was stirring up opposition to the Church in the Kirtland area. In a journal entry written a few weeks after Hurlbut's excommunication, Joseph wrote that after being cut off from the Church, Hurlbut "then sought the destruction of the saints in this place [Kirtland] and more particularly myself and family."[1]

Upon arriving in Perrysburg, Joseph wrote in his journal, "I feel very well in my mind the Lord is with us but [I] have much anxiety about my family."[2] From the context of Doctrine and Covenants 100, it is clear that Joseph and Sidney were also deeply worried over the trials faced by the Saints in Missouri. The Lord addressed all of these concerns and gave them additional instructions in this revelation.[3]

Verse-by-Verse Commentary

1 Verily, thus saith the Lord unto you, my friends Sidney and Joseph, your families are well; they are in mine hands, and I will do with them as seemeth me good; for in me there is all power.

2 Therefore, follow me, and listen to the counsel which I shall give unto you.

3 Behold, and lo, I have much people in this place, in the regions round about; and an effectual door shall be opened in the regions round about in this eastern land.

4 Therefore, I, the Lord, have suffered you to come unto this place; for thus it was expedient in me for the salvation of souls.

With so many pressing concerns in the fall of 1833, Joseph and Sidney could have delegated the mission to Perrysburg to other elders, but the Lord assures Joseph and Sidney that their mission to this place will open "an effectual door into the regions round about" (verse 3). The two leaders stayed in the area from October 12 to November 1 and preached to several large, receptive groups. Among those converted were Freeman Nickerson's two grown sons, Moses and Eleazar. Joseph and Sidney also converted Lydia Bailey, who later married Newel Knight, one of Joseph's first converts and one of his closest friends. A few weeks after Joseph and Sidney went back to Kirtland, Moses Nickerson wrote to Sidney, "Your labors wile [sic] in Canada have been the beginning of a good work: there are 34 members attached to the Church at Mount Pleasant, all of whom appear to live up to their profession, five of whom have spoke[n] in tongues and three who sing in tongues: and we live at the top of the mountain. For my part, I feel that I cannot be thankful enough for that which I have received: the scriptures have been opened to my view beyond account."[4]

The most important harvest from the "effectual door" opened by Joseph and Sidney came two years later, when Parley P. Pratt traveled through the region preaching the gospel. Traveling in company with Freeman Nickerson, Parley traveled on his own to Toronto, where he was instrumental in converting hundreds to the Church. Among these converts were future Church President John Taylor and also Mary Fielding, who later married Hyrum Smith.[5] Mary Fielding became the mother of future Church President Joseph F. Smith, who was in turn the father of future Church President Joseph Fielding Smith. The "effectual door" opened by Joseph and Sidney on this mission eventually became the portal out of which hundreds of Saints and three Church Presidents emerged.[6]

> 5 Therefore, verily I say unto you, lift up your voices unto this people; speak the thoughts that I shall put into your hearts, and you shall not be confounded before men;
>
> 6 For it shall be given you in the very hour, yea, in the very moment, what ye shall say.
>
> 7 But a commandment I give unto you, that ye shall declare whatsoever thing ye declare in my name, in solemnity of heart, in the spirit of meekness, in all things.
>
> 8 And I give unto you this promise, that inasmuch as ye do this the Holy Ghost shall be shed forth in bearing record unto all things whatsoever ye shall say.

As Joseph and Sidney preached in Perrysburg, the Lord's promises in verses 5, 6, and 8 were fulfilled. The experiences of Lydia Goldthwaite Bailey Knight, who was converted during Joseph and Sidney's mission to the area, were part of that fulfillment. Lydia later recorded that as she heard Joseph Smith tell of the coming forth of the Book of Mormon, she "saw his face become white and shining[,] glow seemed to beam from every feature."[7] Lydia's biography records that when she was baptized a few days later, she cried out while standing in the freezing water, "Glory to God in the highest. Thanks be to His holy name that I have lived to see this day."[8] At a meeting held the night of her baptism, Lydia was caught up in the Spirit and spoke in tongues. According to her biography, "She was enveloped as with a flame, and, unable longer to retain her seat, she arose and her mouth was filled with the praises of God and His glory. The spirit of tongues was upon her, and she was clothed in a shining light, so bright that all present saw it with great distinctness above the light of the fire and the candles."[9]

Lydia had earlier been abandoned by her husband, and she wondered about her place in this new church. As recorded in her biography, before his departure Joseph Smith told her and others present, "I have been pondering on Sister Lydia's lonely condition, and wondering why it is that she has passed through so much sorrow and affliction and is thus separated from all her relatives. I now understand it. The Lord has suffered it even as he allowed Joseph of old to be afflicted, who was sold by his brethren as a slave to a far country, and through that became a savior to his house and country. Even so shall it be with her, the hand of the Lord will overrule it for good to her and her father's family." Joseph then spoke to Lydia directly, saying, "Sister Lydia, great are your blessings. The Lord, your Savior, loves you and will overrule all your past afflictions for good unto you."[10]

A few years later Lydia moved to Kirtland, where she met and fell in love with Newel Knight, one of Joseph Smith's close friends. Their marriage was personally performed by Joseph Smith. During the ceremony, Joseph told them that marriage "was an institution of heaven first solemnized in the garden of Eden by God himself, by the authority of everlasting priesthood."[11] Lydia and Newel remained close companions and had seven children together before Newel's death in 1847 during the trek west. She died in the faith in St. George in 1880.[12] Lydia Knight's conversion is one of the best examples during Joseph and Sidney's mission that demonstrates the Lord's assurance that "the Holy Ghost shall be shed forth in bearing record" (verse 8).

> 9 And it is expedient in me that you, my servant Sidney, should be a spokesman unto this people; yea, verily, I will ordain you unto this calling, even to be a spokesman unto my servant Joseph.
>
> 10 And I will give unto him power to be mighty in testimony.
>
> 11 And I will give unto thee power to be mighty in expounding all scriptures, that thou mayest be a spokesman unto him, and he shall be a revelator unto thee, that thou mayest know the certainty of all things pertaining to the things of my kingdom on the earth.

12 Therefore, continue your journey and let your hearts rejoice; for behold, and lo, I am with you even unto the end.

In verse 9 the Lord gives Sidney Rigdon the blessing to be a "spokesman unto my servant Joseph." This blessing must have been reassuring for Sidney given the considerable trauma he had suffered the year before when he was badly beaten and injured during a mob attack at the John Johnson farm. Sidney was a remarkably gifted preacher and leader and a vital part of the Restoration. George Q. Cannon later wrote, "Those who knew Sidney Rigdon, know how wonderfully God inspired him, and with what wonderful eloquence he declared the word of God to the people. He was a mighty man in the hands of God, as a spokesman, as long as the prophet lived, or up to a short time before his death."[13]

Several scriptural commentators have called Sidney's blessing to serve as a spokesman for Joseph Smith a fulfillment of an ancient prophesy made by Joseph, the son of Israel. In the Book of Mormon, Joseph is recorded as saying, "And the Lord said unto me also: I will raise up unto the fruit of thy loins; and I will make for him a spokesman" (2 Nephi 3:18).[14] This prophecy, however, may have multiple fulfillments: Oliver Cowdery (see Doctrine and Covenants 28:2–3) and Hyrum Smith (see Doctrine and Covenants 124:95) also acted as an Aaron to Joseph Smith, the Moses of our dispensation. Passages like the ones mentioned in this paragraph emphasize the divine power of God in raising up not only a prophet to restore the gospel but also a generation of men and women prepared to build the kingdom along with him.

13 And now I give unto you a word concerning Zion. Zion shall be redeemed, although she is chastened for a little season.

14 Thy brethren, my servants Orson Hyde and John Gould, are in my hands; and inasmuch as they keep my commandments they shall be saved.

15 Therefore, let your hearts be comforted; for all things shall work together for good to them that walk uprightly, and to the sanctification of the church.

16 For I will raise up unto myself a pure people, that will serve me in righteousness;

17 And all that call upon the name of the Lord, and keep his commandments, shall be saved. Even so. Amen.

Orson Hyde and John Gould (see verse 14) were dispatched in early August to Missouri to find out more information on the plight of the Saints there.[15] The two elders traveled in a realm of uncertainty and violence, and it is clear from verse 14 that Joseph and Sidney worried for their safety. The sufferings of the Saints in Zion weighed heavily on them during this time. But rather than simply waiting and worrying in Kirtland for word from Missouri, Joseph and Sidney's mission to Perrysburg showed their determination to do good when and where they could. Their time in the area was well spent, and their efforts were well rewarded with a rich harvest of souls. Sometimes the best medicine for coping with serious problems that we have limited control over is diving into the service of others.

The experiences Joseph and Sidney had in and around Perrysburg left the Prophet with a special love for the Saints in the area. In a letter written just a few weeks after returning to Kirtland, Joseph wrote to his friends in Perrysburg, "I remember brother Freeman [Eleazer Freeman Nickerson] and Wife, Ransom also, and sister Lydia [Goldthwaite Bailey], and little Charles, with all the brethren and sisters. I intreat for an interest in all your prayers before the throne of mercy in the name of Jesus. I hope that the Lord will grant that I may see you all again, and above all that we may overcome and sit down together in the Kingdom of our Father."[16]

Joseph also returned home to find that all was as the Lord had promised: "Your families are well; they are in mine hands" (Doctrine and Covenants 100:1). The Prophet recorded his gratitude for this fulfilled promise, writing in his journal, "Friday, November 1. [Left] Buffalo, N. Y. at 8 o'clock A.M. and arrived at home Monday the 4th [November 1833] at 10, A.M. found my family all well according to the promise of the Lord, for which blessings I feel to thank his holy name; Amen."[17]

End Notes

1. Journal, 1832–1834, 50, josephsmithpapers.org.
2. Journal 1832–1834, 6–12 October 1833, 7, josephsmithpapers.org.
3. See "Historical Introduction," Revelation, 12 October 1833 [D&C 100], josephsmithpapers.org.
4. *The Evening and the Morning Star,* Feb. 1834, 134.
5. See Terryl L. Givens and Matthew J. Grow, *Parley P. Pratt: The Apostle Paul of Mormonism* (Oxford: Oxford University Press, 2011), 83–97.
6. See Stephen E. Robinson and H. Dean Garrett, *A Commentary on the Doctrine and Covenants* (Salt Lake City, UT: Deseret Book, 2000), 3:253–54.
7. William G. Hartley, *Stand by My Servant Joseph: Story of the Joseph Knight Family and the Restoration* (Salt Lake City, UT: Joseph Fielding Smith Institute, 2003), 214.
8. Hartley, *Stand by My Servant Joseph,* 215.
9. Hartley, *Stand by My Servant Joseph,* 216.
10. Hartley, *Stand by My Servant Joseph,* 217.
11. Hartley, *Stand by My Servant Joseph,* 224.
12. See "Biography: McClellan, Lydia Goldthwaite," accessed Feb. 19, 2023, https://www.josephsmithpapers.org/person/lydia-goldthwaite-mcclellan.
13. George Q. Cannon, in *Journal of Discourses,* 25:126.
14. See Bruce R. McConkie, *A New Witness for the Articles of Faith* (Salt Lake City, UT: Deseret Book, 1985), 425–27; Joseph Fielding McConkie and Craig J. Ostler, *Revelations of the Restoration* (Salt Lake City, UT: Deseret Book, 2000), 725; and Robinson and Garrett, *A Commentary on the Doctrine and Covenants,* 3:253–54.
15. See History, 1838–1856, volume A-1 [23 December 1805–30 August 1834], 344, josephsmithpapers.org.
16. Letter to Moses Nickerson, 19 November 1833, 65, josephsmithpapers.org.
17. Journal, 1832–1834, 18, josephsmithpapers.org.

Doctrine and Covenants Section 101

Zion Shall Not Be Moved out of Her Place

Historical Context

AFTER THE ATTACK ON THE CHURCH PRINTING PRESS AND THE TARRING and feathering of Edward Partridge and Charles Allen in July 1833, Church leaders in Missouri signed a tentative agreement to leave Jackson County. The leaders of the Church agreed to leave in two different phases: the first group was to leave in January 1834, and the second in April 1834. When Joseph Smith heard about the mobbing, he counseled the Saints "that not one foot of land purchased should be given to the enemies of God or sold to them."[1] Church leaders in Missouri sought legal recourse to gain back their rights and their property. They appealed to Daniel Dunklin, the governor of Missouri, for protection against their persecutors. The Missouri Saints also sought out legal representation to assist them as they worked to obtain justice in local courts.

When mob members in Jackson County became aware that the Saints were seeking legal solutions to their problems, they became incensed and launched a new series of attacks on the Saints that began on October 31, 1833. In the midst of this conflict, Lieutenant Governor Lilburn Boggs called out the militia to disarm both sides in the fighting. However, Parley P. Pratt noted that "among this militia (so called,) were embodied the most conspicuous characters of the mob," and only the Saints were forced to give up their weapons. With no choice but to surrender, the Saints began preparing to leave the county in the worsening conditions of the coming winter.[2]

On November 25, 1833, Joseph Smith heard of the renewed mob attacks from Orson Hyde and John Gould, two elders who had been dispatched from Kirtland the previous August to see how to assist the Saints in Missouri.[3] Upon hearing the sufferings of the Saints in Missouri, Church leaders in Kirtland were overwhelmed with sorrow. Lucy Mack Smith remembered that "upon hearing this [news], Joseph was overwhelmed with grief; he burst into tears, and sobbed aloud: 'Oh my brethren! my brethren!' he exclaimed[,] would that I had been with you to have shared your fate— Oh my God, what shall I do in such a trial as this."[4] Oliver Cowdery was also overwhelmed upon hearing the news. His wife, Elizabeth, was still in Missouri, and Oliver did not know if she was alive or dead. He penned an emotional letter to her, though he did not know her location, writing, "God only knows the feelings of my heart as I address a few lines to you. . . . My prayers ascend daily and hourly to God that you and I may be spared, and yet enjoy each other's society in this life, in peace."[5]

In response to the plight of the Saints, the Prophet wrote an emotional letter to Edward Partridge and other Church leaders in Jackson County. He wrote, "I cannot learn from any communication by the spirit to me that Zion has forfeited her claim to a celestial crown notwithstanding the Lord has caused her to be thus afflicted." He added, "Now there are two things of which I am ignorant and the Lord will not show me—perhaps for a wise purpose in himself. I mean in some respect, and they are these, Why God hath suffered so great calamity to come upon Zion; or what the great moving cause of this great affliction is, and again by what means he will return her back to her inheritance with songs of everlasting joy upon her head."[6]

A few days later, the revelation in section 101 came in response to the pleadings of Church leaders in Kirtland. We know little about the precise circumstances under which the revelation was given. Ira Ames, a Church member living in Kirtland at the time, later said that the revelation came to

Joseph Smith and Oliver Cowdery over the course of one night. According to Ames, he and Martin Harris came to Joseph's home in Kirtland and found Joseph and Oliver eating breakfast. Oliver greeted the pair by saying, "Good morning Brethren, we have just received news from heaven."[7] Ames did not give the precise date that this encounter took place, but when the revelation was copied by John Whitmer into Revelation Book 1, Whitmer dated it as December 16–17, 1833.[8] The revelation provides some firm answers regarding why the persecutions in Jackson County were taking place and what course of action the Saints in Kirtland should take.[9]

Verse-by-Verse Commentary

1 Verily I say unto you, concerning your brethren who have been afflicted, and persecuted, and cast out from the land of their inheritance—

2 I, the Lord, have suffered the affliction to come upon them, wherewith they have been afflicted, in consequence of their transgressions;

3 Yet I will own them, and they shall be mine in that day when I shall come to make up my jewels.

4 Therefore, they must needs be chastened and tried, even as Abraham, who was commanded to offer up his only son.

5 For all those who will not endure chastening, but deny me, cannot be sanctified.

6 Behold, I say unto you, there were jarrings, and contentions, and envyings, and strifes, and lustful and covetous desires among them; therefore by these things they polluted their inheritances.

7 They were slow to hearken unto the voice of the Lord their God; therefore, the Lord their God is slow to hearken unto their prayers, to answer them in the day of their trouble.

8 In the day of their peace they esteemed lightly my counsel; but, in the day of their trouble, of necessity they feel after me.

Verses 1–8 of the revelation addresses the question that had been weighing on the hearts and minds of the Saints, and especially of the Prophet: "Why [hath] God . . . suffered so great calamity to come upon Zion?"[10] The Lord provides two clear answers for this calamity. First, "they [the Saints in Missouri] have been afflicted, in consequence of their transgressions" (verse 2). This statement speaks to the actions of the Saints collectively, not individually. There were many among the Saints in Zion who were striving with all their power to keep the commandments. But as the Lord declares, there were also many who were guilty of "jarrings, and contentions, and envyings, and strifes, and lustful and covetous desires" (verse 6). Documents from the years leading up to the expulsion of the Saints from Jackson County show that there were many disagreements among the Saints and their neighbors.

Second, the Lord declared that the Saints "must needs be chastened and tried, even as Abraham" (verse 4). The test the Lord gave to Abraham—sacrificing Abraham's beloved son, Isaac—is among the most heartbreaking stories in all of scripture. Abraham was not guilty of any great sins, but he was put through his ordeal as a trial of his faith. The Saints in Missouri were guilty of certain transgressions, but trials also came to test their patience and faith. In a letter written near the time section 101 was given, Church leaders declared, "The days of tribulation are fast approaching, and the time to test the fidelity of the Saints, has come.—Rumor with her ten thousand tongues is diffusing her uncertain sounds in almost every ear: but in these times of sore trial, let the saints be patient and see the salvation of God. Those who cannot endure persecution and stand in the day of affliction, cannot stand in the day when the Son of God shall burst the veil, and appear in all the glory of his Father with the holy angels."[11]

> 9 Verily I say unto you, notwithstanding their sins, my bowels are filled with compassion towards them. I will not utterly cast them off; and in the day of wrath I will remember mercy.
>
> 10 I have sworn, and the decree hath gone forth by a former commandment which I have given unto you, that I would let fall the sword of mine indignation in behalf of my people; and even as I have said, it shall come to pass.
>
> 11 Mine indignation is soon to be poured out without measure upon all nations; and this will I do when the cup of their iniquity is full.

12 And in that day all who are found upon the watch-tower, or in other words, all mine Israel, shall be saved.

13 And they that have been scattered shall be gathered.

14 And all they who have mourned shall be comforted.

15 And all they who have given their lives for my name shall be crowned.

In speaking frankly to the Saints about their shortcomings, the Lord was not condoning the actions of the Jackson County mob. The mob members had acted illegally and cruelly in their expulsion of the Saints. In verse 11 the Lord promises to pour out His judgments upon the wicked once the measure of their iniquity is full. But in the meantime, the Savior offers comfort and consolation to the Saints in Zion who are struggling amid their sorrows.

Even while the Saints were making their way out of Jackson County, manifestations of the Lord's mercy appeared among them. Philo Dibble, who was so badly wounded in a skirmish with a mob that a surgeon announced he had no chance of living, later wrote:

David Whitmer, however, sent me word that I should live and not die, but I could see no possible chance to recover. After the surgeon had left me, Brother Newel Knight came to see me, and sat down on the side of my bed. He laid his right hand on my head, but never spoke. I felt the Spirit resting upon me at the crown of my head before his hand touched me, and I knew immediately that I was going to be healed. It seemed to form like a ring under the skin, and followed down my body. When the ring came to the wound, another ring formed around the first bullet hole, also the second and third. Then a ring formed on each shoulder and on each hip, and followed down to the ends of my fingers and toes and left me. I immediately arose and discharged three quarts of blood or more, with some pieces of my clothes that had been driven into my body by the bullets.

I then dressed myself and went outdoors and saw the falling of the stars, which so encouraged the Saints and frightened their enemies. It was one of the grandest sights I ever beheld. From that time not a drop of blood came from me and I never afterwards felt the slightest pain or inconvenience from my wounds, except that I was somewhat weak from the loss of blood. The next day I walked around the field, and the day following I mounted a horse and rode eight miles, and went three miles on foot.[12]

The "falling of stars" that Philo refers to was a meteor shower in November 1833 that the Saints witnessed in Kirtland and Missouri. Edward Partridge wrote to Joseph Smith about the celestial wonders, noting that from one to two o'clock on the morning of November 13, "there appeared an extraordinary phenomenon. The heavens were literally filled with meteors or shooting stars[,] as they are called."[13] Bishop Partridge's daughter Eliza, who also witnessed the meteor shower, later recalled, "I saw the stars fall. They came down almost as thick as snowflakes and could be seen till the daylight hid them from sight. Some of our enemies thought the day of judgment had come and were very much frightened but the Saints rejoiced and considered it as one of the signs of the Latter days."[14] At least one Jackson County resident, Josiah Gregg, agreed with the Saints' interpretation of the heavenly display. He later recalled that the meteor shower caused many of his neighbors "to wonder whether, after all, the Mormons might not be in the right; and whether this was not a sign sent from heaven as a remonstrance for the injustice they had been guilty of towards that chosen sect."[15]

> 16 Therefore, let your hearts be comforted concerning Zion; for all flesh is in mine hands; be still and know that I am God.
>
> 17 Zion shall not be moved out of her place, notwithstanding her children are scattered.
>
> 18 They that remain, and are pure in heart, shall return, and come to their inheritances, they and their children, with songs of everlasting joy, to build up the waste places of Zion—
>
> 19 And all these things that the prophets might be fulfilled.
>
> 20 And, behold, there is none other place appointed than that which I have appointed; neither shall there be any other place appointed than that which I have appointed, for the work of the gathering of my saints—
>
> 21 Until the day cometh when there is found no more room for them; and then I have other places which I will appoint unto them, and they shall be called stakes, for the curtains or the strength of Zion.

In this passage, the Lord answers another question that had been weighing on the minds of the Saints: Was Jackson County still the place for the City of Zion? The Lord declares unequivocally in verse 20 that "there is none other place appointed than that which I have appointed." The city of Zion will still be built in the same location designated by the Lord, the present-day site of Independence, Missouri (see Doctrine and Covenants 57:1–3). In the Lord's due time, the way will be opened for the city to be built. This does not mean that the city that is eventually built will follow precisely the plans laid down by the Saints in Joseph Smith's time. The designs for the temples that were to be built in the city of Zion, for example, had no provisions for modern lighting or indoor plumbing, which were both unheard of in 1833. When the city is built, the Saints will take advantage of all the modern advances the Lord has blessed us with.

In the meantime, the question of building Zion is not one of geography but one of purity. The Lord has declared that "Zion is the pure in heart" (Doctrine and Covenants 97:21). When the Saints are sufficiently pure and humble, the Lord will open the way for them to return to Jackson County and build the city of Zion. In the meantime, stakes of Zion will continue to rise in different places around the globe, serving as gathering places for the lost sheep of the house of Israel.

> 22 Behold, it is my will, that all they who call on my name, and worship me according to mine everlasting gospel, should gather together, and stand in holy places;

> 23 And prepare for the revelation which is to come, when the veil of the covering of my temple, in my tabernacle, which hideth the earth, shall be taken off, and all flesh shall see me together.

> 24 And every corruptible thing, both of man, or of the beasts of the field, or of the fowls of the heavens, or of the fish of the sea, that dwells upon all the face of the earth, shall be consumed;

> 25 And also that of element shall melt with fervent heat; and all things shall become new, that my knowledge and glory may dwell upon all the earth.

> 26 And in that day the enmity of man, and the enmity of beasts, yea, the enmity of all flesh, shall cease from before my face.

> 27 And in that day whatsoever any man shall ask, it shall be given unto him.

28 And in that day Satan shall not have power to tempt any man.

29 And there shall be no sorrow because there is no death.

30 In that day an infant shall not die until he is old; and his life shall be as the age of a tree;

31 And when he dies he shall not sleep, that is to say in the earth, but shall be changed in the twinkling of an eye, and shall be caught up, and his rest shall be glorious.

Doctrine and Covenants 101:22–42 contains some of the most detailed descriptions in scripture of the nature of life during the Millennium. The veil will be rent. The Lord will remove the condition that prevents us from perceiving the larger universe that God reigns over, and all people will see their place in the larger works of God. Because the veil separating the living and the deceased will be taken away, it is likely that God will accelerate temple work during the Millennium. Brigham Young taught that during the Millennium, the Saints "will have revelations to know our forefathers clear back to Father Adam and Mother Eve, and we will enter into the temples of God and officiate for them. Then [children] will be sealed to [parents] until the chain is made perfect back to Adam, so that there will be a perfect chain of Priesthood from Adam to the winding-up scene."[16]

During this time, the earth will "be renewed and received her paradisiacal glory" (Articles of Faith 1:10). All corruptible things, meaning those things of a telestial order, will be consumed, and the earth will once again achieve a terrestrial status. At the end of the Millennium, the earth will die and be resurrected as a celestial world, the eternal home of the righteous (see Doctrine and Covenants 88:25–26). Most notably, death will cease to exist. Mortal men and women will still live on the earth during the Millennium, but when they reach a certain age, they will be changed from mortality to immortality in an instant. This age is given generally in verse 30 "as the age of a tree," which Isaiah identified as one hundred years (see Isaiah 65:20). Most importantly, Satan, having been bound by the angel of God, will lose his power to tempt man (see Revelation 20:1–2). He will be kept in check by the righteousness of the people (see 1 Nephi 22:26).

32 Yea, verily I say unto you, in that day when the Lord shall come, he shall reveal all things—

33 Things which have passed, and hidden things which no man knew, things of the earth, by which it was made, and the purpose and the end thereof—

34 Things most precious, things that are above, and things that are beneath, things that are in the earth, and upon the earth, and in heaven.

35 And all they who suffer persecution for my name, and endure in faith, though they are called to lay down their lives for my sake yet shall they partake of all this glory.

36 Wherefore, fear not even unto death; for in this world your joy is not full, but in me your joy is full.

Another great blessing of living in the Millennium will be the abundance of knowledge made available during this time. The prophet Habakkuk declared that "the earth shall be filled with the knowledge of the glory of the Lord, as the waters cover the sea" (Habakkuk 2:14). All people will fully comprehend the complexity of their origins and their place in the great creation of God. Many of the questions asked by men and women since the dawn of time—questions about dinosaurs, ancient civilizations, the origins of the universe, and the worlds beyond our own—will find answers at last. Even questions we now lack the knowledge to ask, questions about "hidden things which no man knew" (verse 33), will be answered.

There is no conflict between being curious and being a believer. The Lord delights in answering our questions. But He provides answers in His own time and for His own purposes. The universe is a wondrous place, and men and women are endowed with minds that are designed to seek answers. The Millennium will be a time when earnest seekers of truth will find themselves dining at a table overflowing with answers to the deep and mysterious things of the universe.

37 Therefore, care not for the body, neither the life of the body; but care for the soul, and for the life of the soul.

38 And seek the face of the Lord always, that in patience ye may possess your souls, and ye shall have eternal life.

39 When men are called unto mine everlasting gospel, and covenant with an everlasting covenant, they are accounted as the salt of the earth and the savor of men;

40 They are called to be the savor of men; therefore, if that salt of the earth lose its savor, behold, it is thenceforth good for nothing only to be cast out and trodden under the feet of men.

41 Behold, here is wisdom concerning the children of Zion, even many, but not all; they were found transgressors, therefore they must needs be chastened—

42 He that exalteth himself shall be abased, and he that abaseth himself shall be exalted.

The Savior hearkens back to the Sermon on the Mount and His sermon at the temple as He explains the role of the Saints in the world by comparing them to salt. Salt cannot lose its savor with age, only through mixing or contaminating it with another substance. In the time of the New Testament, if salt lost its usefulness for seasoning or preserving food, it was thrown out into the streets and trodden under the foot of men. Just like salt, we need to keep ourselves clean from the impurities of sin. The Lord in verse 41 declares that "many, but not all" of the Saints in Zion were guilty of transgression.

Unfortunately, at times the sins of others also affect those who have committed no transgression. Recognizing the plight of the faithful, Joseph Smith wrote to the Saints in Missouri:

When I contemplate upon all things that have been manifested, I am sensible that I ought not to murmur and do not murmur only in this, that those who are innocent are compelled to suffer for the iniquities of the guilty; and I cannot account for this, only on this wise, that the saying of the Savior has not been strictly observed: If thy right eye offend thee pluck it out. and cast it from thee or if thy right arm offend thee pluck it of[f] and cast it from thee. Now the fact is, if any of the members of our body are disordered, the rest of our body will be affected with them and then all is brought into bondage together. And yet notwithstanding all this, it is with difficulty that I can restrain my feelings; when I know that you my brethren with whom I have had so many happy hours, sitting as it were in heavenly places in Christ Jesus. and also having the witness which I feel, and even have felt, of the purity of your motives—are cast out, and are as strangers and pilgrims on the earth, exposed to hunger, cold, nakedness peril, sword &c I say when I contemplate this, it is with difficulty that I can keep from complaining and murmurings against this dispensation; but I am sensible that this is not right, and may God grant that notwithstanding your great afflictions and sufferings there may not anything separate us from the Love of Christ.[17]

43 And now, I will show unto you a parable, that you may know my will concerning the redemption of Zion.

44 A certain nobleman had a spot of land, very choice; and he said unto his servants: Go ye unto my vineyard, even upon this very choice piece of land, and plant twelve olive trees;

45 And set watchmen round about them, and build a tower, that one may overlook the land round about, to be a watchman upon the tower, that mine olive trees may not be broken down when the enemy shall come to spoil and take upon themselves the fruit of my vineyard.

46 Now, the servants of the nobleman went and did as their lord commanded them, and planted the olive trees, and built a hedge round about, and set watchmen, and began to build a tower.

47 And while they were yet laying the foundation thereof, they began to say among themselves: And what need hath my lord of this tower?

48 And consulted for a long time, saying among themselves: What need hath my lord of this tower, seeing this is a time of peace?

49 Might not this money be given to the exchangers? For there is no need of these things.

50 And while they were at variance one with another they became very slothful, and they hearkened not unto the commandments of their lord.

51 And the enemy came by night, and broke down the hedge; and the servants of the nobleman arose and were affrighted, and fled; and the enemy destroyed their works, and broke down the olive trees.

52 Now, behold, the nobleman, the lord of the vineyard, called upon his servants, and said unto them, Why! what is the cause of this great evil?

53 Ought ye not to have done even as I commanded you, and—after ye had planted the vineyard, and built the hedge round about, and set watchmen upon the walls thereof—built the tower also, and set a watchman upon the tower, and watched for my vineyard, and not have fallen asleep, lest the enemy should come upon you?

54 And behold, the watchman upon the tower would have seen the enemy while he was yet afar off; and then ye could have made ready and kept the enemy from breaking down the hedge thereof, and saved my vineyard from the hands of the destroyer.

During His earthly ministry, the Savior often spoke in parables. Parables can have multiple interpretations, but in this instance at least one interpretation of the story in verses 43–54 seems clear. The choice spot of land mentioned in verse 44 is the location for the city of Zion, and the nobleman is the Lord Himself. Twelve is a number often associated with the house of Israel and the Church, and the twelve olive trees represent the Saints in Jackson County. Later in the parable, the watchmen (the leaders of the Church in Missouri) failed to build the tower (the temple) as they were commanded. As a consequence, the enemy was able to ransack the orchard.

Beyond laying the foundation stones to mark the site, the Saints in Missouri did little to promote the work of building the temple. This neglect might be justifiable, given that many of the Saints were emigrants with families and farms to look after. However, the parable identifies a deeper problem among the Saints in Missouri. In the parable, the servants of the nobleman began to question the need for having a tower in the first place; they suggest that the resources for the tower could be used for more worldly things (see verses 46–50). This detail from the parable suggests that even if the Saints had possessed the time and resources to construct the temple, they would still have neglected to carry out the work. Because they wavered in their desire to even begin work on the temple, the Saints failed to gain the spiritual foresight that might have prevented their enemies from destroying their work. Likewise, in our own lives, if we place spiritual things first, we will find more joy and success in all areas of life.

55 And the lord of the vineyard said unto one of his servants: Go and gather together the residue of my servants, and take all the strength of mine house, which are my warriors, my young men,

and they that are of middle age also among all my servants, who are the strength of mine house, save those only whom I have appointed to tarry;

56 And go ye straightway unto the land of my vineyard, and redeem my vineyard; for it is mine; I have bought it with money.

57 Therefore, get ye straightway unto my land; break down the walls of mine enemies; throw down their tower, and scatter their watchmen.

58 And inasmuch as they gather together against you, avenge me of mine enemies, that by and by I may come with the residue of mine house and possess the land.

59 And the servant said unto his lord: When shall these things be?

60 And he said unto his servant: When I will; go ye straightway, and do all things whatsoever I have commanded you;

61 And this shall be my seal and blessing upon you—a faithful and wise steward in the midst of mine house, a ruler in my kingdom.

62 And his servant went straightway, and did all things whatsoever his lord commanded him; and after many days all things were fulfilled.

The second part of the parable, verses 55–62, hints at a commandment that was not given until several months later. After consulting with leaders who had just arrived from Missouri in February 1834, Joseph Smith received a revelation instructing him to lead a relief mission to the Saints in Zion (see Doctrine and Covenants 103). Gathering together a small but dedicated group of men and women, Joseph Smith marched to Missouri a few months later. The expedition, known as "Zion's Camp," ultimately failed to return the Saints to their homes in Jackson County, but it served as a rich training ground for future Church leaders, including Brigham Young, Wilford Woodruff, Parley P. Pratt, and others.

It is interesting that when the concept of a march to Zion is brought up in these verses, the servant's first response is to ask, "When will these things be?" The Lord provides an ambiguous answer, only saying, "When I will; go ye straightway and do all things whatsoever I have commanded you" (verse 59). The road to redeeming Zion was going to be much longer and more complex than any of the Saints in 1833 could have imagined.

> 63 Again, verily I say unto you, I will show unto you wisdom in me concerning all the churches, inasmuch as they are willing to be guided in a right and proper way for their salvation—

> 64 That the work of the gathering together of my saints may continue, that I may build them up unto my name upon holy places; for the time of harvest is come, and my word must needs be fulfilled.

> 65 Therefore, I must gather together my people, according to the parable of the wheat and the tares, that the wheat may be secured in the garners to possess eternal life, and be crowned with celestial glory, when I shall come in the kingdom of my Father to reward every man according as his work shall be;

> 66 While the tares shall be bound in bundles, and their bands made strong, that they may be burned with unquenchable fire.

> 67 Therefore, a commandment I give unto all the churches, that they shall continue to gather together unto the places which I have appointed.

> 68 Nevertheless, as I have said unto you in a former commandment, let not your gathering be in haste, nor by flight; but let all things be prepared before you.

> 69 And in order that all things be prepared before you, observe the commandment which I have given concerning these things—

> 70 Which saith, or teacheth, to purchase all the lands with money, which can be purchased for money, in the region round about the land which I have appointed to be the land of Zion, for the beginning of the gathering of my saints;

> 71 All the land which can be purchased in Jackson county, and the counties round about, and leave the residue in mine hand.

> 72 Now, verily I say unto you, let all the churches gather together all their moneys; let these things be done in their time, but not in haste; and observe to have all things prepared before you.

73 And let honorable men be appointed, even wise men, and send them to purchase these lands.

74 And the churches in the eastern countries, when they are built up, if they will hearken unto this counsel they may buy lands and gather together upon them; and in this way they may establish Zion.

75 There is even now already in store sufficient, yea, even an abundance, to redeem Zion, and establish her waste places, no more to be thrown down, were the churches, who call themselves after my name, willing to hearken to my voice.

One of the reasons that the mob leaders in Jackson County openly cited for persecuting the Saints was that "since the arrival of the first of them [the Saints] they have been daily increasing in numbers."[18] The calamities and persecutions that fell upon the Saints in Zion might have caused an impulse in the Church to cease the practice of gathering to one place. But in Doctrine and Covenants 101:63–74 the Lord emphasizes the importance of continuing the gathering to "build them [the Saints] up unto my name upon holy places" and to prepare them for the time of harvesting, a likely reference to the Second Coming (see Doctrine and Covenants 101:64). The Lord also asks the Saints to purchase land in Zion with money and to not respond to persecution with violence. This counsel echoes the earlier counsel He gave to the Saints to obtain the land for Zion peacefully (see Doctrine and Covenants 63:27–31). In a revelation given a few months later to the Saints in Zion's Camp, the Lord reiterates the need to obtain the land through peaceful means (see Doctrine and Covenants 105:29).

While the Lord continued to command the Saints to gather to Zion, He also urged them to not gather in haste; the Saints were to ensure that they had enough money to provide for themselves before moving (see verse 72). Failure to follow this commandment led to an overflow of Saints gathering to Kirtland without the resources to establish themselves. In an attempt to help, Church leaders established the Kirtland Safety Society, a bank which later collapsed. The fall of the Kirtland Safety Society led to a major apostasy in Kirtland, and Kirtland eventually ceased to be a meaningful Church center.

76 And again I say unto you, those who have been scattered by their enemies, it is my will that they should continue to impor-

tune for redress, and redemption, by the hands of those who are placed as rulers and are in authority over you—

77 According to the laws and constitution of the people, which I have suffered to be established, and should be maintained for the rights and protection of all flesh, according to just and holy principles;

78 That every man may act in doctrine and principle pertaining to futurity, according to the moral agency which I have given unto him, that every man may be accountable for his own sins in the day of judgment.

79 Therefore, it is not right that any man should be in bondage one to another.

80 And for this purpose have I established the Constitution of this land, by the hands of wise men whom I raised up unto this very purpose, and redeemed the land by the shedding of blood.

Throughout their trials in Missouri and elsewhere, the Saints sought peaceful redress of their wrongs through legal means. The Lord in verse 80 explains that the Constitution of the United States was created by wise men whom the Lord had "raised up unto this very purpose." Joseph Smith at one point proclaimed, "I am the greatest advocate of the Constitution of [the] U.S. [that] there is on the earth."[19] The Prophet also saw a need for the US Constitution to be amended and enforced justly. In a discourse given to the Council of Fifty on April 11, 1844, Joseph Smith taught, "There is only two or three things lacking in the constitution of the United States. If they had said all men [are] born equal, and not only that but they shall have their rights, they shall be free, or the armies of the government should be compelled to enforce those principles of liberty. . . . And when a Governor or president will not protect his subjects he ought to be put away from his office."[20] This was, in part, why Joseph Smith was running for president in 1844—to ensure that the rights of the Constitution extended to all peoples.

The Lord's statement that "it is not right that any man should be in bondage one to another" powerfully refutes slavery and racism (verse 79). President Oaks used this passage to disaffirm those who would use the scriptures to justify racism and discrimination. He taught:

Some religious people have sought to justify practices of racism by references to the Bible, as I will discuss later. Nevertheless, the proper understanding of scriptures—ancient and modern—and recent prophetic statements help us to see that racism, as defined, is not consistent with the revealed word of God. We know that God created all mortals and we are all children of God. Moreover, God created us with the differences that identify races. Therefore, any *personal attitudes* or *official practices* of racism involve one group whom God created exercising authority or advantage over another group God created, both groups having God-given qualities they cannot change. So understood, neither group should think or behave as if God created them as first-class children and others as second-class children. Yet that is how racism affects thinking and practices toward others. Members of the Church of Jesus Christ must remember that all such attitudes and official practices were outlawed for us by the Lord's 1833 revelation to the Prophet Joseph Smith that "it is not right that any man should be in bondage one to another" (Doctrine and Covenants 101:79).[21]

81 Now, unto what shall I liken the children of Zion? I will liken them unto the parable of the woman and the unjust judge, for men ought always to pray and not to faint, which saith—

82 There was in a city a judge which feared not God, neither regarded man.

83 And there was a widow in that city, and she came unto him, saying: Avenge me of mine adversary.

84 And he would not for a while, but afterward he said within himself: Though I fear not God, nor regard man, yet because this widow troubleth me I will avenge her, lest by her continual coming she weary me.

85 Thus will I liken the children of Zion.

86 Let them importune at the feet of the judge;

87 And if he heed them not, let them importune at the feet of the governor;

88 And if the governor heed them not, let them importune at the feet of the president;

89 And if the president heed them not, then will the Lord arise and come forth out of his hiding place, and in his fury vex the nation;

271

90 And in his hot displeasure, and in his fierce anger, in his time, will cut off those wicked, unfaithful, and unjust stewards, and appoint them their portion among hypocrites, and unbelievers;

91 Even in outer darkness, where there is weeping, and wailing, and gnashing of teeth.

92 Pray ye, therefore, that their ears may be opened unto your cries, that I may be merciful unto them, that these things may not come upon them.

93 What I have said unto you must needs be, that all men may be left without excuse;

94 That wise men and rulers may hear and know that which they have never considered;

95 That I may proceed to bring to pass my act, my strange act, and perform my work, my strange work, that men may discern between the righteous and the wicked, saith your God.

96 And again, I say unto you, it is contrary to my commandment and my will that my servant Sidney Gilbert should sell my storehouse, which I have appointed unto my people, into the hands of mine enemies.

97 Let not that which I have appointed be polluted by mine enemies, by the consent of those who call themselves after my name;

98 For this is a very sore and grievous sin against me, and against my people, in consequence of those things which I have decreed and which are soon to befall the nations.

99 Therefore, it is my will that my people should claim, and hold claim upon that which I have appointed unto them, though they should not be permitted to dwell thereon.

100 Nevertheless, I do not say they shall not dwell thereon; for inasmuch as they bring forth fruit and works meet for my kingdom they shall dwell thereon.

101 They shall build, and another shall not inherit it; they shall plant vineyards, and they shall eat the fruit thereof. Even so. Amen.

In verses 81–101 of the revelation, the Lord references the parable of the woman and the unjust judge, found in Luke 18:1–8. The parable can be interpreted in different ways, but the parable's central message seems to be to continue enduring when engaged in a just cause. Like the unjust judge, the unjust officials in Missouri refused for a long time to help the Saints. However, it was still important to seek redress and reparations through legal means rather than through force and violence. Joseph Smith wrote to the Saints in Missouri:

> Therefore this is my counsel[:] that you retain your land; even unto the uttermost, and seek every lawful means to seek redress of your enemies, &c, &c, and pray to God, day and night, to return you in peace and in safety to the Lands of your inheritance; and when the Judge fails you, appeal unto the executive; and when the executive fails you[,] appeal unto the President; and when the President fails you, and all laws fail you, and the humanity of the people fails you, and all things else fail you but God alone, and you continue to weary him with your importunings, as the poor woman did the unjust Judge, he will not fail to execute Judgment upon your enemies, and to avenge his own elect that cry unto him day and night.[22]

The Lord also makes an ominous promise to "vex the nation" if the leaders of the federal and state governments refuse to help the Saints (verse 89). The hint of coming judgement upon the United States, later stated even more directly in Doctrine and Covenants 105:15, is a dark thread in the revelations in the Doctrine and Covenants. Eventually, judgment in the form of the American Civil War did come upon the land because of its callous disregard for human rights.

End Notes

1. Letter to Church Leaders in Jackson County, Missouri, 18 August 1833, 3, josephsmithpapers.org.
2. See Parley P. Pratt et al., "'The Mormons' So Called," 12 December 1833, 2, josephsmithpapers.org.
3. See History, 1838–1856, volume A-1 [23 December 1805–30 August 1834], 344, josephsmithpapers.org.
4. Lucy Mack Smith History, 1845, 221, josephsmithpapers.org.
5. Quoted in Milton V. Backman, *The Heavens Resound: A History of the Latter-Day Saints in Ohio, 1830–1838* (Salt Lake City, UT: Deseret Book, 1983), 167.
6. Letter to Edward Partridge and Others, 10 December 1833, 71–72, josephsmithpapers.org.
7. Ira Ames, Autobiography and Journal, 1858, CHL MS 6055; cited in "Historical Introduction," Revelation, 16–17 December 1834 [D&C 101], footnote 10, josephsmithpapers.org.
8. See Revelation Book 1, 183, josephsmithpapers.org.
9. See "Historical Introduction," Revelation, 16–17 December 1833 [D&C 101], josephsmithpapers.org.
10. Letter to Edward Partridge and Others, 10 December 1833, 71–72, josephsmithpapers.org.
11. Letter to the Church, not after 18 December 1833, 120, josephsmithpapers. org.
12. Philo Dibble, "Early Scenes in Church History," in *Four Faith Promoting Classics: A String of Pearls, Fragments of Experience, Gems for the Young Folks, Early Scenes in Church History* (Salt Lake City, UT: Bookcraft, 1968), 74–96.
13. Letter from Edward Partridge, between 14 and 19 November 1833, 1, josephsmithpapers.org.
14. Letter from Edward Partridge, between 14 and 19 November 1833, 1, footnote 12, josephsmithpapers.org.
15. Letter from Edward Partridge, between 14 and 19 November 1833, 1, footnote 12, josephsmithpapers.org.
16. *Teachings of Presidents of the Church: Brigham Young* (1997), 334.
17. Letter to Edward Partridge and Others, 10 December 1833, 71–72, josephsmithpapers.org.
18. Letter from John Whitmer, 29 July 1833, 53, josephsmithpapers.org.

19. Discourse, 15 October 1843, as Reported by Willard Richards, 128, josephsmithpapers.org.
20. Council of Fifty, Minutes, March 1844–January 1846; Volume 1, 10 March 1844–1 March 1845, 122, josephsmithpapers.org; emphasis in original.
21. Dallin H. Oaks, "Racism and Other Challenges" (Brigham Young University devotional, Oct. 27, 2020), 4, speeches.byu.edu.
22. Joseph Smith, in History, 1838–1856, volume A-1 [23 December 1805–30 August 1834], 395, josephsmithpapers.org.

Doctrine and Covenants Section 102

The Redemption of Zion Must Needs Come by Power

Historical Context

DOCTRINE AND COVENANTS 102 CONSISTS OF THE MINUTES TAKEN AT A meeting of priesthood holders on February 17, 1834. The minutes clarify the functions of the "Presidents Church Council" in Kirtland, Ohio and contain instructions about how councils are to be conducted in the Church. At a council held a few days earlier on February 12, Joseph Smith expressed concerns about the way councils were being conducted and told those present that "in ancient days councils were conducted with such strict propriety, that no one was allowed to whisper, be weary, leave the room, or get uneasy in the least, until the voice of the Lord, by revelation, or by the voice of the Council by the spirit was obtained."[1] Joseph chastised the council in Kirtland because, as he noted, "generally, one would be uneasy, another asleep, one praying another not; one's mind on the business of the Council and another thinking on something else."[2] He emphasized the importance of councils by teaching, "Our acts are recorded, and at a future day they will be laid before us, and if we should fail to judge right and injure our fellow beings, they may there perhaps condemn us."[3]

Five days later, the council met again, this time presided over by the First Presidency of the Church, who also served as the stake presidency in Kirtland. Orson Hyde and Oliver Cowdery recorded the minutes of the meeting, and Joseph Smith significantly revised them two days later, on February 19.[4] Several months later, after traveling to Missouri with Zion's Camp, the Prophet also organized another high council in Missouri on July 3, 1834. The stake presidency of the Church in Missouri presided over this high council.[5] At the time, there were only two stakes in the Church—one in Ohio and one in Missouri. As the Church grew and new stakes were created, high councils serving under stake presidencies were organized according to this pattern.

Though this section is not a formal revelation, the patterns and procedures were revealed to Joseph Smith. Speaking to the council, Joseph explained "the order of Councils in ancient days as shown to him by vision. The law by which to govern the Council in the Church of Christ. Jerusalem was the seat of the Church Council in ancient days. The apostle, Peter, was the president of the Council and held the Keys of the Kingdom of God, on the Earth was appointed to this office by the voice of the Savior and acknowledged in it by the voice of the Church."[6] The minutes were placed in the 1835 edition of the Doctrine and Covenants. They remain an important guide for how councils are to be conducted in the Church.[7]

$\mathcal{V}$erse-by-$\mathcal{V}$erse $\mathcal{C}$ommentary

1 This day a general council of twenty-four high priests assembled at the house of Joseph Smith, Jun., by revelation, and proceeded to organize the high council of the church of Christ, which was to consist of twelve high priests, and one or three presidents as the case might require.

2 The high council was appointed by revelation for the purpose of settling important difficulties which might arise in the church, which could not be settled by the church or the bishop's council to the satisfaction of the parties.

3 Joseph Smith, Jun., Sidney Rigdon and Frederick G. Williams were acknowledged presidents by the voice of the council; and Joseph Smith, Sen., John Smith, Joseph Coe, John Johnson, Martin Harris, John S. Carter, Jared Carter, Oliver Cowdery, Samuel H. Smith, Orson Hyde, Sylvester Smith, and Luke Johnson, high priests, were chosen to be a standing council for the church, by the unanimous voice of the council.

4 The above-named councilors were then asked whether they accepted their appointments, and whether they would act in that office according to the law of heaven, to which they all answered that they accepted their appointments, and would fill their offices according to the grace of God bestowed upon them.

5 The number composing the council, who voted in the name and for the church in appointing the above-named councilors were forty-three, as follows: nine high priests, seventeen elders, four priests, and thirteen members.

6 Voted: that the high council cannot have power to act without seven of the above-named councilors, or their regularly appointed successors are present.

7 These seven shall have power to appoint other high priests, whom they may consider worthy and capable to act in the place of absent councilors.

8 Voted: that whenever any vacancy shall occur by the death, removal from office for transgression, or removal from the bounds of this church government, of any one of the above-named councilors, it shall be filled by the nomination of the president or presidents, and sanctioned by the voice of a general council of high priests, convened for that purpose, to act in the name of the church.

The high council in Kirtland was unique because the First Presidency also presided over it as a stake presidency. As the first high council in the Church, the Kirtland high council was established before wards came into existence. Today the Church has a different system in which a stake presidency presides over a group of high priests that constitute the high council for that stake. Modern high councils assist stake presidencies in carrying out the Lord's work in the various wards of each stake. The Kirtland high council was established as a "standing council" (verse 3), meaning that it was responsible for a specific geographical area designated as a stake but consisting largely of branches. Beginning with the Quorum of the Twelve Apostles, traveling councils not limited by any geographic area were established by later revelations (see Doctrine and Covenants 107:23). Using terminology common in the Church today, we refer to standing councils as *local* or *area authorities* and those councils with no specific geographic responsibility as *General Authorities*. In addition to a high council, section 102 also refers to a "bishop's council" (verse 2).

The establishment of councils in the early Church was an important step toward disseminating the divine power first given to Joseph Smith and Oliver Cowdery. Today councils remain one of the most important methods for receiving revelation in the Church. Stephen L Richards, a member of the First Presidency under David O. McKay, taught:

> As I conceive it, the genius of our Church government is government through *councils*. The Council of the Presidency, the Council of the Twelve, the Council of the Stake Presidency . . . the Council of the Bishopric. . . . I have had enough experience to know the value of councils. . . . I see the wisdom, God's wisdom, in creating councils: to govern his Kingdom. In the spirit under which we labor, men can get together with seemingly divergent views and far different backgrounds, and under the operation of that spirit, by counseling together, they can arrive at an accord.[8]

9 The president of the church, who is also the president of the council, is appointed by revelation, and acknowledged in his administration by the voice of the church.

10 And it is according to the dignity of his office that he should preside over the council of the church; and it is his privilege to be assisted by two other presidents, appointed after the same manner that he himself was appointed.

11 And in case of the absence of one or both of those who are appointed to assist him, he has power to preside over the council without an assistant; and in case he himself is absent, the other presidents have power to preside in his stead, both or either of them.

12 Whenever a high council of the church of Christ is regularly organized, according to the foregoing pattern, it shall be the

duty of the twelve councilors to cast lots by numbers, and thereby ascertain who of the twelve shall speak first, commencing with number one and so in succession to number twelve.

Verses 9–12 explain the procedures for holding a Church membership council. As noted in Doctrine and Covenants 102:2, these councils convene to deal with difficult cases that cannot be resolved by a bishop's council. Most repentance is handled between an individual, the Lord, and sometimes those who have been affected by the individual's sins. More serious sins are resolved with the assistance of a bishop, who holds the keys to act as a judge in Israel. Church membership councils, which have also been known as Church courts or Church disciplinary councils, deal with sins for which a membership council is required and usually involve a person who has made temple covenants or who holds an important position of trust in the Church.[9]

Church membership councils are generally held for three reasons. First, they are held to help protect others. As the *General Handbook* states, "Sometimes a person poses a physical or spiritual threat. Predatory behaviors, physical harm, sexual abuse, substance abuse, fraud, and apostasy are some of the ways this can occur. With inspiration, a bishop or stake president acts to protect others when someone poses a threat in these and other serious ways (see Alma 5:59–60)."[10]

Second, a Church membership council may be held to help a person access the redeeming power of Jesus Christ through repentance. "Through this process, he or she may again become clean and worthy to receive all of God's blessings."[11] When serious sin has occurred, these councils can help individuals come to terms with what has occurred, use the power of Jesus Christ to overcome their sins, and repair the damage done to themselves and the important relationships in their lives. These councils are conducted in the spirit of love—every involved individual seeks to do what is best for the individual who has fallen into transgression.

Finally, Church membership councils are held to protect the integrity of the Church. "Restricting or withdrawing a person's Church membership may be necessary if his or her conduct significantly harms the Church (see Alma 39:11). The integrity of the Church is not protected by concealing or minimizing serious sins—but by addressing them."[12]

13 Whenever this council convenes to act upon any case, the twelve councilors shall consider whether it is a difficult one or

not; if it is not, two only of the councilors shall speak upon it, according to the form above written.

14 But if it is thought to be difficult, four shall be appointed; and if more difficult, six; but in no case shall more than six be appointed to speak.

15 The accused, in all cases, has a right to one-half of the council, to prevent insult or injustice.

16 And the councilors appointed to speak before the council are to present the case, after the evidence is examined, in its true light before the council; and every man is to speak according to equity and justice.

17 Those councilors who draw even numbers, that is, 2, 4, 6, 8, 10, and 12, are the individuals who are to stand up in behalf of the accused, and prevent insult and injustice.

18 In all cases the accuser and the accused shall have a privilege of speaking for themselves before the council, after the evidences are heard and the councilors who are appointed to speak on the case have finished their remarks.

According to the instructions given in section 102, when a Church membership council is convened, high councilors draw lots numbered from one to twelve. Those who draw even-numbered lots are asked to represent the needs of the accused, ensuring that the individual is treated fairly in the council. This does not mean that those who draw even lots act as defense attorneys and those who draw odd-numbered lots act as prosecutors. In these councils, all who are present are simply seeking for the truth and for the best way forward for the accused. This is another procedure followed by councils today found in example of the councils held in the early Church.

Joseph Smith explained:

It was not the order of heaven in ancient councils to plead for and against the guilty as in our judicial courts (so called) but that every counselor when he arose to speak, should speak precisely according to evidence and according to the teaching of the spirit of the Lord, that no counselor should attempt to screen the guilty when his guilt was manifest[.] That the person accused before the high council had a right to one half the members of the council to plead his cause, in order that his case might be fairly presented before the president that a decision might be rendered according to truth and righteousness.[13]

When it came to the rights of the accused, Joseph explained, "In all cases, the accuser and the accused have a perfect right to speak for themselves before the council."[14] In most cases, when individuals appear before a Church membership council, they have already spoken with their bishop and stake president. The council is held to allow individuals to make a full accounting of their sins and to allow the council members to use their collective wisdom to assist in finding the best way forward for the individual.

> 19 After the evidences are heard, the councilors, accuser and accused have spoken, the president shall give a decision according to the understanding which he shall have of the case, and call upon the twelve councilors to sanction the same by their vote.

> 20 But should the remaining councilors, who have not spoken, or any one of them, after hearing the evidences and pleadings impartially, discover an error in the decision of the president, they can manifest it, and the case shall have a re-hearing.

> 21 And if, after a careful re-hearing, any additional light is shown upon the case, the decision shall be altered accordingly.

> 22 But in case no additional light is given, the first decision shall stand, the majority of the council having power to determine the same.

> 23 In case of difficulty respecting doctrine or principle, if there is not a sufficiency written to make the case clear to the minds of the council, the president may inquire and obtain the mind of the Lord by revelation.

Once the evidence has been presented in a Church membership council, the councilors and the stake presidency discuss the case and seek to "obtain the mind of the Lord by revelation" (verse 23). In most councils, those present—especially the presiding officers—will make the outcome a matter of prayer. When revelation comes to the presiding officer, members of the council are asked to offer their sustaining vote or engage in further discussion.

Church membership councils have three possible outcomes: individuals remain in good standing with the Church, they have formal membership restrictions placed on them, or they have their Church membership withdrawn. In cases in which members remain in good standing, the members may be deemed innocent or may have already repented sincerely. Thus, they do not require further council actions. At times members are kept in good standing but are asked by the council to continue counseling with their bishop or stake president.[15]

In other situations, leaders may find it necessary to formally restrict a person's membership. This outcome is usually associated with sins that are very serious but do not require a withdrawal of Church membership. Membership restrictions could include asking the individual to not attend the temple, exercise priesthood authority, partake of the sacrament, or hold a calling in the Church. These restrictions usually remain in effect for at least one year, though they may be in place longer. At the end of the period of probation, the council reconvenes to determine if membership restrictions should be removed or continued.[16]

In the most serious cases, a person's membership in the Church may be withdrawn. This outcome is required in extreme cases in which murder, plural marriage, or incest may be involved. When a person is judged to be a danger to others or to have committed a very serious sin, or when a person does not demonstrate repentance for serious sins or commits serious sins that harm the Church, their membership records may also be withdrawn. Those who have had their membership withdrawn may be considered for baptism and readmission to the Church after one year and after a Church membership council has met to consider their repentance.[17] Withdrawing an individual's Church membership is intended not as a punishment but as a measure to protect the vulnerable and to withdraw the expectations of sacred covenants from a person who is not able to keep them.

> 24 The high priests, when abroad, have power to call and organize a council after the manner of the foregoing, to settle difficulties, when the parties or either of them shall request it.
>
> 25 And the said council of high priests shall have power to appoint one of their own number to preside over such council for the time being.
>
> 26 It shall be the duty of said council to transmit, immediately, a copy of their proceedings, with a full statement of the testimony accompanying their decision, to the high council of the seat of the First Presidency of the Church.

27 Should the parties or either of them be dissatisfied with the decision of said council, they may appeal to the high council of the seat of the First Presidency of the Church, and have a re-hearing, which case shall there be conducted, according to the former pattern written, as though no such decision had been made.

28 This council of high priests abroad is only to be called on the most difficult cases of church matters; and no common or ordinary case is to be sufficient to call such council.

29 The traveling or located high priests abroad have power to say whether it is necessary to call such a council or not.

30 There is a distinction between the high council or traveling high priests abroad, and the traveling high council composed of the twelve apostles, in their decisions.

31 From the decision of the former there can be an appeal; but from the decision of the latter there cannot.

32 The latter can only be called in question by the general authorities of the church in case of transgression.

33 Resolved: that the president or presidents of the seat of the First Presidency of the Church shall have power to determine whether any such case, as may be appealed, is justly entitled to a re-hearing, after examining the appeal and the evidences and statements accompanying it.

34 The twelve councilors then proceeded to cast lots or ballot, to ascertain who should speak first, and the following was the result, namely: 1, Oliver Cowdery; 2, Joseph Coe; 3, Samuel H. Smith; 4, Luke Johnson; 5, John S. Carter; 6, Sylvester Smith; 7, John Johnson; 8, Orson Hyde; 9, Jared Carter; 10, Joseph Smith, Sen.; 11, John Smith; 12, Martin Harris.

After prayer the conference adjourned.

OLIVER COWDERY,
ORSON HYDE,
CLERKS

Verses 30–32 were added in the 1835 edition of the Doctrine and Covenants under the direction of Joseph Smith. Joseph called the first Quorum of the Twelve Apostles in 1835, making it necessary to amend these instructions. The decision to add these verses effectively places the Quorum of the Twelve over stake high councils in authority. As instructed in verse 31, a decision made by a lower council can be appealed to a higher council.

A later revelation specifies that "the most important business of the church, and the most difficult cases of the church, inasmuch as there is not satisfaction upon the decision of the bishop or judges, it shall be handed over and carried up unto the council of the church, before the Presidency of the High Priesthood" (Doctrine and Covenants 107:78). For instance, "the First Presidency has final authority over all Church membership restrictions and withdrawal."[18] A later revelation also specifies that there is no appeal beyond the authority of the First Presidency, declaring, "And after this decision it shall be had in remembrance no more before the Lord; for this is the highest council of the church of God, and a final decision upon controversies in spiritual matters. There is not any person belonging to the church who is exempt from this council of the church" (Doctrine and Covenants 107:80–81).

End Notes

1. Minutes, 12 February 1834, 27–28, josephsmithpapers.org.
2. Minutes, 12 February 1834, 28, josephsmithpapers.org.
3. Minutes, 12 February 1834, 28, josephsmithpapers.org.
4. For comparison, see Minutes, 17 February 1834, josephsmithpapers.org.
5. See Minutes, 3 July 1834, 43, josephsmithpapers.org.
6. Minutes, 17 February 1834, 29–20, josephsmithpapers.org.
7. See "Historical Introduction," Revised Minutes, 18–19 February 1834 [D&C 102], josephsmithpapers.org.
8. Stephen L Richards, in Conference Report, Oct. 1953, 86.
9. For a list of situations that require the convening of a Church membership council, see *General Handbook: Serving in The Church of Jesus Christ of Latter-day Saints*, 32.6.1, Gospel Library. For a list of situations in which a Church membership council is not normally necessary, see *General Handbook*, 32.6.4.1.
10. *General Handbook*, 32.2.1.
11. *General Handbook*, 32.2.2.
12. *General Handbook*, 32.2.3.
13. Minutes, 17 February 1834, 30, josephsmithpapers.org.
14. Minutes, 17 February 1834, 30, josephsmithpapers.org.
15. See *General Handbook*, 32.11.1, 32.11.2.
16. See *General Handbook*, 32.11.3.
17. See *General Handbook*, 32.11.4.
18. *General Handbook*, 32.11.6.

Doctrine and Covenants Section 103

The Redemption of Zion

Historical Context

In November 1833 the Saints in Jackson County, Missouri, were driven out of their homes. Most of the Saints escaped to nearby Clay County, where they labored to find adequate shelter and sustenance before winter came. Parley P. Pratt notes, "Hundreds of people were seen in every direction, some in tents and some in the open air around their fires, while the rain descended in torrents. Husbands were inquiring for their wives, wives for their husbands; parents for children, and children for parents. . . . The scene was indescribable, and, I am sure, would have melted the hearts of any people on the earth, except our blind oppressors, and a blind and ignorant community."[1] Lyman Wight recalls, "I saw one hundred and ninety women and children driven thirty miles across the prairie, with three decrepit men only in their company, in the month of Nov[ember], the ground thinly crusted with sleet, and I could easily follow on their trail by the blood that flowed from their lacerated feet . . . on the stubble of the burnt prairie."[2]

A conference was held among the Saints in Missouri, who decided to send Parley P. Pratt and Lyman Wight to Kirtland to inform Church leadership of the Saints' situation. Joseph received section 103 the same day that the two men reported on the crisis to the high council in Kirtland. During the high council meeting, Pratt and Wight asked "how and by what means Zion was to be redeemed from our enemies."[3] The minutes of the meeting reveal that "Bro. Joseph arose and said that he was going to Zion to assist in redeeming it."[4] Joseph called for volunteers to go with him, and around thirty to forty of those present offered to go. The council then nominated Joseph to serve as "the Commander in Chief of the Armies of Israel and the leader of those who volunteered to go and assist in the redemption of Zion."[5] It is not known if section 103 was given before, during, or after the high council meeting in which Joseph volunteered to travel to Zion.

Church leadership immediately began acting on the commandments given in section 103. Just two days after Joseph received them, he and Parley P. Pratt left home to begin recruiting volunteers to go to Missouri. In the following weeks, Orson Pratt, Orson Hyde, Hyrum Smith, and Frederick G. Williams all joined in the recruiting efforts. Parley later notes that "our mission resulted in the assembling of about two hundred men at Kirtland, with teams, baggage, provisions, arms, etc. for a march of one thousand miles, for the purpose of carrying some supplies to the afflicted and persecuted Saints in Missouri, and to reinforce and strengthen them, and, if possible, to influence the Governor of the State to call out sufficient additional force to cooperate in restoring them to their rights. This little army was led by President Joseph Smith in person."[6] In records from Joseph's time, this group was referred to as the "Camp of Israel." It was later known by the name "Zion's Camp."[7]

Verse-by-Verse Commentary

1 Verily I say unto you, my friends, behold, I will give unto you a revelation and commandment, that you may know how to act in the discharge of your duties concerning the salvation and

redemption of your brethren, who have been scattered on the land of Zion;

2 Being driven and smitten by the hands of mine enemies, on whom I will pour out my wrath without measure in mine own time.

3 For I have suffered them thus far, that they might fill up the measure of their iniquities, that their cup might be full;

4 And that those who call themselves after my name might be chastened for a little season with a sore and grievous chastisement, because they did not hearken altogether unto the precepts and commandments which I gave unto them.

The Lord provides two reasons why the Saints in Jackson County were allowed to be persecuted. First, the Lord allowed the wicked to "fill up the measure of their iniquities" (verse 3). The Book of Mormon records a similar situation in which Alma and Amulek are forced to watch the cold-blooded murder of innocent men, women, and children at the hands of the wicked. When Amulek asks Alma to use the power of the priesthood to end the bloodshed, Alma replies that he was constrained from acting by the influence of the Spirit. He then teaches Amulek that the Lord "doth suffer that they may do this thing, or that the people may do this thing unto them, according to the hardness of their hearts, that the judgments which he shall exercise upon them in his wrath may be just; and the blood of the innocent shall stand as a witness against them, yea, and cry mightily against them at the last day" (Alma 14:11).

Second, the Lord allowed the Saints to be persecuted to chasten them "because they did not hearken altogether unto the precepts and commandments which I gave unto them" (verse 4). The Lord here simply emphasizes what was given in an earlier revelation: the Saints "polluted their inheritances" because of "jarrings, and contentions, and envying, and strifes, and lustful and covetous desires among them" (Doctrine and Covenants 101:6). But although the Saints in Jackson County were guilty of transgression, they were not cast off. The Lord had more for them to do. The primary purpose of section 103 is to rally the rest of the Church to help the suffering Saints in Missouri.

5 But verily I say unto you, that I have decreed a decree which my people shall realize, inasmuch as they hearken from this very

hour unto the counsel which I, the Lord their God, shall give unto them.

6 Behold they shall, for I have decreed it, begin to prevail against mine enemies from this very hour.

7 And by hearkening to observe all the words which I, the Lord their God, shall speak unto them, they shall never cease to prevail until the kingdoms of the world are subdued under my feet, and the earth is given unto the saints, to possess it forever and ever.

8 But inasmuch as they keep not my commandments, and hearken not to observe all my words, the kingdoms of the world shall prevail against them.

9 For they were set to be a light unto the world, and to be the saviors of men;

10 And inasmuch as they are not the saviors of men, they are as salt that has lost its savor, and is thenceforth good for nothing but to be cast out and trodden under foot of men.

Even during this time of suffering, the Lord still extends His hand toward the Saints, if they will hearken "from this very hour unto the counsel" He gives to them (verse 5). The Lord holds high expectations for the Saints and declares their purpose to be "a light unto the world, and to be the saviors of men" (verse 9). Note that the Saints are given the title of "saviors" with a lowercase s; they are not on the same level as the Savior, Jesus Christ. The title "saviors" is linked to the prophecy of Obadiah that "saviors shall come up on mount Zion" (Obadiah 1:20). This prophecy and the concept of the Saints becoming "saviors" would gain greater importance as the theology of the Restoration, specifically the role of temple ordinances, was revealed to Joseph Smith.

The tribulations of the Saints in Ohio and Missouri were soul-rending, but they helped refine the Saints and bring them closer toward being a people who could truly act as "saviors on mount Zion" to the rest of the human race.

11 But verily I say unto you, I have decreed that your brethren which have been scattered shall return to the lands of their inheritances, and shall build up the waste places of Zion.

12 For after much tribulation, as I have said unto you in a former commandment, cometh the blessing.

13 Behold, this is the blessing which I have promised after your tribulations, and the tribulations of your brethren—your redemption, and the redemption of your brethren, even their restoration to the land of Zion, to be established, no more to be thrown down.

14 Nevertheless, if they pollute their inheritances they shall be thrown down; for I will not spare them if they pollute their inheritances.

15 Behold, I say unto you, the redemption of Zion must needs come by power;

16 Therefore, I will raise up unto my people a man, who shall lead them like as Moses led the children of Israel.

17 For ye are the children of Israel, and of the seed of Abraham, and ye must needs be led out of bondage by power, and with a stretched-out arm.

18 And as your fathers were led at the first, even so shall the redemption of Zion be.

19 Therefore, let not your hearts faint, for I say not unto you as I said unto your fathers: Mine angel shall go up before you, but not my presence.

20 But I say unto you: Mine angels shall go up before you, and also my presence, and in time ye shall possess the goodly land.

In verse 15 the Lord declares that "the redemption of Zion must needs come by power." This prophecy will come to pass, though we do not know the time frame. The Savior says specifically that He "will raise up unto my people a man, who shall lead them like as Moses led the children of Israel" (Doctrine and Covenants 107:16). For the identity of this modern Moses, we need look no further than Doctrine and Covenants 107:91, in which the Lord declares that "the President of the office of the High Priesthood is [called] to preside over the whole church, and to be like Moses." When the redemption of Zion is at last brought to pass, it will be under the direction of the President of the Church, whoever it will be in that day.

The Lord further identifies the Saints with the children of Israel and the seed of Abraham, telling them that they will be led "even as your fathers were led" (verse 18). The day of the redemption of Zion will be a time of miracles. Just as the Israelites witnessed the parting of the Red Sea, followed a pillar of fire, and ate manna from heaven, so will their latter-day descendants see similar miracles. At the same time, when we compare the building of Zion to the exodus of the children of Israel from Egypt, we should also take into account the Lord's emphasis on purity among His people. The Lord allowed the children of Israel to wander for forty years before they were ready to move into their promised land. We do not know how long the period of purification for the Latter-day Saints will be before we can finally build the Lord's holy city.

21 Verily, verily I say unto you, that my servant Joseph Smith, Jun., is the man to whom I likened the servant to whom the Lord of the vineyard spake in the parable which I have given unto you.

22 Therefore let my servant Joseph Smith, Jun., say unto the strength of my house, my young men and the middle aged— Gather yourselves together unto the land of Zion, upon the land which I have bought with money that has been consecrated unto me.

23 And let all the churches send up wise men with their moneys, and purchase lands even as I have commanded them.

24 And inasmuch as mine enemies come against you to drive you from my goodly land, which I have consecrated to be the land of Zion, even from your own lands after these testimonies, which ye have brought before me against them, ye shall curse them;

25 And whomsoever ye curse, I will curse, and ye shall avenge me of mine enemies.

26 And my presence shall be with you even in avenging me of mine enemies, unto the third and fourth generation of them that hate me.

27 Let no man be afraid to lay down his life for my sake; for whoso layeth down his life for my sake shall find it again.

28 And whoso is not willing to lay down his life for my sake is not my disciple.

The Lord identifies Joseph Smith as the servant referred to in the parable of the redemption of Zion (see Doctrine and Covenants 101:55). Though the Lord told the Saints that the redemption of Zion would come "by power" (Doctrine and Covenants 103:15), this phrase does not refer to violence on the part of the Saints. A quick review of the revelations in the Doctrine and Covenants will show that the Saints were continually instructed to purchase the lands in Zion (see verse 23) and obtain the land through peaceful and legal means (see Doctrine and Covenants 42:5; 45:65–66; 48:4–5; 57:4–6; 58:49–52; 63:27–30; 101:70–71; 105:28–30).

None of the men who chose to travel with Zion's Camp were asked to fire a shot in anger. The most significant conflict the expedition experienced came when they arrived at Fishing River, just ten miles away from the beleaguered Missouri Saints. As the members of Zion's Camp pitched their tents, five men rode into the camp. The visitors waved their weapons and announced that more than three hundred men were coming to destroy the Saints. Alarmed by this visit, Joseph posted guards around the area, and one member of the camp begged the Prophet to attack the mob first. Instead, Joseph told the group to "stand still and see the salvation of God."[8]

Shortly after Joseph's declaration, dark clouds gathered overhead. Nathan Baldwin, a member of the camp, recalls, "A small black cloud appeared in the west and increased in size until shortly the whole blue arch was draped in black, presenting a vengeful appearance, while the rain descended in torrents, the winds bellowed[,] and such vivid flashes of lightning and such peals of thunder are seldom seen and heard."[9]

A rainstorm of overwhelming fury burst upon the camp, driving the members of Zion's Camp from their tents in search of better shelter. Many of the camp members huddled in a small church nearby. As they huddled inside the building, Joseph Smith entered, shaking the water from his hat and clothes. He looked around and exclaimed with exuberance, "Boys, there is some meaning to this—God is in this storm!" As the storm continued to rage, the men remained huddled in the church, singing hymns throughout the night. Nathan Baldwin later wrote, "The Lord had previously said He would fight the battles of His saints, and it seemed as though the mandate had gone forth from His presence, to ply the artillery of Heaven in defense of His servants."[10]

When they emerged in the morning, camp members found that their belongings were scattered, but nothing was damaged beyond repair. In addition, the river separating them from their enemies had risen dramatically overnight, cutting them off from a possible attack. In a later history, Joseph Smith recalls that their enemies "declared that if that was the way God fought for the Mormons, they might as well go about their business."[11]

29 It is my will that my servant Sidney Rigdon shall lift up his voice in the congregations in the eastern countries, in preparing the churches to keep the commandments which I have given unto them concerning the restoration and redemption of Zion.

30 It is my will that my servant Parley P. Pratt and my servant Lyman Wight should not return to the land of their brethren, until they have obtained companies to go up unto the land of Zion, by tens, or by twenties, or by fifties, or by an hundred, until they have obtained to the number of five hundred of the strength of my house.

31 Behold this is my will; ask and ye shall receive; but men do not always do my will.

32 Therefore, if you cannot obtain five hundred, seek diligently that peradventure you may obtain three hundred.

33 And if ye cannot obtain three hundred, seek diligently that peradventure ye may obtain one hundred.

34 But verily I say unto you, a commandment I give unto you, that ye shall not go up unto the land of Zion until you have obtained a hundred of the strength of my house, to go up with you unto the land of Zion.

35 Therefore, as I said unto you, ask and ye shall receive; pray earnestly that peradventure my servant Joseph Smith, Jun., may go with you, and preside in the midst of my people, and organize my kingdom upon the consecrated land, and establish the children of Zion upon the laws and commandments which have been and which shall be given unto you.

36 All victory and glory is brought to pass unto you through your diligence, faithfulness, and prayers of faith.

37 Let my servant Parley P. Pratt journey with my servant Joseph Smith, Jun.

38 Let my servant Lyman Wight journey with my servant Sidney Rigdon.

39 Let my servant Hyrum Smith journey with my servant Frederick G. Williams.

40 Let my servant Orson Hyde journey with my servant Orson Pratt, whithersoever my servant Joseph Smith, Jun., shall counsel them, in obtaining the fulfilment of these commandments which I have given unto you, and leave the residue in my hands. Even so. Amen.

Though the Lord in verse 30 instructed Church leaders that they could recruit as many as 500 men for the expedition to Zion, in the end Zion's Camp numbered about 205 men and approximately 25 women and children.[12] On May 3, 1834, Joseph Smith led the main party from Kirtland. A smaller group left the Michigan Territory on May 5 under the leadership of Lyman Wight and Hyrum Smith.

Joseph Smith had faith in the Lord and the charge given to him to lead the camp, but he also worried over the size of their group. A month into the expedition he wrote to his wife, Emma, "All the Camp is in as good a situation as could be expected; but our numbers and means are altogether too small for the accomplishment of such a great enterprise."[13] Still, Joseph had hope for a miracle to redeem Zion. "We believe the hand of the Lord is in it," he wrote to Emma. "Now is the time for the Church abroad to come to Zion. It is our prayer day and night that God will open the heart of the Churches to pour in men and means to assist us, for the redemption and upbuilding of Zion."[14]

End Notes

1. Parley P. Pratt, *Autobiography of Parley P. Pratt (Revised and Enhanced)* (Salt Lake City, UT: Deseret Book, 2000), 102.
2. Lyman Wight, in "Trial of Joseph Smith," *Times and Seasons,* July 15, 1843, 264.
3. Minutes, 24 January 1834, 41, josephsmithpapers.org.
4. Minutes, 24 January 1834, 42, josephsmithpapers.org.
5. Minutes, 24 January 1834, 42, josephsmithpapers.org.
6. Parley P. Pratt, *Autobiography of Parley P. Pratt*, 102.
7. "Camp of Israel," Joseph Smith Papers, accessed Feb. 20, 2024, https://www.josephsmithpapers.org/topic/camp-of-israel. See also "Historical Introduction," Revelation, 24 February 1834 [D&C 103], josephsmithpapers.org.
8. *Saints: The Story of the Church of Jesus Christ in the Latter Days,* vol. 1, *The Standard of Truth, 1815–1846,* 2018, 203–4.
9. Matthew C. Godfrey, "The Acceptable Offering of Zion's Camp," in *Revelations in Context* (2016), 216.
10. Godfrey, "The Acceptable Offering of Zion's Camp," 216.
11. Joseph Smith, in History, 1838–1856, volume A-1 [23 December 1805–30 August 1834], 15–16 (addenda), josephsmithpapers.org.
12. See Matthew C. Godfrey, "The Acceptable Offering of Zion's Camp," 214.
13. Letter to Emma Smith, 4 June 1834, 57, josephsmithpapers.org.
14. Letter to Emma Smith, 4 June 1834, 57, josephsmithpapers.org.

$\mathcal{D}$octrine and $\mathcal{C}$ovenants Section 104

An Everlasting Order for the Benefit of My Church

$\mathcal{H}$istorical $\mathcal{C}$ontext

IN APRIL 1834, EVEN AS JOSEPH SMITH WAS PREPARING TO TRAVEL TO AS-
sist the Saints in Missouri, he was also attempting to reorganize the financial
affairs of the Church. The reorganization was necessary because the expulsion of the Saints from Zion seriously impacted Church finances. Many
Church assets and businesses in Ohio and Missouri were overseen by the
United Firm, which was organized in 1832 (see Doctrine and Covenants
78:3; 82:11–12). Mob attacks in Missouri put several elements of the United
Firm, including the printshop operated by William W. Phelps and the store
operated by Sidney Gilbert, out of business. Around the same time, an apostate member of the Church in Kirtland, Doctor Philastus Hurlbut, began
bringing lawsuits against Church leaders. Hurlbut was attempting to obtain
property owned by the United Firm, and fighting his continuous lawsuits
brought further legal fees and travel expenses.

In the midst of these difficulties, Joseph Smith became concerned: unless the situation in Kirtland was remedied, he might not be able to travel to Missouri to assist the Saints there. In a letter to Orson Hyde written on April 7, 1834, Joseph lamented that "unless we can obtain help I myself cannot go to Zion, and if I do not go it will be impossible to get my brethren in Kirtland[,] any of them[,] to go[,] and if we do not go it is in vain for our eastern brethren to think of going."[1] During this time, Joseph met in prayer with Oliver Cowdery, Newel K. Whitney, Heber C. Kimball, and Frederick G. Williams to pray for guidance. Joseph wrote that they "met in the council room, and bowed down before the Lord, and prayed that he would furnish the means to deliver the Firm from debt, that they might be set at liberty; also that I might prevail against that wicked man, Hurlburt [Doctor Philastus Hurlbut], and that he might be put to shame."[2] A few days later, Hurlbut lost his lawsuit, was placed under a bond to keep the peace, and was ordered to pay all legal costs.[3]

The question still remained as to how to save the United Firm. On April 10 members of the United Firm met and agreed that the firm should be dissolved and that each member should have their stewardship given to them as private property.[4] In hopes of obtaining funds to make the dissolution unnecessary, firm members delayed two weeks. On April 23, members of the firm met again and received Doctrine and Covenants 104. This revelation directed Church leaders to reorganize the firm into two separate orders, one in Ohio and the other in Missouri. The Lord also instructed them concerning the Church's properties and how to deal with debts incurred by Church members. An unpublished revelation given five days later declared that the Kirtland branch of the firm was "free from the firm of Zion."[5] Members of the original order still received their individual stewardships.

When section 104 was later published in the 1835 edition of the Doctrine and Covenants, the named leaders were given code names, and the references to the "United Firm" were replaced with "united order."[6] On the surface, Doctrine and Covenants 104 appears to address the very specific circumstances of the Saints in Kirtland. However, many of the principles of finance found in this revelation concerning stewardships, resources, and avoiding debt became important to Church leaders and still guide the Church in its financial matters today.[7]

*V*erse-by-*V*erse *C*ommentary

1 Verily I say unto you, my friends, I give unto you counsel, and a commandment, concerning all the properties which belong to the order which I commanded to be organized and established, to be a united order, and an everlasting order for the benefit of my church, and for the salvation of men until I come—

2 With promise immutable and unchangeable, that inasmuch as those whom I commanded were faithful they should be blessed with a multiplicity of blessings;

3 But inasmuch as they were not faithful they were nigh unto cursing.

4 Therefore, inasmuch as some of my servants have not kept the commandment, but have broken the covenant through covetousness, and with feigned words, I have cursed them with a very sore and grievous curse.

5 For I, the Lord, have decreed in my heart, that inasmuch as any man belonging to the order shall be found a transgressor, or, in other words, shall break the covenant with which ye are bound, he shall be cursed in his life, and shall be trodden down by whom I will;

6 For I, the Lord, am not to be mocked in these things—

7 And all this that the innocent among you may not be condemned with the unjust; and that the guilty among you may not escape; because I, the Lord, have promised unto you a crown of glory at my right hand.

8 Therefore, inasmuch as you are found transgressors, you cannot escape my wrath in your lives.

9 Inasmuch as ye are cut off for transgression, ye cannot escape the buffetings of Satan until the day of redemption.

10 And I now give unto you power from this very hour, that if any man among you, of the order, is found a transgressor and repenteth not of the evil, that ye shall deliver him over unto the

buffetings of Satan; and he shall not have power to bring evil upon you.

The commandment that the Lord refers to in verse 4 is most likely a reference to Doctrine and Covenants 98:20–22. In that revelation, given about eight months earlier, the Lord expressed His displeasure toward the Saints in Kirtland, saying:

> For they do not forsake their sins, and their wicked ways, the pride of their hearts, and their covetousness, and all their detestable things, and observe the words of wisdom and eternal life which I have given unto them.
>
> Verily I say unto you, that I, the Lord, will chasten them and will do whatsoever I list, if they do not repent and observe all things whatsoever I have said unto them.
>
> And again I say unto you, if ye observe to do whatsoever I command you, I, the Lord, will turn away all wrath and indignation from you, and the gates of hell shall not prevail against you.

Doctrine and Covenants 104 declares that members of the order were guilty of covetousness. Entering into the united order came at considerable sacrifice, and many of the Saints struggled to have faith that the Lord would provide for them. Brigham Young later recalls:

> In the fall of 1833, many of the brethren had gathered to Kirtland, and not finding suitable employment, and having some difficulty in getting their pay after they had labored, several went off to Willoughby, Painesville and Cleveland. I told them I had gathered to Kirtland because I was so directed by the Prophet of God, and I was not going away to Willoughby, Painesville, Cleveland, nor anywhere else to build up the Gentiles, but I was going to stay here and seek the things that pertained to the kingdom of God by listening to the teachings of his servants, and I should work for my brethren and trust in God and them that I would be paid. I labored for Brother Cahoon and finished his house, and although he did not know he could pay me when I commenced, before I finished he had me paid in full. I then went to work for Father John Smith and others, who paid me, and sustained myself in Kirtland, and when the brethren who had gone out to work for the Gentiles returned, I had means, though some of them were scant.[8]

Based on this revelation, the Saints had not fully committed to working and serving among their own community. This lack of commitment kept them from fully living the principles of the law of consecration. Because of their "feigned words" (verse 4), the order was cursed and did not prosper.

> 11 It is wisdom in me; therefore, a commandment I give unto you, that ye shall organize yourselves and appoint every man his stewardship;
>
> 12 That every man may give an account unto me of the stewardship which is appointed unto him.
>
> 13 For it is expedient that I, the Lord, should make every man accountable, as a steward over earthly blessings, which I have made and prepared for my creatures.
>
> 14 I, the Lord, stretched out the heavens, and built the earth, my very handiwork; and all things therein are mine.
>
> 15 And it is my purpose to provide for my saints, for all things are mine.
>
> 16 But it must needs be done in mine own way; and behold this is the way that I, the Lord, have decreed to provide for my saints, that the poor shall be exalted, in that the rich are made low.

The Lord in verse 11 directs the members of the order to take the order's collective assets and divide them into individual stewardships. The original publication of the revelation (and in part until the 1981 edition of the Doctrine and Covenants) referred to those who were to be given these stewardships by code names. These code names may have been used in part to protect individuals from litigation by enemies of the Church.

Beyond the division of property in Kirtland, the revelation highlights the importance of stewardships in the law of consecration. From the time the law was first revealed, the Lord has emphasized stewardship alongside community sacrifice (see Doctrine and Covenants 42:32). While members in Kirtland sacrificed to elevate the situation of the poor and the needy, they were also given the commandment to manage their individual stewardships, which were essentially considered private property. At the same time, the use of the word *steward* served as a reminder to the Saints that everything they owned really belonged to God. To become good stewards, we must be led by God to find ways to use our temporal and spiritual blessings to bless the lives of others.

17 For the earth is full, and there is enough and to spare; yea, I prepared all things, and have given unto the children of men to be agents unto themselves.

18 Therefore, if any man shall take of the abundance which I have made, and impart not his portion, according to the law of my gospel, unto the poor and the needy, he shall, with the wicked, lift up his eyes in hell, being in torment.

The creations of God are given to us to provide for our welfare and help us progress and grow. When the Lord teaches in verse 17 that "the earth is full, and there is enough and to spare," this does not mean that we can recklessly use our resources in any way that we choose. The very next phrase, "[I] have given unto the children of men to be agents unto themselves" (verse 17), shows that the Lord intends for us to be wise stewards over the precious resources we possess. It is not a scarcity of resources but a mismanagement of them that causes most of the poverty and suffering in the world.

In verses 17–18, the Lord alludes to the parable of the rich man and Lazarus (see Luke 16:19–31). In the parable, the rich man refuses to help Lazarus, a beggar who lives in the most difficult conditions. After both their lives end, the rich man looks up from hellfire toward Lazarus, who is content in Abraham's bosom. When the rich man begs for relief, Abraham tells him, "Son, remember that thou in thy lifetime receivedst thy good things, and likewise Lazarus evil things: but now he is comforted and thou art tormented" (Luke 16:25). The message is clear. Money is neither good nor evil; we determine our eternal fate in part by how we use it. Those who hide and hoard their blessings like the rich man will find themselves in torment. Meanwhile, those who give of their abundance and seek to find ways to lift and help everyone around them will find themselves rewarded with blessings in the next life, where money is meaningless.

19 And now, verily I say unto you, concerning the properties of the order—

20 Let my servant Sidney Rigdon have appointed unto him the place where he now resides, and the lot of the tannery for his stewardship, for his support while he is laboring in my vineyard, even as I will, when I shall command him.

21 And let all things be done according to the counsel of the order, and united consent or voice of the order, which dwell in the land of Kirtland.

22 And this stewardship and blessing, I, the Lord, confer upon my servant Sidney Rigdon for a blessing upon him, and his seed after him;

23 And I will multiply blessings upon him, inasmuch as he will be humble before me.

24 And again, let my servant Martin Harris have appointed unto him, for his stewardship, the lot of land which my servant John Johnson obtained in exchange for his former inheritance, for him and his seed after him;

25 And inasmuch as he is faithful, I will multiply blessings upon him and his seed after him.

26 And let my servant Martin Harris devote his moneys for the proclaiming of my words, according as my servant Joseph Smith, Jun., shall direct.

27 And again, let my servant Frederick G. Williams have the place upon which he now dwells.

28 And let my servant Oliver Cowdery have the lot which is set off joining the house, which is to be for the printing office, which is lot number one, and also the lot upon which his father resides.

29 And let my servants Frederick G. Williams and Oliver Cowdery have the printing office and all things that pertain unto it.

30 And this shall be their stewardship which shall be appointed unto them.

31 And inasmuch as they are faithful, behold I will bless, and multiply blessings upon them.

32 And this is the beginning of the stewardship which I have appointed them, for them and their seed after them.

33 And, inasmuch as they are faithful, I will multiply blessings upon them and their seed after them, even a multiplicity of blessings.

34 And again, let my servant John Johnson have the house in which he lives, and the inheritance, all save the ground which has been reserved for the building of my houses, which pertains to that inheritance, and those lots which have been named for my servant Oliver Cowdery.

35 And inasmuch as he is faithful, I will multiply blessings upon him.

36 And it is my will that he should sell the lots that are laid off for the building up of the city of my saints, inasmuch as it shall be made known to him by the voice of the Spirit, and according to the counsel of the order, and by the voice of the order.

37 And this is the beginning of the stewardship which I have appointed unto him, for a blessing unto him and his seed after him.

38 And inasmuch as he is faithful, I will multiply a multiplicity of blessings upon him.

39 And again, let my servant Newel K. Whitney have appointed unto him the houses and lot where he now resides, and the lot and building on which the mercantile establishment stands, and also the lot which is on the corner south of the mercantile establishment, and also the lot on which the ashery is situated.

40 And all this I have appointed unto my servant Newel K. Whitney for his stewardship, for a blessing upon him and his seed after him, for the benefit of the mercantile establishment of my order which I have established for my stake in the land of Kirtland.

41 Yea, verily, this is the stewardship which I have appointed unto my servant N. K. Whitney, even this whole mercantile establishment, him and his agent, and his seed after him.

42 And inasmuch as he is faithful in keeping my commandments, which I have given unto him, I will multiply blessings upon him and his seed after him, even a multiplicity of blessings.

43 And again, let my servant Joseph Smith, Jun., have appointed unto him the lot which is laid off for the building of my house, which is forty rods long and twelve wide, and also the inheritance upon which his father now resides;

44 And this is the beginning of the stewardship which I have appointed unto him, for a blessing upon him, and upon his father.

45 For behold, I have reserved an inheritance for his father, for his support; therefore he shall be reckoned in the house of my servant Joseph Smith, Jun.

46 And I will multiply blessings upon the house of my servant Joseph Smith, Jun., inasmuch as he is faithful, even a multiplicity of blessings.

In verses 19–46, the Lord divides the properties of the United Firm into individual stewardships among its members. For the most part, the assets of the firm described here were deeded to members who were already living on those properties. The legal ownership changed from the United Firm to the individual. As mentioned earlier, when this revelation was first published, this section contained code names to keep the members of the firm "from unnecessary scrutiny by a sometimes unfriendly public and peering creditors."[9] The Church used fifty-four code names for the names of officers, business properties, and places. Perhaps the most significant change was that the words "United Firm" were changed to "united order." The practice of using code names to protect Church individuals was followed in other revelations as well.[10]

The changes to the firm reflected the flexibility of the principles of the law of consecration. The United Firm played an important role in its time, but when section 104 was received, the needs of the Church were changing. One scholar notes, "The firm, while applying the principles of consecration and stewardship, was the means by which the infant Church tried to achieve its temporal mission. Thus, the Prophet used its board of managers to help build the Kingdom before the quorums of high-level leadership were developed to assist him in his work."[11] In the months following this revelation, the councils of the Church began to take over the work of the United Firm. This began first with the high council organized in Kirtland (see Doctrine and Covenants 102) and continued to the organization of a Presiding Bishopric, the Quorum of the Twelve, and Quorums of the Seventy (see Doctrine and

Covenants 107). The men listed in this revelation, despite their flaws, deserve recognition and gratitude for the role they played in helping assist the Church while its presiding quorums were still being revealed.

> 47 And now, a commandment I give unto you concerning Zion, that you shall no longer be bound as a united order to your brethren of Zion, only on this wise—
>
> 48 After you are organized, you shall be called the United Order of the Stake of Zion, the City of Kirtland. And your brethren, after they are organized, shall be called the United Order of the City of Zion.
>
> 49 And they shall be organized in their own names, and in their own name; and they shall do their business in their own name, and in their own names;
>
> 50 And you shall do your business in your own name, and in your own names.
>
> 51 And this I have commanded to be done for your salvation, and also for their salvation, in consequence of their being driven out and that which is to come.
>
> 52 The covenants being broken through transgression, by covetousness and feigned words—
>
> 53 Therefore, you are dissolved as a united order with your brethren, that you are not bound only up to this hour unto them, only on this wise, as I said, by loan as shall be agreed by this order in council, as your circumstances will admit and the voice of the council direct.

Before Doctrine and Covenants 104 was received, the United Firm represented the interests of the Church in both Ohio and Missouri. In this revelation, the Lord commanded the leaders to separate the United Firm into two separate branches, one in Kirtland and the other in Missouri. The Lord explains that this separation was "commanded to be done for your salvation," referring to the financial salvation of the Church (verse 51). In addition, the losses incurred by the Missouri order were so great that they threatened to bankrupt the entire Church. The Lord intended for the Saints to pay their debts (see Doctrine and Covenants 104:78), and the legal separation gave the Saints in Kirtland more time to raise the funds to pay for the debts incurred by the Missouri Saints (see Doctrine and Covenants 104:84–85).[12]

54 And again, a commandment I give unto you concerning your stewardship which I have appointed unto you.

55 Behold, all these properties are mine, or else your faith is vain, and ye are found hypocrites, and the covenants which ye have made unto me are broken;

56 And if the properties are mine, then ye are stewards; otherwise ye are no stewards.

57 But, verily I say unto you, I have appointed unto you to be stewards over mine house, even stewards indeed.

58 And for this purpose I have commanded you to organize yourselves, even to print my words, the fulness of my scriptures, the revelations which I have given unto you, and which I shall, hereafter, from time to time give unto you—

59 For the purpose of building up my church and kingdom on the earth, and to prepare my people for the time when I shall dwell with them, which is nigh at hand.

60 And ye shall prepare for yourselves a place for a treasury, and consecrate it unto my name.

61 And ye shall appoint one among you to keep the treasury, and he shall be ordained unto this blessing.

62 And there shall be a seal upon the treasury, and all the sacred things shall be delivered into the treasury; and no man among you shall call it his own, or any part of it, for it shall belong to you all with one accord.

63 And I give it unto you from this very hour; and now see to it, that ye go to and make use of the stewardship which I have appointed unto you, exclusive of the sacred things, for the purpose of printing these sacred things as I have said.

64 And the avails of the sacred things shall be had in the treasury, and a seal shall be upon it; and it shall not be used or taken out of the treasury by any one, neither shall the seal be loosed

which shall be placed upon it, only by the voice of the order, or by commandment.

65 And thus shall ye preserve the avails of the sacred things in the treasury, for sacred and holy purposes.

66 And this shall be called the sacred treasury of the Lord; and a seal shall be kept upon it that it may be holy and consecrated unto the Lord.

In a commandment that highlights the importance of the scriptures, the Lord directs Church leaders to create two treasuries, a "sacred treasury" and "another treasury" (verses 66–67). The sacred treasury was intended to house "sacred things" published by the Church and the "avails" or profits from the sales of these publications.[13] The "fulness of my scriptures" (verse 58) most likely refers to the Prophet's work to produce a new translation of the Bible. In 1835 Joseph Smith wrote a letter to the Saints, saying, "We are now commencing to prepare and print the New Translation, together with all the revelations which God has been pleased to give us in these last days, and as we are in want of funds to go on with so great and glorious a work, brethren we want you should [sic] donate and loan us all the means or money you can that we may be enable[d] to accomplish the work as a great means towards the salvation of Men."[14]

Unfortunately, persecution and lack of financial support from the Saints prevented Joseph Smith from publishing his new translation of the Bible during his lifetime. However, this command to set apart a sacred treasury highlights the commission given to the Saints to put the scriptures before the world. A large part of the resources of the Church are devoted to ensuring that "the fulness of my scriptures, the revelations which I have given unto you, and which I shall, hereafter, from time to time give unto you" are widely available (verse 58). In the early Restoration, following this commandment meant printing physical books; in our time, Church resources are used to share the word of God in a wide variety of settings and mediums, including films, online resources, social media, and in-person missionary work.

67 And again, there shall be another treasury prepared, and a treasurer appointed to keep the treasury, and a seal shall be placed upon it;

68 And all moneys that you receive in your stewardships, by improving upon the properties which I have appointed unto you, in houses, or in lands, or in cattle, or in all things save it be the holy and sacred writings, which I have reserved unto myself for holy and sacred purposes, shall be cast into the treasury as fast as you receive moneys, by hundreds, or by fifties, or by twenties, or by tens, or by fives.

69 Or in other words, if any man among you obtain five dollars let him cast them into the treasury; or if he obtain ten, or twenty, or fifty, or an hundred, let him do likewise;

70 And let not any among you say that it is his own; for it shall not be called his, nor any part of it.

71 And there shall not any part of it be used, or taken out of the treasury, only by the voice and common consent of the order.

72 And this shall be the voice and common consent of the order—that any man among you say to the treasurer: I have need of this to help me in my stewardship—

73 If it be five dollars, or if it be ten dollars, or twenty, or fifty, or a hundred, the treasurer shall give unto him the sum which he requires to help him in his stewardship—

74 Until he be found a transgressor, and it is manifest before the council of the order plainly that he is an unfaithful and an unwise steward.

75 But so long as he is in full fellowship, and is faithful and wise in his stewardship, this shall be his token unto the treasurer that the treasurer shall not withhold.

76 But in case of transgression, the treasurer shall be subject unto the council and voice of the order.

77 And in case the treasurer is found an unfaithful and an unwise steward, he shall be subject to the council and voice of the order, and shall be removed out of his place, and another shall be appointed in his stead.

The other treasury designated by the Lord was to consist of money gained from the wise use of individual stewardships. No single member of the firm was given power to use the profits generated from this fund. Instead, the Lord directed members of the United Firm to use the law of common consent to govern the use of this fund (see verse 71), and He gives strict warnings to the treasurers chosen to manage these funds.

While finance is traditionally not seen as a spiritual field, the Lord uses the words "faithful" and "wise" to describe those called to manage finances. Both faith and wisdom are gifts of the Spirit (Doctrine and Covenants 46:14, 17–18). When calling Church officers to work in finance, the *General Handbook* of the Church offers the following guidance: "All clerks should have unquestionable integrity and demonstrate a willingness to follow the Lord's commandments. They should be honest and careful record keepers. They should also be capable teachers and administrators. The clerk who is assigned to finances should be qualified to handle financial matters. Calling clerks who meet these qualifications will help ensure that they have the Spirit of the Lord with them as they work with Church finances and records."[15]

> 78 And again, verily I say unto you, concerning your debts—behold it is my will that you shall pay all your debts.
>
> 79 And it is my will that you shall humble yourselves before me, and obtain this blessing by your diligence and humility and the prayer of faith.
>
> 80 And inasmuch as you are diligent and humble, and exercise the prayer of faith, behold, I will soften the hearts of those to whom you are in debt, until I shall send means unto you for your deliverance.
>
> 81 Therefore write speedily to New York and write according to that which shall be dictated by my Spirit; and I will soften the hearts of those to whom you are in debt, that it shall be taken away out of their minds to bring affliction upon you.
>
> 82 And inasmuch as ye are humble and faithful and call upon my name, behold, I will give you the victory.
>
> 83 I give unto you a promise, that you shall be delivered this once out of your bondage.
>
> 84 Inasmuch as you obtain a chance to loan money by hundreds, or thousands, even until you shall loan enough to deliver yourself from bondage, it is your privilege.

85 And pledge the properties which I have put into your hands, this once, by giving your names by common consent or otherwise, as it shall seem good unto you.

86 I give unto you this privilege, this once; and behold, if you proceed to do the things which I have laid before you, according to my commandments, all these things are mine, and ye are my stewards, and the master will not suffer his house to be broken up. Even so. Amen.

In verses 83–84, and elsewhere in the Doctrine and Covenants, the Lord refers to excessive debt as "bondage" (Doctrine and Covenants 19:35). The Church at times has struggled with debt due to past persecutions. However, Church leaders today strive to follow the principles given here to avoid debt. Explaining the financial principles that guide the Church, President Hinckley has said:

> In the financial operations of the Church, we have observed two basic and fixed principles: One, the Church will live within its means. It will not spend more than it receives. Two, a fixed percentage of the income will be set aside to build reserves against what might be called a possible "rainy day." For years, the Church has taught its membership the principle of setting aside a reserve of food, as well as money, to take care of emergency needs that might arise. We are only trying to follow the same principle for the Church as a whole.[16]

End Notes

1. Letter to Orson Hyde, 7 April 1834, 83, josephsmithpapers.org.
2. Joseph Smith, in History, 1838–1856, volume A-1 [23 December 1805–30 August 1834], 450, josephsmithpapers.org.
3. See History, 1838–1856, volume A-1 [23 December 1805–30 August 1834], 452, josephsmithpapers.org.
4. See Journal, 1832–1834, 71–72, josephsmithpapers.org.
5. See Revelation Book 2, 111, josephsmithpapers.org.
6. See Doctrine and Covenants, 1835, 240, josephsmithpapers.org.
7. See "Historical Introduction," Revelation, 23 April 1834 [D&C 104], josephsmithpapers.org.
8. *Manuscript History of Brigham Young, 1801–1844,* comp. Elden Jay Watson (1968), 7.
9. Max H. Parkin, "Joseph Smith and the United Firm," *BYU Studies* 46, no. 3 (2007): 58.
10. See Parkin, "Joseph Smith and the United Firm," 58. The other scriptures with code names are Doctrine and Covenants 78:4, 8; 82:11, 20; 92:1–2; and 96:2, 4, 6, 8.
11. Parkin, "Joseph Smith and the United Firm," 66.
12. See Stephen E. Robinson and H. Dean Garrett, *A Commentary on the Doctrine and Covenants* (Salt Lake City, UT: Deseret Book, 2000), 3:301.
13. See "Historical Introduction," Revelation, 23 April 1834 [D&C 104], josephsmithpapers.org.
14. Letter to Church Brethren, 15 June 1835, 1, josephsmithpapers.org.
15. *General Handbook: Serving in The Church of Jesus Christ of Latter-day Saints,* 33.2, Gospel Library.
16. Gordon B. Hinckley, "The State of the Church," *Ensign,* May 1991, 54.

Doctrine and Covenants Section 105

The Principles of the Law of the Celestial Kingdom

Historical Context

FROM EARLY MAY TO JUNE 1834 JOSEPH SMITH MARCHED TO MISSOURI with the Camp of Israel, or Zion's Camp, in an attempt to bring help to the beleaguered Saints in Zion. Once the relief expedition arrived in Missouri, however, they discovered that Daniel Dunklin, the governor of Missouri, was reluctant to call out the state militia to assist Zion's Camp in helping the Saints return to their homes in Jackson County. One local resident informed the camp leaders that "should they cross the river" in Jackson County, "there will be a battle, and probably much blood shed."[1] With tensions rising, Joseph Smith and other Church leaders issued a declaration stating, "It is not our intentions to commence hostilities against any man or body of men; it is not our intention to injure any ma[n]'s person or property, except in defending ourselves." They added, "We are anxious for a settlement of the difficulties existing between us upon honorable and constitutional principles."[2]

The day after this declaration was issued, Joseph Smith called a council to determine the next steps they should take. Some of the men of the camp were anxious to fight; others were hesitant to go forward without the help of the governor and the local militia. During the council, Joseph Smith received this revelation that provided guidance to the men and women of the camp. The Lord counseled the camp members that Zion could not be redeemed with violence and instructed them instead to dissolve the camp and make preparations to return to Kirtland.[3]

Verse-by-Verse Commentary

1 Verily I say unto you who have assembled yourselves together that you may learn my will concerning the redemption of mine afflicted people—

2 Behold, I say unto you, were it not for the transgressions of my people, speaking concerning the church and not individuals, they might have been redeemed even now.

3 But behold, they have not learned to be obedient to the things which I required at their hands, but are full of all manner of evil, and do not impart of their substance, as becometh saints, to the poor and afflicted among them;

4 And are not united according to the union required by the law of the celestial kingdom;

5 And Zion cannot be built up unless it is by the principles of the law of the celestial kingdom; otherwise I cannot receive her unto myself.

Speaking to Church members collectively, the Lord declares that they are not yet ready to redeem Zion. The revelation directly states that "Zion cannot be built up unless it is by the principles of the law of the celestial kingdom" (verse 4). As evidence of their inability to build Zion, the Lord cited that the Saints had failed to impart of their substance to the poor and afflicted among them (see verse 3). This was not a condemnation of all the Saints, especially the men and women who sacrificed to travel with Zion's

Camp, but many members of the Church were not living the principles of Zion and therefore were not ready to build Zion.

While we do not condemn the Saints of the time for their failings, it is clear that in several ways they fell short. First, while the Lord had originally called for as many as five hundred men to assist in Zion's Camp, Joseph Smith set out with barely one hundred men, gathering a final total of around two hundred. There were contentions and problems along the way to Missouri, and eventually a scourge of cholera came upon the camp.[4]

Some of the Saints in Missouri also failed to impart of their substance to the members of Zion's Camp. Heber C. Kimball relates an experience that occurred when the members of the camp were suffering from an outbreak of cholera:

> While we were here [Clay County, Missouri], the brethren being in want of some refreshment, Brother Luke Johnson went to Brother Burgett to get a fowl, asking him for one to make a broth for Elder Wilcox and others; but Brother Burgett denied him it, saying "in a few days we expect to return back into Jackson County, and I shall want them when I get there." When Brother Johnson returned he was so angry at Burgett for refusing him, he said, "I have a great mind to take my rifle and go back and shoot his horse." I told Luke to never mind, that such actions never fail to bring their reward.
>
> Judge how we felt, after having left the society of our beloved families, taking our lives in our hands and traveling about one thousand miles through scenes of suffering and sorrow, for the benefit of our brethren, and after all to be denied of a small fowl to make a little soup for brethren in the agonies of death. Such things never fail to bring their reward, and it would do well for the saints never to turn away a brother who is penniless and in want, or a stranger, lest they may one day or other want a friend themselves.[5]

6 And my people must needs be chastened until they learn obedience, if it must needs be, by the things which they suffer.

7 I speak not concerning those who are appointed to lead my people, who are the first elders of my church, for they are not all under this condemnation;

8 But I speak concerning my churches abroad—there are many who will say: Where is their God? Behold, he will deliver them

in time of trouble, otherwise we will not go up unto Zion, and will keep our moneys.

9 Therefore, in consequence of the transgressions of my people, it is expedient in me that mine elders should wait for a little season for the redemption of Zion—

10 That they themselves may be prepared, and that my people may be taught more perfectly, and have experience, and know more perfectly concerning their duty, and the things which I require at their hands.

11 And this cannot be brought to pass until mine elders are endowed with power from on high.

12 For behold, I have prepared a great endowment and blessing to be poured out upon them, inasmuch as they are faithful and continue in humility before me.

13 Therefore it is expedient in me that mine elders should wait for a little season, for the redemption of Zion.

It is possible that the "little season" (verse 13) referred to here may have been only two years, or until the time the Kirtland Temple was dedicated in March 1836. The endowment of power referred to in verse 11 consisted of the washings and anointings given to the elders of the Church when the Kirtland Temple was dedicated. Later the Lord gave the fulness of the endowment to Joseph Smith before the Nauvoo Temple was built, and then the endowment ceremony was offered to the larger membership of the Church. In addition, a Pentecostal outpouring at the time of the Kirtland Temple's dedication strengthened the Saints.

If the Saints had managed to build on the blessings given during the dedication of the Kirtland Temple and its accompanying version of the endowment, it is possible that the redemption of Zion may have come much sooner. However, soon after the Kirtland Temple was dedicated, contention and strife disrupted the Church in Kirtland. Many Kirtland members fell into apostasy, and the Saints in Ohio who remained faithful to the Church were forced to flee to Missouri for sanctuary.

14 For behold, I do not require at their hands to fight the battles of Zion; for, as I said in a former commandment, even so will I fulfil—I will fight your battles.

15 Behold, the destroyer I have sent forth to destroy and lay waste mine enemies; and not many years hence they shall not be left to pollute mine heritage, and to blaspheme my name upon the lands which I have consecrated for the gathering together of my saints.

16 Behold, I have commanded my servant Joseph Smith, Jun., to say unto the strength of my house, even my warriors, my young men, and middle-aged, to gather together for the redemption of my people, and throw down the towers of mine enemies, and scatter their watchmen;

17 But the strength of mine house have not hearkened unto my words.

18 But inasmuch as there are those who have hearkened unto my words, I have prepared a blessing and an endowment for them, if they continue faithful.

19 I have heard their prayers, and will accept their offering; and it is expedient in me that they should be brought thus far for a trial of their faith.

The Lord's declaration that He would "fight the battles of Zion" (verse 14) was met with mixed emotions among the members of the camp. William Cahoon recalls, "Many in the camp murmured because we were not permitted at this time to restore our Brethren & Sisters to their Homes and defend them there at all hazards."[6] George A. Smith, a future apostle, remarked that "several of the brethren apostatized because they were not going to have the privilege of fighting."[7] Nathan Tanner, another camp member, recalls that some declared "they had rather die than to return without a fight" and then "gave vent to their wrath on a patch of pawpaw brush" some distance from the camp, mowing it "down like grass."[8] But to Nathan, this revelation "was the most acceptable to [him] of anything [he] had ever heard before, the gospel being the exception."[9]

The prophecy about the "destroyer" who is sent forth to lay waste to the enemies of the Church (verse 15) was partially fulfilled during the Civil War. Church Historian B. H. Roberts cites a history of the Civil War in Missouri by a local clergyman, W. M. Leftwich, who writes, "The warfare at home [Missouri] presented scenes of outrage and horror unsurpassed by anything in the annals of civilized warfare, if, indeed, there can be such a thing as civilized warfare, for everything about it is intensely savage. . . . Between the 'jayhawkers' of Kansas and the 'bushwackers' of Missouri some whole counties were plundered, some were desolated by fire and sword, and some were almost depopulated."[10] Although Missouri never seceded from the Union during the Civil War, two significant battles took place in Independence, Missouri.[11] Some of the bloodiest fighting in the second battle of Independence took place on the temple lot itself.[12]

> 20 And now, verily I say unto you, a commandment I give unto you, that as many as have come up hither, that can stay in the region round about, let them stay;
>
> 21 And those that cannot stay, who have families in the east, let them tarry for a little season, inasmuch as my servant Joseph shall appoint unto them;
>
> 22 For I will counsel him concerning this matter, and all things whatsoever he shall appoint unto them shall be fulfilled.
>
> 23 And let all my people who dwell in the regions round about be very faithful, and prayerful, and humble before me, and reveal not the things which I have revealed unto them, until it is wisdom in me that they should be revealed.
>
> 24 Talk not of judgments, neither boast of faith nor of mighty works, but carefully gather together, as much in one region as can be, consistently with the feelings of the people;
>
> 25 And behold, I will give unto you favor and grace in their eyes, that you may rest in peace and safety, while you are saying unto the people: Execute judgment and justice for us according to law, and redress us of our wrongs.
>
> 26 Now, behold, I say unto you, my friends, in this way you may find favor in the eyes of the people, until the army of Israel becomes very great.

The Lord counsels the Saints to be cautious in their dealings with the local settlers. He instructs the members of Zion's Camp to "talk not of judgment, neither boast of faith, nor of mighty works," to "carefully gather together," and to act "consistently with the feelings of the people" (verse 24). Shortly after this revelation was given, the Lord meted out His punishment upon Zion's Camp because of their disobedience. Joseph Smith later wrote:

While we were refreshing ourselves and teams, about the middle of the day, I got up on a wagon wheel, called the people together, and said that I would deliver a prophecy. After giving the brethren much good advice, exhorting them to faithfulness and humility; I said the Lord had revealed to me that there would a scourge come upon the camp in consequence of the fractious and unruly spirits that appeared among them, and they should die like sheep with the rot: still, if they would repent and humble themselves before the Lord, the scourge, in a great measure, might be turned away; but, as the Lord lives, this camp will-suffer for giving way to their unruly temper.[13]

Just a few days after Doctrine and Covenants 105 was given, the scourge appeared in the form of a cholera epidemic that swept through the camp. For Heber C. Kimball, this was the most harrowing part of the march of Zion's Camp. "The destroyer came upon us as we had been warned by the servant of God," he later recalled. "About 12 o'clock at night we began to hear the cries of those who were seized with the cholera, and they fell before the destroyer. Even those on guard fell with their guns in their hands to the ground, and we had to exert ourselves considerably to attend to the sick, for they fell on every hand." Kimball later recorded:

At this scene my feelings were beyond expression. Those only who witnessed it, can realize any thing of the nature of our sufferings, and I felt to weep and pray to the Lord, that he would spare my life that I might behold my dear family again. I felt to covenant with my brethren, and I felt in my heart never to commit another sin while I lived. We felt to sit and weep over our brethren, and so great was our sorrow that we could have washed them with our tears, to realize that they had travelled 1000 miles through so much fatigue to lay down their lives for our brethren.[14]

By the time the epidemic subsided, thirteen members of the camp died as well as two other members of the Church who were living in Missouri.[15] Among those who died were Jesse J. Smith, a young cousin of the Prophet; Phebe Murdock, the daughter of John Murdock (see Doctrine and Covenants 99); and Algernon Sidney Gilbert, one of the key leaders of the Church in Missouri (see Doctrine and Covenants 53).[16]

27 And I will soften the hearts of the people, as I did the heart of Pharaoh, from time to time, until my servant Joseph Smith, Jun., and mine elders, whom I have appointed, shall have time to gather up the strength of my house,

28 And to have sent wise men, to fulfil that which I have commanded concerning the purchasing of all the lands in Jackson county that can be purchased, and in the adjoining counties round about.

29 For it is my will that these lands should be purchased; and after they are purchased that my saints should possess them according to the laws of consecration which I have given.

30 And after these lands are purchased, I will hold the armies of Israel guiltless in taking possession of their own lands, which they have previously purchased with their moneys, and of throwing down the towers of mine enemies that may be upon them, and scattering their watchmen, and avenging me of mine enemies unto the third and fourth generation of them that hate me.

Even after the Saints were driven out of Jackson County through violent means, the Lord stood firm in His instructions that the lands of Zion should be obtained through the peaceful means of legal purchases. He also mentions that the land would be obtained through following the "laws of consecration" (verse 29), or the principles of cooperation and sacrifice given throughout the revelations. The Lord intended for the armies of Israel to be guiltless in obtaining the land. They were not to resort to the same kind of violence that their enemies had used against them.

For modern Saints, the question of the recovery of Zion is about more than just recapturing the lands belonging to our forebears—it is a question of the soul. Elder Orson F. Whitney teaches, "The redemption of Zion is more than the purchase or recovery of lands, the building of cities, or even the founding of nations. It is the conquest of the heart, the subjugation of the soul, the sanctifying of the flesh, the purifying and ennobling of the passions."[17]

31 But first let my army become very great, and let it be sanctified before me, that it may become fair as the sun, and clear as the moon, and that her banners may be terrible unto all nations;

32 That the kingdoms of this world may be constrained to acknowledge that the kingdom of Zion is in very deed the kingdom of our God and his Christ; therefore, let us become subject unto her laws.

SECTION 105

33 Verily I say unto you, it is expedient in me that the first elders of my church should receive their endowment from on high in my house, which I have commanded to be built unto my name in the land of Kirtland.

34 And let those commandments which I have given concerning Zion and her law be executed and fulfilled, after her redemption.

The day after Doctrine and Covenants 105 was given, Joseph Smith sought to fulfill the commandment of the Lord to give the elders the endowment. He records in his history, "A council of High Priests assembled in fulfillment of the revelation given the day previous, and the following individuals were called and chosen as they were made manifest unto me by the voice of the Spirit, and Revelation, to receive their endowment."[18] The men chosen were Edward Partridge, William W. Phelps, Isaac Morley, John Corrill, John Whitmer, David Whitmer, A. Sidney Gilbert, Peter Whitmer Jr., Simeon Carter, Newel Knight, Parley P. Pratt, Christian Whitmer, Solomon Hancock, Thomas B. Marsh, and Lyman Wight.[19]

35 There has been a day of calling, but the time has come for a day of choosing; and let those be chosen that are worthy.

36 And it shall be manifest unto my servant, by the voice of the Spirit, those that are chosen; and they shall be sanctified;

37 And inasmuch as they follow the counsel which they receive, they shall have power after many days to accomplish all things pertaining to Zion.

The march of Zion's Camp was indeed a day of calling. As noted, some who went on the journey fell into apostasy, and others saw the journey as a great time of learning. Future leaders of the Church had the opportunity to see the hand of God in their lives and learn directly from the Prophet Joseph Smith. In an 1853 discourse, Brigham Young declared:

When I returned from that mission [Zion's Camp] to Kirtland, a brother said to me, "Brother Brigham, what have you gained by this journey?" I replied, "Just what we went for; but I would not exchange the knowledge I have received this season for the whole of Geauga County; for property and mines of wealth are not to be compared to the worth of knowledge." Ask those brethren and sisters who have passed through scenes of affliction and suffering for years in this Church, what they would take in exchange for their experience, and be placed back where they were, were it possible.

323

I presume they would tell you, that all the wealth, honors, and riches of the world could not buy the knowledge they had obtained, could they barter it away. Let the brethren be contented, and if you have trials, and must see hard times, learn to acknowledge the hand of the Lord in it all.[20]

Another future president of the Church, Wilford Woodruff, echoed Brigham's feelings. In an 1869 discourse, he said:

When the members of Zion's Camp were called, many of us had never beheld each other's faces; we were strangers to each other and many had never seen the prophet. We had been scattered abroad, like corn sifted in a sieve, throughout the nation. We were young men, and were called upon in that early day to go up and redeem Zion, and what we had to do we had to do by faith. We assembled together from the various States at Kirtland and went up to redeem Zion, in fulfillment of the commandment of God unto us. God accepted our works as He did the works of Abraham. We accomplished a great deal, though apostates and unbelievers many times asked the question, "What have you done?" We gained an experience that we never could have gained in any other way. We had the privilege of beholding the face of the prophet, and we had the privilege of traveling a thousand miles with him, and seeing the workings of the Spirit of God with him, and the revelations of Jesus Christ unto him and the fulfillment of those revelations. Had I not gone up with Zion's Camp I should not have been here today.[21]

Though Zion's Camp ultimately failed in its aim to reinstate the members of the Church in homes in Jackson County, it was an important proving ground for the future leadership of the Church.

38 And again I say unto you, sue for peace, not only to the people that have smitten you, but also to all people;

39 And lift up an ensign of peace, and make a proclamation of peace unto the ends of the earth;

40 And make proposals for peace unto those who have smitten you, according to the voice of the Spirit which is in you, and all things shall work together for your good.

41 Therefore, be faithful; and behold, and lo, I am with you even unto the end. Even so. Amen.

When the outbreak of cholera occurred among the members of Zion's Camp, Joseph Smith was affected also. He later wrote:

At the commencement [of the cholera outbreak] I attempted to lay on hands for their recovery, but I quickly learned by painful experience that when the Great Jehovah decrees destruction upon any people, and makes known his determination, man must not attempt to stay his hand. The moment I attempted to rebuke the disease, I was attacked, it seized upon me like the talons of a hawk, and I said to the brethren if I had my work done, you have had to tumble me into the ground without a coffin and had I not desisted. I must have saved the life of my brother by the sacrifice of my own.[22]

Joseph's brush with mortality during the journey with Zion's Camp may have caused him to begin thinking about who would continue God's work if his life was taken. The winter after he arrived back in Kirtland, he called together the priesthood holders of the Church, many of whom had been members of Zion's Camp. Joseph Young, one of the men present, recalls the following words of Joseph Smith: "Brethren, some of you are angry with me, because you did not fight in Missouri; but let me tell you, God did not want you to fight. He could not organize his kingdom with twelve men to open the gospel door to the nations of the earth, and with seventy men under their direction to follow in their tracks, unless he took them from a body of men who had offered their lives, and who had made as great a sacrifice as did Abraham."[23]

Nine of the original Apostles in the first Quorum of the Twelve Apostles were members of Zion's Camp. All seven presidents of the Quorum of the Seventy, and sixty-three other members of that Quorum, marched with Zion's Camp. Joseph Young remembered Joseph Smith declaring, "Now, the Lord has got his Twelve and his Seventy, and there will be other quorums of Seventies called, who will make the sacrifice, and those who have not made their sacrifices and their offerings now, will make them hereafter."[24]

End Notes

1. "Historical Introduction," Revelation 22 June 1834 [D&C 105], josephsmithpapers.org.

2. Declaration, 21 June 1834, 1, josephsmithpapers.org.

3. See "Historical Introduction," Revelation, 22 June 1834 [D&C 105], josephsmithpapers.org.

4. See Matthew C. Godfrey, "The Acceptable Offering of Zion's Camp," in *Revelations in Context* (20160, 213–17.

5. Orson F. Whitney, *Life of Heber C. Kimball* (Salt Lake City, UT: Bookcraft, 1973), 62–63.

6. William F. Cahoon, Autobiography, 43, 1878, CHL MS 8433, cited in "Historical Introduction," Revelation, 22 June 1834 [D&C 105], footnote 6, josephsmithpapers.org.

7. George A. Smith, Autobiography, 38, CHL MS 1322, box 1, fd. 2, cited in "Historical Introduction," Revelation, 22 June 1834 [D&C 105], footnote 14, josephsmithpapers.org.

8. Nathan Tanner, Address, no date, CHL MS 2815, cited in "Historical Introduction," Revelation, 22 June 1834 [D&C 105], footnote 15, josephsmithpapers.org.

9. See Matthew C. Godfrey, "The Acceptable Offering of Zion's Camp," 213–17.

10. B. H. Roberts, *Comprehensive History of the Church of Jesus Christ of the Latter Day Saints* (Provo, UT: Brigham Young University Press, 1965), 1:547.

11. See "Civil War on the Western Border: The Missouri-Kansas Conflict,1855–1865," Kansas City Public Library, accessed May 8, 2021, https://civilwaronthewesternborder.org/timeline/first-battle-independence.

12. See Kyle S. Sinisi, *The Last Hurrah: Sterling Price's Missouri Expedition of 1864* (Washington, DC: Rowman & Littlefield Publishers, 2020), 209–10.

13. Joseph Smith, in History, 1838–1856, volume A-1 [23 December 1805–30 August 1834], 5 (addenda), josephsmithpapers.org.

14. Orson F. Whitney, *Life of Heber C. Kimball,* 59–61.

15. See Matthew W. Godfrey, "'We Believe the Hand of the Lord Is in It': Memories of Divine Intervention in the Zion's Camp Expedition," *BYU Studies Quarterly* 56, no. 4 (2017): 117.

16. See Revelation, 22 June 1834 [D&C 105], 100, footnote 16, josephsmithpapers.org.

17. Orson F. Whitney, *Life of Heber C. Kimball,* 65.

18. Joseph Smith, in History, 1838–1856, volume A-1 [23 December 1805–30 August 1834], 503–4, josephsmithpapers.org.

19. See History, 1838–1856, volume A-1 [23 December 1805–30 August 1834], 503–4, josephsmithpapers.org.

20. Brigham Young, in *Journal of Discourses*, 2:10.

21. Wilford Woodruff, in *Journal of Discourses*, 13:158.

22. Joseph Smith, in History, 1838–1856, volume A-1 [23 December 1805–30 August 1834], 505, josephsmithpapers.org.

23. Quoted in Joseph Young Sr., *History of the Organization of the Seventies* (Salt Lake City, UT: Deseret News Press, 1878), 14.

24. Young, *History of the Organization of the Seventies*, 14.

$\mathcal{D}$octrine and $\mathcal{C}$ovenants
Section 106
The Laborer Is Worthy of His Hire

$\mathcal{H}$istorical $\mathcal{C}$ontext

IN THE SPRING OF 1834 JOSEPH SMITH TRAVELED TO FREEDOM, NEW YORK, to help recruit men for the march of Zion's Camp. At that time, Joseph stayed in the home of Warren Cowdery, the older brother of Oliver Cowdery. Joseph wrote in his journal that during his stay with Warren, his group had received the "full enjoyment of all the blessings[,] both temporal and spiritual."[1] Sometime after Joseph's visit, between May and September 1834, a small branch of the Church was set up in Freedom and Warren Cowdery was baptized. After his baptism, Warren wrote to Oliver, requesting "a preacher of our order" to "do us good, by strengthening and building us up in the most holy faith."[2]

In October 1834 Warren wrote to Oliver. Warren shared his hope of being "useful in the vineyard of the Lord" and told his brother that he "had thoughts of requesting you to enquire what is the will of the Lord concerning me."[3] Section 106 was given in response to Warren's request.

In Joseph Smith's official history, the Prophet noted how busy he was during this time, writing, "No month ever found me more busily engaged than November; but as, my life consisted of activity and unyielding exertion, I made this my rule, when the Lord commands, do it. . . . I continued my labors daily, preparing for the school, &c and received the following: [Doctrine and Covenants 106]."[4]

Verse-by-Verse Commentary

1 It is my will that my servant Warren A. Cowdery should be appointed and ordained a presiding high priest over my church, in the land of Freedom and the regions round about;

2 And should preach my everlasting gospel, and lift up his voice and warn the people, not only in his own place, but in the adjoining counties;

3 And devote his whole time to this high and holy calling, which I now give unto him, seeking diligently the kingdom of heaven and its righteousness, and all things necessary shall be added thereunto; for the laborer is worthy of his hire.

4 And again, verily I say unto you, the coming of the Lord draweth nigh, and it overtaketh the world as a thief in the night—

5 Therefore, gird up your loins, that you may be the children of light, and that day shall not overtake you as a thief.

6 And again, verily I say unto you, there was joy in heaven when my servant Warren bowed to my scepter, and separated himself from the crafts of men;

7 Therefore, blessed is my servant Warren, for I will have mercy on him; and, notwithstanding the vanity of his heart, I will lift him up inasmuch as he will humble himself before me.

8 And I will give him grace and assurance wherewith he may stand; and if he continue to be a faithful witness and a light unto

the church I have prepared a crown for him in the mansions of my Father. Even so. Amen.

Warren Cowdery was appointed as a high priest in this revelation (see verse 1). Commentary later published in the December 1834 issue of the *Latter-day Saints' Messenger and Advocate* listed Warren as "the presiding elder of the church at Freedom, N.Y."[5] Warren Cowdery is not well known in the Church today, but he made several important contributions to the Church in his time. Warren worked as a clerk for Joseph Smith and in the publishing office in Kirtland, where he helped edit a newspaper published by the Church. He also served as a member of the high council of the Church in Kirtland.[6] The Lord recognized Warren's struggles to join the Church when he told him, "There was joy in heaven when my servant Warren bowed to my scepter, and separated himself from the crafts of men" (verse 6). He also tenderly counseled Warren when he added, "Blessed is my servant Warren, for I will have mercy on him; and, notwithstanding the vanity of his heart, I will lift him up inasmuch as he will humble himself before me" (verse 7).[7]

Warren's service as the presiding elder in Freedom was marred when, a year later, he was accused of writing a letter containing "reports derogatory to the character and teaching of the twelve."[8] In the letter, Warren told Church leaders that the Twelve had failed to provide instruction to the members of the Church at Freedom about the need to donate funds for the construction of the Kirtland Temple.[9] In response, the Twelve charged Warren with "unchristian conduct."[10] The matter was dropped when Warren "confessed his mistake" in a meeting with the Twelve on March 5, 1836.[11]

Like his brother Oliver, Warren Cowdery was a gifted writer and scribe. Warren eventually moved to Kirtland, where he served as the editor for the *Latter-day Saints' Messenger and Advocate* and as a bookbinder in the Church's printing office in Kirtland. Warren even assisted in writing the dedicatory prayer for the Kirtland Temple (see Doctrine and Covenants 109). Unfortunately, Warren was swept up in the tumult that overthrew the Church in Kirtland and became disaffected with Church leadership in 1838. The excommunication of Oliver Cowdery (which occurred in April 1838) undoubtedly affected Warren's feelings toward Church leadership. He stayed behind after most active Church members left Kirtland. According to an 1850 census, he was living with his wife and six children in Kirtland in 1850, and he passed away in 1851. Unlike his brother Oliver, he never returned to the Church in his lifetime.[12]

End Notes

1. Journal, 1832–1834, 60, josephsmithpapers.org.
2. "Warren Cowdery, Freedom, NY, to Oliver Cowdery, Kirtland, OH, 1 Sept. 1834," *The Evening and the Morning Star*, Sept. 1834, 189.
3. "Warren Cowdery, Freedom, NY, to Oliver Cowdery, [Kirtland, OH], 28 Oct. 1834," *Latter-day Saints' Messenger and Advocate*, Nov. 1834, 1:22.
4. See "Historical Introduction," Revelation, 25 November 1834 [D&C 106], josephsmithpapers.org.
5. "A Summary," *Latter-day Saints' Messenger and Advocate*, Dec. 1834, 1:45.
6. See "Biography: Cowdery, Warren A.," Joseph Smith Papers, accessed Feb. 19, 2023, https://www.josephsmithpapers.org/person/warren-a-cowdery.
7. See Lisa Olsen Tait, "Warren Cowdery," in *Revelations in Context* (2016), 219–223.
8. Minutes, 26 September 1835, 119, josephsmithpapers.org.
9. See Letter to Quorum of the Twelve, 4 August 1835, 90, josephsmithpapers.org.
10. Journal, 1835–1836, 121, josephsmithpapers.org.
11. "Historical Introduction," Letter to Quorum of the Twelve, 4 August 1835, 90, josephsmithpapers.org.
12. See "Biography: Cowdery, Warren A.," Joseph Smith Papers, accessed Feb. 19, 2023, https://www.josephsmithpapers.org/person/warren-a-cowdery.

$\mathcal{D}$octrine and $\mathcal{C}$ovenants Section 107

The Holy Priesthood after the Order of the Son of God

$\mathcal{H}$istorical $\mathcal{C}$ontext

DOCTRINE AND COVENANTS 107 CONSISTS OF SEVERAL DIFFERENT REVELA-
tions woven together that were first published in the 1835 Doctrine and
Covenants. The first revelation was received on November 11, 1831, most
likely in Hiram, Ohio.[1] This portion of section 107 consists of verses 59–
100. Joseph Smith revised this revelation prior to its publication in the
1835 Doctrine and Covenants, adding verses 61, 70, 73, 76–77, 88, 90, and
93–98.[2] While as a whole, verses 59–100 address the needs of the Saints
in Missouri, these verses also represent an important milestone in the development of the Saints' understanding of the priesthood, particularly the
Melchizedek, or higher, Priesthood. At a conference held around the time
this revelation was received, Joseph Smith taught "that the order of the High
priesthood is that they have power given them to seal up the Saints unto

eternal life." He added that "it was the privilege of every Elder present to be ordained to the High priesthood."[3]

Another part of section 107 was received on December 18, 1833, when Joseph Smith gave a blessing to his father and mother. Parts of this blessing are found in verses 53–55. This revelation speaks about the office of evangelist, or patriarch; links the practice of patriarchal blessings to the first patriarch, Adam; and reveals that Jesus Christ appeared in Adam-ondi-Ahman three years prior to the death of Adam. In the fall of 1835 Joseph added to the original blessing that he gave his parents before he included it in the 1835 Doctrine and Covenants.[4]

The final part of section 107 that was revealed, constituting verses 1–58, was written sometime between March 1 and May 4, 1835. This period was around the time that the first Quorum of the Twelve Apostles in this dispensation was called, along with the original Presidency of the Seventy and many other members of the Seventy.[5] We do not know exactly when the revelation was received, but it appears to have come in answer to several questions raised in a meeting of the Twelve held on February 27, 1835. In the meeting, Joseph Smith asked the Twelve to discuss the question "What importance is attached to the callings of these twelve apostles different from the other callings and offices of the church?" During the same meeting, Joseph also taught the Apostles that they "are called to a travelling high council to preside over all the churches of the saints."[6] Since Doctrine and Covenants 107 provides clarifications and answers to many of these questions, it was likely received after this time but before the Twelve departed from Kirtland in May 1835 on their first mission.

Doctrine and Covenants 107 provides vital instructions to the governing quorums of the Church, including the First Presidency, the Quorum of the Twelve Apostles, the office and callings of the Seventy, and the Presiding Bishopric. The revelations that make up this section together constitute another milestone in the growing government of the Church. Earlier revelations established the governing structure for a branch of the Church (see Doctrine and Covenants 20) and the basic functions of the priesthood (see Doctrine and Covenants 13, 84), but section 107 establishes a structure of councils sufficient to govern a Church of thousands and eventually millions.[7]

Verse-by-Verse Commentary

1 There are, in the church, two priesthoods, namely, the Melchizedek and Aaronic, including the Levitical Priesthood.

2 Why the first is called the Melchizedek Priesthood is because Melchizedek was such a great high priest.

3 Before his day it was called *the Holy Priesthood, after the Order of the Son of God.*

4 But out of respect or reverence to the name of the Supreme Being, to avoid the too frequent repetition of his name, they, the church, in ancient days, called that priesthood after Melchizedek, or the Melchizedek Priesthood.

5 All other authorities or offices in the church are appendages to this priesthood.

6 But there are two divisions or grand heads—one is the Melchizedek Priesthood, and the other is the Aaronic or Levitical Priesthood.

In an instruction on the priesthood, which was read in the October 1840 general conference, Joseph Smith provided further commentary on this passage, stating:

There are two priesthoods spoken of in the scriptures, viz, the Melchizedek and the Aaronic or Levitical[.] Although there are two priesthoods, yet the Melchizedek priesthood comprehends the Aaronic or Levitical priesthood and is the Grand head and holds the highest authority which pertains to the priesthood— the keys of the Kingdom of God in all ages of the world to the latest posterity on the earth— and is the channel through which all knowledge, doctrine, the plan of salvation[,] and every important truth is revealed from heaven. Its institution was prior to "the foundation of this earth or the morning stars sang together or the sons of God shouted for joy," it is the highest and holiest priesthood and is after the order of the Son [of] God, and all other priesthoods are only parts, ramifications, powers[,] and blessings belonging to the same and are held controlled and directed by it. It is the channel through which the Almighty commenced revealing his glory at the beginning of the creation of this earth and through which he has continued to reveal himself to the children of men to the present time and through which he will make known his purposes to the end of time.[8]

This quote indicates that the Aaronic Priesthood is considered an appendage of the Melchizedek Priesthood, which is the authority of Jesus Christ Himself. On another occasion, Joseph Smith taught simply, "All priesthood is Melchizedek; but there are different portions or degrees of it."[9]

7 The office of an elder comes under the priesthood of Melchizedek.

8 The Melchizedek Priesthood holds the right of presidency, and has power and authority over all the offices in the church in all ages of the world, to administer in spiritual things.

9 The Presidency of the High Priesthood, after the order of Melchizedek, have a right to officiate in all the offices in the church.

10 High priests after the order of the Melchizedek Priesthood have a right to officiate in their own standing, under the direction of the presidency, in administering spiritual things, and also in the office of an elder, priest (of the Levitical order), teacher, deacon, and member.

11 An elder has a right to officiate in his stead when the high priest is not present.

12 The high priest and elder are to administer in spiritual things, agreeable to the covenants and commandments of the church; and they have a right to officiate in all these offices of the church when there are no higher authorities present.

Every person ordained to an office in the Melchizedek Priesthood holds the same priesthood, regardless of their office or calling. Thus, the offices of elder, high priest, Seventy, and Apostle all hold the same priesthood. All officers of the Church, male or female, hold priesthood authority to operate within their calling. The "right of presidency" mentioned in verse 8 refers to the keys of the priesthood, or the authority to direct the work of the Church. In the modern Church, "the Presidency of the High Priesthood" (verse 9), or the First Presidency, holds all priesthood keys and has the right to direct all other Church officers who hold priesthood offices and priesthood authority, whether it be a group of elders or the Relief Society.

As noted in section 107, the work of the Melchizedek Priesthood is to administer in spiritual things (see verses 8, 12). This work contrasts with that of the Aaronic Priesthood, which is tasked with administering in "outward ordinances" (Doctrine and Covenants 107:14), such as the sacrament, baptism, and so forth. Though the priesthood is hierarchical, with high priests occupying a position above the elders, it is not dictatorial. In a letter written to John S. Carter in April 1833, Joseph Smith taught, "The duty of a high priest is to administer spiritual and holy things and to hold communion with God but not to exercise monarchial government or to appoint meetings for the Elders without their consent[,] and again it is the high priests duty to be bet[t]er qualified to teach principles and doctrines than the Elder[,] for the office of Elders is an appendage to the high priesthood."[10]

> 13 The second priesthood is called the Priesthood of Aaron, because it was conferred upon Aaron and his seed, throughout all their generations.
>
> 14 Why it is called the lesser priesthood is because it is an appendage to the greater, or the Melchizedek Priesthood, and has power in administering outward ordinances.
>
> 15 The bishopric is the presidency of this priesthood, and holds the keys or authority of the same.
>
> 16 No man has a legal right to this office, to hold the keys of this priesthood, except he be a literal descendant of Aaron.
>
> 17 But as a high priest of the Melchizedek Priesthood has authority to officiate in all the lesser offices, he may officiate in the office of bishop when no literal descendant of Aaron can be found, provided he is called and set apart and ordained unto this power by the hands of the Presidency of the Melchizedek Priesthood.

In the modern Church, the "bishopric" referred to in verse 15 is interpreted to refer to the Presiding Bishopric. In the Church today, local bishops hold the keys of the Aaronic Priesthood and preside over the Aaronic Priesthood holders in their ward or branch. Though the office of bishop is a part of the Aaronic Priesthood, in practice it is always held by a high priest who acts as the bishop and the presiding high priest over a ward. The revelation explains that high priests can function in the offices of the Aaronic Priesthood (see verses 10, 17).

As explained in verse 16, a literal descendant of Aaron has a "legal right" to the office of bishop, though this only refers to the office of bishop and not to the position of a ward bishop. A lineal connection to Aaron does not guarantee an appointment to the office of bishop; a candidate must still be worthy and receive their calling through the proper channels of authority (see commentary for Doctrine and Covenants 68:13–21). For a literal descendant of Aaron to hold the office of Presiding Bishop, he must first be identified and found worthy by the First Presidency, who preside over the Aaronic Priesthood.

> 18 The power and authority of the higher, or Melchizedek Priesthood, is to hold the keys of all the spiritual blessings of the church—
>
> 19 To have the privilege of receiving the mysteries of the kingdom of heaven, to have the heavens opened unto them, to commune with the general assembly and church of the Firstborn, and to enjoy the communion and presence of God the Father, and Jesus the mediator of the new covenant.
>
> 20 The power and authority of the lesser, or Aaronic Priesthood, is to hold the keys of the ministering of angels, and to administer in outward ordinances, the letter of the gospel, the baptism of repentance for the remission of sins, agreeable to the covenants and commandments.

Currently only the presiding high priest (i.e., the President of the Church) can hold and exercise all the keys of the priesthood that the Lord has delegated to him as President of the Church. Similarly, the modern Church believes that all members of the Church who qualify have the "privilege of receiving the mysteries of the kingdom of heaven" (verse 19). For men to receive these mysteries, they must first be found worthy and receive the higher priesthood (see Doctrine and Covenants 84:33–39). Several years later, in Nauvoo, Joseph Smith revealed that women and men must both enter into the fulness of the everlasting covenant to receive these blessings (see Doctrine and Covenants 132:19–24). The promise is then given to both men and women that they may become part of the Church of the Firstborn (see Doctrine and Covenants 93:22) and receive the presence of the Father and the Son (see Doctrine and Covenants 107:19). Every person may receive these blessings as quickly as they can qualify.

The Aaronic Priesthood enables people to receive the higher blessings mentioned in verse 19 by administering the outward ordinances necessary to return to God, referred to here as the "letter of the gospel" (verse 20). Ordinances such as baptism act as doorways for a deeper connection with God. For example, the cleansing baptism of fire comes upon people through the power of the Holy Ghost only after they are baptized. Implied in verse 20 is the teaching of Paul that "the letter killeth, but the spirit giveth life" (2 Corinthians 3:6). Simply going through the motions when it comes to the outward ordinances of the gospel, such as baptism and the covenants of the sacrament, does not produce exaltation.

> 21 Of necessity there are presidents, or presiding officers growing out of, or appointed of or from among those who are ordained to the several offices in these two priesthoods.
>
> 22 Of the Melchizedek Priesthood, three Presiding High Priests, chosen by the body, appointed and ordained to that office, and upheld by the confidence, faith, and prayer of the church, form a quorum of the Presidency of the Church.
>
> 23 The twelve traveling councilors are called to be the Twelve Apostles, or special witnesses of the name of Christ in all the world—thus differing from other officers in the church in the duties of their calling.
>
> 24 And they form a quorum, equal in authority and power to the three presidents previously mentioned.
>
> 25 The Seventy are also called to preach the gospel, and to be especial witnesses unto the Gentiles and in all the world—thus differing from other officers in the church in the duties of their calling.
>
> 26 And they form a quorum, equal in authority to that of the Twelve special witnesses or Apostles just named.

Verses 21–26 establish the three presiding quorums of the Church, specifically the First Presidency, the Quorum of the Twelve, and the Quorum of the Seventy. While this passage states several times that these quorums are "equal in authority and power," this phrase does not mean that the Church is governed by three different but equal quorums. Elder Hyrum M. Smith and Janne M. Sjodhal explained, "It should be understood that this condition of equality could prevail only when the ranking quorum is no longer in existence, through death or otherwise. When the First Presidency becomes disorganized on the death of the President then the Apostles become the presiding quorum, or council of the Church, with all the power to organize again the First Presidency, when they fall back again as the second ranking quorum of the Church."[11] As time went on and the Church expanded, the number of stakes increased into the thousands, and the role of the Twelve increased in importance.

The phrase "chosen by the body" (verse 22) refers to when the First Presidency was organized at a council of high priests held in Amherst, Ohio, on January 25, 1832.[12] At that time, the higher quorums of the Church— the Twelve and the Seventy—were not yet restored. The "body" that sustained Joseph Smith as President of the Church consisted of the whole body of the priesthood of the Church present at the Amherst conference. After the Twelve and the Seventy were organized in 1835, the governing councils of the Church consisted of the First Presidency, the Quorum of the Twelve, and the Seventy. In our day, the "body" that sustains the new President of the Church is the Quorum of the Twelve. When a President of the Church dies, the First Presidency is dissolved and the Quorum of the Twelve becomes the highest governing quorum, making the President of the Twelve the highest presiding officer in the Church until a new President is sustained by the Twelve and set apart as the President of the Church. According to the pattern established by the Twelve, they sustain the most senior Apostle to be the new Church President.[13]

In our time, the process of choosing a new president of the Church has become fairly seamless. At the death of the President of the Church, the Twelve briefly become the presiding quorum only for a short time. The Twelve then sustain the new President of the Church. This process at first took several years following the deaths of Joseph Smith and Brigham Young, but it has become a matter of days since the time when Lorenzo Snow became the President of the Church.

Several Church leaders have commented on how this process is not an election but a sustaining. President Joseph Fielding Smith taught, "There is no mystery about the choosing of the successor to the President of the Church. The Lord settled this a long time ago, and the senior apostle automatically becomes the presiding officer of the Church, and he is so sustained by the Council of the Twelve which becomes the presiding body of the Church when there is no First Presidency. The president is not elected, but he has to be sustained both by his brethren of the Council and by the members of the Church."[14]

President Spencer W. Kimball taught a similar principle when he said, "It is reassuring to know that [a new President is] . . . not elected through committees and conventions with all their conflicts, criticisms, and by the vote of men, but [is] called of God and then sustained by the people. . . The pattern divine allows for no errors, no conflicts, no ambitions, no ulterior motives. The Lord has reserved for himself the calling of his leaders over his church."[15] President Hinckley also testified, "At [the president of the Church's] passing, that authority becomes operative in the senior Apostle, who is then named, set apart, and ordained a prophet and President by his associates of the Council of the Twelve. There is no electioneering. There is no campaigning. There is only the quiet and simple operation of a divine plan which provides inspired and tested leadership."[16]

27 And every decision made by either of these quorums must be by the unanimous voice of the same; that is, every member in each quorum must be agreed to its decisions, in order to make their decisions of the same power or validity one with the other—

28 A majority may form a quorum when circumstances render it impossible to be otherwise—

29 Unless this is the case, their decisions are not entitled to the same blessings which the decisions of a quorum of three presidents were anciently, who were ordained after the order of Melchizedek, and were righteous and holy men.

30 The decisions of these quorums, or either of them, are to be made in all righteousness, in holiness, and lowliness of heart, meekness and long-suffering, and in faith, and virtue, and knowledge, temperance, patience, godliness, brotherly kindness and charity;

31 Because the promise is, if these things abound in them they shall not be unfruitful in the knowledge of the Lord.

32 And in case that any decision of these quorums is made in unrighteousness, it may be brought before a general assembly of the several quorums, which constitute the spiritual authori-

ties of the church; otherwise there can be no appeal from their decision.

The Lord's directive in verse 27 that decisions in the presiding quorums must be unanimous does not mean that there is always absolute agreement. The leaders of the Church come from different backgrounds and bring different gifts and experience to their service. Though there can be spirited discussions among the leaders of the Church over the best course to pursue, Church leaders and members are instructed to seek unanimity in their counsels through a spirit of meekness and gentle persuasion (see Doctrine and Covenants 121:41–43). When President Henry B. Eyring first witnessed a discussion among the leaders of the Church, he later recalled thinking, "This is the strangest. . . . Here are the prophets of God, and they're disagreeing in an openness that I had never seen in business. . . . I watched this process of them disagreeing and I thought, 'Good heavens!' It was more open than anything I had ever seen with all the groups I had seen in business."

However, as the meeting went on, President Eyring witnessed what he later called a miracle. The Spirit began to work on every person in the room, each came to see the right path, and a spirit of unity prevailed. "I saw the most incredible thing," President Eyring recalled, "I have seen a miracle! I have seen unity!" But then he saw President Harold B. Lee, who was chairing the meeting, pause the discussion and say, "Wait a minute, I think we will bring this matter up again some other time. I sense there is someone in the room who is not yet settled." When the meeting ended, President Eyring saw someone from the meeting thank President Lee for recognizing their feelings and holding off on making the decision. President Eyring was moved by what he saw, saying later, "This is what it claims to be. This is the true Church of Jesus Christ. Revelation is real, even in business settings."[17]

The Lord's expectation of unanimity might slow the process of decision-making in the Church, but it is another indelible example of how the Holy Spirit helps lead and guide Church councils.

> 33 The Twelve are a Traveling Presiding High Council, to officiate in the name of the Lord, under the direction of the Presidency of the Church, agreeable to the institution of heaven; to build up the church, and regulate all the affairs of the same in all nations, first unto the Gentiles and secondly unto the Jews.

34 The Seventy are to act in the name of the Lord, under the direction of the Twelve or the traveling high council, in building up the church and regulating all the affairs of the same in all nations, first unto the Gentiles and then to the Jews—

35 The Twelve being sent out, holding the keys, to open the door by the proclamation of the gospel of Jesus Christ, and first unto the Gentiles and then unto the Jews.

In verses 33–35 the Lord establishes the Twelve and the Seventy primarily as traveling authorities and charges them "to regulate all the affairs of the same in all nations, first unto the Gentiles and secondly unto the Jews" (verses 33–34). The Twelve were originally intended to act as a traveling high council, working to solve differences and problems in the branches of the Church that were not part of an organized stake and thus had no high council or stake presidency to assist them. As time went on and the Church expanded, the number of stakes increased into the thousands, making the role of the Twelve increase in importance.

Members of the Twelve spend much of their time traveling to assist in regulating and governing the work of the Church. President Packer, an Apostle for several decades, gave this accounting of his travels: "I am no different from the Brethren of the Twelve . . . when I tell you that the records show I have been in Mexico and Central and South America more than 75 times, in Europe over 50 times, Canada 25 times, the islands of the Pacific 10 times, Asia 10 times, and Africa 4 times; also China twice; to Israel, Saudi Arabia, Bahrain, the Dominican Republic, India, Pakistan, Egypt, Indonesia, and many, many other places around the globe. Others have traveled even more than that."[18]

36 The standing high councils, at the stakes of Zion, form a quorum equal in authority in the affairs of the church, in all their decisions, to the quorum of the presidency, or to the traveling high council.

37 The high council in Zion form a quorum equal in authority in the affairs of the church, in all their decisions, to the councils of the Twelve at the stakes of Zion.

38 It is the duty of the traveling high council to call upon the Seventy, when they need assistance, to fill the several calls for preaching and administering the gospel, instead of any others.

When verses 36–37 state that the standing, or local, high councils in the Church are equal in authority to the Twelve and the Seventy, this statement must be taken in historical context. At the time this revelation was given, there were only two stake high councils, one in Ohio and one in Missouri. The high council in Kirtland was presided over by Joseph Smith and the members of the First Presidency (see Doctrine and Covenants 102:3). The stake presidency in Zion was presided over by David Whitmer, William W. Phelps, and John Whitmer.[19] The simple fact that there were only two high councils, with one led by the First Presidency, increased these councils' importance in managing the affairs of the Church.

Today stakes of the Church number in the thousands and exist on every continent except Antarctica. While stake presidencies and stake high councils play a vital role in the local communities in which they are found, they are not treated as a separate quorum on the same level of authority as the First Presidency, the Twelve, or the Seventy. This difference in authority does not undermine the importance of local stake high councils in any sense. As the Church has grown, distinguishing between "general" authorities, who have no specific area assigned to them, and "area" authorities, who act as a standing high council in their own communities, is important. Members of the Church are asked to sustain both the General Officers and local authorities of the Church.[20]

> 39 It is the duty of the Twelve, in all large branches of the church, to ordain evangelical ministers, as they shall be designated unto them by revelation—
>
> 40 The order of this priesthood was confirmed to be handed down from father to son, and rightly belongs to the literal descendants of the chosen seed, to whom the promises were made.
>
> 41 This order was instituted in the days of Adam, and came down by lineage in the following manner:
>
> 42 From Adam to Seth, who was ordained by Adam at the age of sixty-nine years, and was blessed by him three years previous to his (Adam's) death, and received the promise of God by his father, that his posterity should be the chosen of the Lord, and that they should be preserved unto the end of the earth;
>
> 43 Because he (Seth) was a perfect man, and his likeness was the express likeness of his father, insomuch that he seemed to be like

unto his father in all things, and could be distinguished from him only by his age.

44 Enos was ordained at the age of one hundred and thirty-four years and four months, by the hand of Adam.

45 God called upon Cainan in the wilderness in the fortieth year of his age; and he met Adam in journeying to the place Shedolamak. He was eighty-seven years old when he received his ordination.

46 Mahalaleel was four hundred and ninety-six years and seven days old when he was ordained by the hand of Adam, who also blessed him.

47 Jared was two hundred years old when he was ordained under the hand of Adam, who also blessed him.

48 Enoch was twenty-five years old when he was ordained under the hand of Adam; and he was sixty-five and Adam blessed him.

49 And he saw the Lord, and he walked with him, and was before his face continually; and he walked with God three hundred and sixty-five years, making him four hundred and thirty years old when he was translated.

50 Methuselah was one hundred years old when he was ordained under the hand of Adam.

51 Lamech was thirty-two years old when he was ordained under the hand of Seth.

52 Noah was ten years old when he was ordained under the hand of Methuselah.

The Twelve are charged as part of their duties to seek out evangelists to serve in all the large branches of the Church (see verse 39). "This order of the priesthood" is the patriarchal priesthood, which Joseph Smith later explained more extensively and linked to the ordinances of the temple that were revealed in Nauvoo.[21] The patriarchal order should be considered not as an order separate from the Melchizedek Priesthood but as an appendage to the higher priesthood, like the Aaronic Priesthood. Evangelists are chosen to provide patriarchal blessings.

Joseph Smith taught, "An Evangelist is a Patriarch[,] even the oldest man of the blood of Joseph or of the seed of Abraham, wherever the Church of Christ is established in the Earth, there should be a Patriarch for the benefit of the posterity of the Saints as it was with Jacob, in giving his patriarchal blessing unto his sons."[22] In most stakes a stake patriarch provides these blessings. Patriarchal blessings are a great source of comfort, guidance, and connection for Latter-day Saints.[23]

> 53 Three years previous to the death of Adam, he called Seth, Enos, Cainan, Mahalaleel, Jared, Enoch, and Methuselah, who were all high priests, with the residue of his posterity who were righteous, into the valley of Adam-ondi-Ahman, and there bestowed upon them his last blessing.
>
> 54 And the Lord appeared unto them, and they rose up and blessed Adam, and called him Michael, the prince, the archangel.
>
> 55 And the Lord administered comfort unto Adam, and said unto him: I have set thee to be at the head; a multitude of nations shall come of thee, and thou art a prince over them forever.
>
> 56 And Adam stood up in the midst of the congregation; and, notwithstanding he was bowed down with age, being full of the Holy Ghost, predicted whatsoever should befall his posterity unto the latest generation.
>
> 57 These things were all written in the book of Enoch, and are to be testified of in due time.

Doctrine and Covenants 107:53–55 was originally received as part of a blessing Joseph Smith Jr. gave to his father and mother on December 18, 1833. Joseph later revised the wording of the blessing in the fall of 1835. In the blessing, Joseph Jr. declared that his father was given the "keys of the patriarchal priesthood over the kingdom of God on earth."[24] This blessing is tied directly to Joseph Sr.'s ordination as the Patriarch to the Church in December 1834.[25] The blessing also declared that Lucy Mack Smith "shall be a partaker with my father in all his patriarchal blessings."

The blessing to Joseph Sr. begins with these words: "Blessed of the Lord is my father, for he shall stand in the midst of his posterity and shall be comforted by their blessings when he is old and bowed down with years, and shall be called a prince over them, and shall be numbered among those who hold the right of patriarchal priesthood, even the keys of that ministry: for he shall assemble together his posterity like unto Adam; and the assembly which he called shall be an ensample for my father, for this it is written of him." The blessing continues with the text of Doctrine and Covenants 107:53–55 in full.[26] Later the blessing mentions Lucy Mack Smith and reads in part:

> So shall it be with my father: he shall be called a prince over his posterity, holding the keys of the patriarchal priesthood over the kingdom of God on earth, even the Church of the Latter Day Saints; and he shall sit in the general assembly of patriarchs, even in council with the Ancient of Days when he shall sit and all the patriarchs with him—and shall enjoy his right and authority under the direction of the Ancient of Days.
>
> And blessed, also, is my mother, for she is a mother in Israel, and shall be a partaker with my father in all his patriarchal blessings.
>
> Blessed is my mother, for her soul is ever filled with benevolence and philanthropy; and notwithstanding her age, she shall yet receive strength and be comforted in the midst of her house: and thus saith the Lord, She shall have eternal life.[27]

Joseph Smith Sr. served as the Patriarch to the Church until his death in 1840. As the eldest surviving Smith son, Hyrum Smith succeeded his father as Patriarch to the Church. The office of Patriarch to the Church continued to be passed down through Hyrum's descendants until the death of Elder Eldred G. Smith in 2013. At the October 1979 general conference, Eldred Smith was granted emeritus status, and with his death, the office of Patriarch to the Church was discontinued. At the time Elder Smith was granted emeritus status, President N. Eldon Tanner explained the reason for the change, stating, "Because of the large increase in the number of stake patriarchs and the availability of patriarchal service throughout the world, we now designate Elder Eldred G. Smith as a Patriarch Emeritus, which means that he is honorably relieved of all duties and responsibilities pertaining to the office of Patriarch to the Church."[28] Patriarchs who serve in stakes around the globe now carry on the work first started in this dispensation by Joseph Smith Sr.

> 58 It is the duty of the Twelve, also, to ordain and set in order all the other officers of the church, agreeable to the revelation which says:
>
> 59 To the church of Christ in the land of Zion, in addition to the church laws respecting church business—

60 Verily, I say unto you, saith the Lord of Hosts, there must needs be presiding elders to preside over those who are of the office of an elder;

61 And also priests to preside over those who are of the office of a priest;

62 And also teachers to preside over those who are of the office of a teacher, in like manner, and also the deacons—

63 Wherefore, from deacon to teacher, and from teacher to priest, and from priest to elder, severally as they are appointed, according to the covenants and commandments of the church.

64 Then comes the High Priesthood, which is the greatest of all.

65 Wherefore, it must needs be that one be appointed of the High Priesthood to preside over the priesthood, and he shall be called President of the High Priesthood of the Church;

66 Or, in other words, the Presiding High Priest over the High Priesthood of the Church.

67 From the same comes the administering of ordinances and blessings upon the church, by the laying on of the hands.

Verse 58 in Doctrine and Covenants 107 marks the beginning of an additional revelation that Joseph originally received in Hiram, Ohio, on November 11, 1831.[29] Parts of this revelation—specifically verses 61, 70, 73, 76–77, 88, 90, 93, and 98—were published in a separate section in the 1835 edition of the Doctrine and Covenants. Most of the content of this additional revelation concerns the role of a bishop and its relationship to the lineal descendants of Aaron (see commentary for Doctrine and Covenants 68:13–21).

Verses 58–67 establish the basic principle that quorums of the priesthood are generally presided over by those who hold the same office as the members of a particular quorum—elders over elders, deacons over deacons, and so forth. In the modern Church, a notable exception to this rule is the priests quorum, which is presided over by a ward's bishop, who in turn acts as the presiding officer for the Aaronic Priesthood (see verse 88). Elder Quentin L. Cook explained:

The bishop has a paramount role in serving as a shepherd to guide the rising generation, including young single adults, to Jesus Christ. . . . The bishopric supports parents in watching over and nurturing children and youth in the ward. The bishop and ward Young Women president counsel together. You might ask, "Why is the bishop directed to spend so much time with the youth?" The Lord has organized His Church to accomplish crucial priorities. Accordingly, the organization of His Church has a structure in which the bishop has a dual responsibility. He has doctrinal responsibility for the ward as a whole, but he also has specific doctrinal responsibility for the priests quorum.[30]

In a similar vein, President Nelson taught bishoprics that their "first and foremost responsibility is to care for the young men and young women of [their] ward."[31]

68 Wherefore, the office of a bishop is not equal unto it; for the office of a bishop is in administering all temporal things;

69 Nevertheless a bishop must be chosen from the High Priesthood, unless he is a literal descendant of Aaron;

70 For unless he is a literal descendant of Aaron he cannot hold the keys of that priesthood.

71 Nevertheless, a high priest, that is, after the order of Melchizedek, may be set apart unto the ministering of temporal things, having a knowledge of them by the Spirit of truth;

72 And also to be a judge in Israel, to do the business of the church, to sit in judgment upon transgressors upon testimony as it shall be laid before him according to the laws, by the assistance of his counselors, whom he has chosen or will choose among the elders of the church.

73 This is the duty of a bishop who is not a literal descendant of Aaron, but has been ordained to the High Priesthood after the order of Melchizedek.

74 Thus shall he be a judge, even a common judge among the inhabitants of Zion, or in a stake of Zion, or in any branch of the church where he shall be set apart unto this ministry, until the borders of Zion are enlarged and it becomes necessary to have other bishops or judges in Zion or elsewhere.

75 And inasmuch as there are other bishops appointed they shall act in the same office.

76 But a literal descendant of Aaron has a legal right to the presidency of this priesthood, to the keys of this ministry, to act in the office of bishop independently, without counselors, except in a case where a President of the High Priesthood, after the order of Melchizedek, is tried, to sit as a judge in Israel.

Verses 68–76 contain extensive instructions to the bishops of the Church. At the time this revelation was received, the use of the term *bishop* referred to the role of what we would now call the Presiding Bishop in the Church. Verse 75 points out that if other bishops are called, the same instructions apply to them as well. Today thousands of bishops serve throughout the Church. The Presiding Bishopric plays a vital role in the Church's mission, especially in the temporal affairs of the Church. Elder Quentin L. Cook summarized the responsibilities of local bishops in the modern Church as follows: "The bishop has five principal responsibilities in presiding over a ward: He is the presiding high priest in the ward. He is president of the Aaronic Priesthood. He is a common judge. He coordinates the work of salvation and exaltation, including caring for those in need. And he oversees records, finances, and the use of the meetinghouse. In his role as presiding high priest, the bishop is the ward's 'spiritual leader.' He is a 'faithful disciple of Jesus Christ.'"[32]

77 And the decision of either of these councils, agreeable to the commandment which says:

78 Again, verily, I say unto you, the most important business of the church, and the most difficult cases of the church, inasmuch as there is not satisfaction upon the decision of the bishop or judges, it shall be handed over and carried up unto the council of the church, before the Presidency of the High Priesthood.

79 And the Presidency of the council of the High Priesthood shall have power to call other high priests, even twelve, to assist as counselors; and thus the Presidency of the High Priesthood and its counselors shall have power to decide upon testimony according to the laws of the church.

80 And after this decision it shall be had in remembrance no more before the Lord; for this is the highest council of the church of God, and a final decision upon controversies in spiritual matters.

81 There is not any person belonging to the church who is exempt from this council of the church.

82 And inasmuch as a President of the High Priesthood shall transgress, he shall be had in remembrance before the common council of the church, who shall be assisted by twelve counselors of the High Priesthood;

83 And their decision upon his head shall be an end of controversy concerning him.

84 Thus, none shall be exempted from the justice and the laws of God, that all things may be done in order and in solemnity before him, according to truth and righteousness.

No person in the Church, not even a member of the First Presidency, is exempt from the justice and laws of God (see verse 84). Verse 82 explains that if a member of the First Presidency is found in transgression, he should be tried before "the common council of the church." The head of this "common council" is the head of the "common judges" (verses 74) in Israel, or the Presiding Bishop of the Church. President Joseph Fielding Smith explained, "The bishop is a common judge in Israel, and members are amenable to his jurisdiction. In case of an accusation made against one of the First Presidency, the case would be tried before the presiding bishop and a council of high priests."[33] John A. Widtsoe called this bishop's council "a tribunal extraordinary, from which there is no appeal, to be convened if it should be necessary to try a member of the First Presidency."[34]

Throughout the history of the Church, several members of the First Presidency have been brought before a common council. In August 1834, after the members of Zion's Camp returned from their march to Missouri, Sylvester Smith (no relation to Joseph Smith) accused President Joseph Smith of improper conduct during their journey. George A. Smith, who also traveled with Zion's Camp, remembered the circumstances that led to the trial:

I remember well in Zion's Camp, Levi W. Hancock made a fife, from a joint of sweet elder, Sylvester Smith marched his company to the music of that fife. That fife may be considered almost the introduction of martial music among the "Mormons." A dog came out and barked, when Sylvester Smith was going to kill the dog. Joseph said he was a good watch dog, Sylvester became wrathy and threatened; finally Joseph reproved him sharply, showing him that such a spirit would not conquer or control the human family, that he must get rid of it, and predicted that if he did not get rid of it, the day would come when a dog would gnaw his flesh, and he [would] not have the power to resist it.

Some months after the return to Kirtland, Sylvester Smith preferred a charge against Joseph the Prophet, for having prophesied lies in the name of the Lord, and undertook to substantiate that charge on the ground that the Prophet had said a dog should bite him, if he did not get rid of that spirit, when he had not power to resist. They were three days and parts of nights, with the High Council in Kirtland, in investigating this charge; one person spoke three hours in behalf of the Prophet. Sylvester published a confession which can be seen in the Church History, acknowledging his fault.[35]

Oliver Cowdery, David Whitmer, and Frederick G. Williams were also tried in front of a common council.[36]

> 85 And again, verily I say unto you, the duty of a president over the office of a deacon is to preside over twelve deacons, to sit in council with them, and to teach them their duty, edifying one another, as it is given according to the covenants.

> 86 And also the duty of the president over the office of the teachers is to preside over twenty-four of the teachers, and to sit in council with them, teaching them the duties of their office, as given in the covenants.

> 87 Also the duty of the president over the Priesthood of Aaron is to preside over forty-eight priests, and sit in council with them, to teach them the duties of their office, as is given in the covenants—

> 88 This president is to be a bishop; for this is one of the duties of this priesthood.

> 89 Again, the duty of the president over the office of elders is to preside over ninety-six elders, and to sit in council with them, and to teach them according to the covenants.

> 90 This presidency is a distinct one from that of the seventy, and is designed for those who do not travel into all the world.

> 91 And again, the duty of the President of the office of the High Priesthood is to preside over the whole church, and to be like unto Moses—

92 Behold, here is wisdom; yea, to be a seer, a revelator, a translator, and a prophet, having all the gifts of God which he bestows upon the head of the church.

The Lord specifies the duties of presidents and the general sizes of quorums for deacons, teachers, priests, and elders in the Church. All presidents are directed to "sit in council" with the members of their quorum, seeking insights and revelation from all quorum members (see verses 85–87, 89). This direction emphasizes the principle that presiding officers are not expected to dominate their quorums but to lead wisely and serve those whom they lead. Elder David A. Bednar taught, "I believe the gift of discernment operates more effectively when we're listening as opposed to when we're talking."[37]

In verse 91 the highest presiding officer in the Church (the President) is compared to Moses, not to Christ, because like Moses, the President of the Church ultimately serves under the direction of the Lord. The President of the Church, a modern prophet, presides over modern Israel with all of the gifts, powers, and priesthood held anciently by Moses. When President Hinckley was asked by broadcaster Larry King point-blank, "What is your role? You're the leader of a major religion. What's your role?" President Hinckley replied, "My role is to declare doctrine. My role is to stand as an example before the people. My role is to be a voice in defense of the truth. My role is to stand as a conservator of those values which are important in our civilization and our society. My role is to lead."[38]

93 And it is according to the vision showing the order of the Seventy, that they should have seven presidents to preside over them, chosen out of the number of the seventy;

94 And the seventh president of these presidents is to preside over the six;

95 And these seven presidents are to choose other seventy besides the first seventy to whom they belong, and are to preside over them;

96 And also other seventy, until seven times seventy, if the labor in the vineyard of necessity requires it.

97 And these seventy are to be traveling ministers, unto the Gentiles first and also unto the Jews.

98 Whereas other officers of the church, who belong not unto the Twelve, neither to the Seventy, are not under the responsibility to travel among all nations, but are to travel as their circumstances shall allow, notwithstanding they may hold as high and responsible offices in the church.

99 Wherefore, now let every man learn his duty, and to act in the office in which he is appointed, in all diligence.

100 He that is slothful shall not be counted worthy to stand, and he that learns not his duty and shows himself not approved shall not be counted worthy to stand. Even so. Amen.

The end of section 107 references a "vision showing the order of the Seventy" (verse 93). We do not have a record of this vision, but the reference underscores the fact that God established the government of the Church by revelation. At a meeting on February 14, 1835, the Twelve Apostles received their calling. During the meeting, Joseph Smith declared that he had called the meeting because "God had commanded it and it was made known to him by vision."[39] Joseph Young, who was called as one of the Presidents of the Seventy around the same time, later recalled that a week before the meeting on February 14, Joseph Smith had told him and Brigham Young that he (Joseph Smith) had received a revelation to appoint the Twelve Apostles and to designate the Seventy.[40]

The phrase "the vision showing the order of the Seventy" from verse 93 led Elder Orson F. Whitney to reason:

Now, if he [Joseph Smith] saw the Seventies in vision, why not the Apostles? Why not the First Presidency? Why not the stakes and wards, with their presiding officers, and even the auxiliary organizations? Who can say that he did not see them? Who can say that these quorums of the Priesthood, these auxiliary societies and associations, the Church of God in its entirety as it exists upon the earth, are not a reflex of the Church of God in heaven, so far as it is adapted to our present conditions, so far as it has been found necessary to organize it here; the eventual outcome to be a perfect Church, corresponding in every particular to the Church of the First Born; and this that the will of God may be done upon earth even as it is done in heaven?[41]

End Notes

1. Revelation Book 1, which is most likely the earliest version of this revelation, provides a preface that states, "A Revelation given at Hiram Portage Co. Nov. 11, 1831." Revelation Book 2, also known as the Kirtland Revelation Book, provides this preface: "Revelation given November 1831[,] Cuyahog[a] Co[.,] Ohio[,] regulating the Presidency of the Church." Revelation Book 2 was recorded later than Revelation Book 1, but this insertion makes it possible that this portion of the revelation was given at the conference held in Orange Township, Ohio, Cuyahoga County, on October 25–26, 1831. See Revelation Book 2, 84, josephsmithpapers.org.
2. See Doctrine and Covenants, 1835, 82, josephsmithpapers.org.
3. Minutes, 25–26 October 1831, 11, josephsmithpapers.org.
4. See Appendix 5, Document 1. Blessing to Joseph Smith Sr. and Lucy Mack Smith, between circa 15 and 28 September 1835, Journal, 1832–1834, 33–34, josephsmithpapers.org.
5. See Minutes, Discourse, and Blessings, 14–15 Feb. 1835, josephsmithpapers.org; and Minutes and Blessings, 28 Feb.–1 Mar. 1835, josephsmithpapers.org.
6. Minutes and Discourses, 27 February 1835, as Reported by William E. McLellin, 3, josephsmithpapers.org.
7. See "Historical Introduction," Revelation, 11 November 1831–B [D&C 107 (partial)]; "Historical Introduction," Appendix 5, Document 1; Blessing to Joseph Smith Sr. and Lucy Mack Smith, between circa 15 and 28 September 1835; and "Historical Introduction," Instruction on Priesthood, between circa 1 March and circa 4 May 1835 [D&C 107], josephsmithpapers.org.
8. Instruction on Priesthood, circa 5 October 1840, 1, josephsmithpapers.org.
9. Discourse, 5 January 1841, as Reported by William Clayton, 5, josephsmithpapers.org.
10. Letterbook 1, 30, josephsmithpapers.org.
11. Joseph Smith and Janne M. Sjodahl, *Doctrine and Covenants Commentary* (Salt Lake City, UT: Deseret Book, 1951), 700.
12. See "Presidency of the high priesthood," josephsmithpapers.org.
13. See Harold B. Lee, "The Strength of the Priesthood," *Ensign*, May 1972.
14. Joseph Fielding Smith, *Doctrines of Salvation*, comp. Bruce R. McConkie (1956), 3:156.

15. Spencer W. Kimball, "We Thank Thee, O God, for a Prophet," *Ensign*, Jan. 1973, 33.

16. Gordon B. Hinckley, "Come and Partake," *Ensign*, May 1986, 46–47.

17. CptMni, "Henry B. Eyring: Forget Harvard and Stanford. We're in Another Kind of Thing Here," YouTube video, Jan. 7, 2012, https://www.youtube.com/watch?v=l8tccvnKEy0.

18. Boyd K. Packer, "The Twelve," *Ensign* or *Liahona*, May 2008, 86.

19. See Minutes, 3 July 1834, 43, josephsmithpapers.org.

20. See Russell M. Nelson, "Closing Remarks," *Ensign* or *Liahona*, Nov. 2019, 120–122.

21. See Discourse, 27 August 1843, as Reported by Willard Richards, 74, josephsmithpapers.org. See also History, 1838–1856, volume E-1 [1 July 1843–30 April 1844], 1708, josephsmithpapers.org.

22. Joseph Smith, in History, 1838–1856, volume C-1 [2 November 1838–31 July 1842], 9 [addenda], josephsmithpapers.org.

23. See *General Handbook: Serving in The Church of Jesus Christ of Latter-day Saints*, 18.17–18.17.3, Gospel Library.

24. The first part of this blessing is found in Journal, 1832–1834, 33–34, josephsmithpapers.org. The blessing was expanded in 1835 and can be found in its expanded form in Appendix 5, Document 1. Blessing to Joseph Smith Sr. and Lucy Mack Smith, between circa 15 and 28 September 1835, 9, josephsmithpapers.org.

25. See "Historical Introduction," Appendix 5, Document 1. Blessing to Joseph Smith Sr. and Lucy Mack Smith, between circa 15 and 28 September 1835, josephsmithpapers.org.

26. See Appendix 5, Document 1. Blessing to Joseph Smith Sr. and Lucy Mack Smith, between circa 15 and 28 September 1835, 9, josephsmithpapers.org.

27. Appendix 5, Document 1. Blessing to Joseph Smith Sr. and Lucy Mack Smith, between circa 15 and 28 September 1835, 9, josephsmithpapers.org.

28. N. Eldon Tanner, "The Sustaining of Church Officers," *Ensign*, Nov. 1979, 18.

29. See Revelation, 11 November 1831–B [D&C 107 (partial)], josephsmithpapers.org.

30. Quentin L. Cook, "Bishops—Shepherds over the Lord's Flock," *Liahona*, May 2021, 58.

31. Russell M. Nelson, "Witnesses, Aaronic Priesthood Quorums, and Young Women Classes," *Ensign* or *Liahona*, Nov. 2019, 39.

32. Quentin L. Cook, "Bishops—Shepherds over the Lord's Flock," 58. See also *General Handbook*, 6.1.1–4.

33. Joseph Fielding Smith, *Church History and Modern Revelation* (Salt Lake City, UT: Deseret Book, 1948), 2:21.

34. John A. Widtsoe, *Priesthood and Church Government* (Salt Lake City, UT: Deseret Book, 1939), 212.

35. George A. Smith, in *Journal of Discourses*, 11:7. See also Minutes, 11 August 1834; Minutes, 23 August 1834; Minutes, 28–29 August 1834, josephsmithpapers.org; and Andrew Jenson, "Smith, Sylvester," in *Latter-day Saint Biographical Encyclopedia: A Compilation of Biographical Sketches of Prominent Men and Women in the Church of Jesus Christ of Latter-day Saints* (Salt Lake City, UT: Deseret News Press, 1901), 1:191.

36. See Joseph Fielding Smith, *Church History and Modern Revelation*, 3:21.

37. Quoted in Michael Magleby, "To Sit in Council," *Ensign*, Jan. 2018, 52.

38. Gordon B. Hinckley, "What Are People Asking about Us?," *Ensign*, Nov. 1998, 70.

39. Minutes, Discourse, and Blessings, 14–15 February 1835, 147, josephsmithpapers.org.

40. See Joseph Young Sr., *History of the Organization of the Seventies* (Salt Lake City, UT: Deseret News Press, 1878), 1–2.

41. Orson F. Whitney, in Conference Report, Apr. 1912, 51.

ABOUT THE AUTHOR

CASEY PAUL GRIFFITHS IS AN ASSOCIATE PROFESSOR OF CHURCH HISTORY and Doctrine at Brigham Young University in Provo, Utah. He holds a bachelor's degree in history, a master's degree in religious education, and a PhD in educational leadership and foundations, all from Brigham Young University. He has served as president of the John Whitmer Historical Association and the BYU Education Society. Before coming to BYU he served as a teacher and curriculum writer in the Seminaries and Institutes of Religion department of The Church of Jesus Christ of Latter-day Saints. He also serves as a managing editor of Doctrine and Covenants Central, a website designed to build faith in Jesus Christ by making the Doctrine and Covenants accessible, comprehensible, and defensible to people everywhere. He lives in Saratoga Springs with his wife, Elizabeth, and their four wonderful children.

Scan to visit

https://doctrineandcovenantscentral.org/